CHARGE TO GLORY!

JAMES D. LUNT

Charge to Glory!

HARCOURT, BRACE AND COMPANY

New York

To

ARTHUR SANDEMAN

of

The Central India Horse

Killed in action March 21, 1942

CONTENTS

FOREWORD

THIS is a story about cavalry—the mobile arm in land operations. It is not the complete story, since that would cover the entire history of warfare and require many volumes. My aim has been much more modest. I have sought to portray to the ordinary reader, and not to the military expert who knows it all already, those qualities of dash and daring which have so often been described as the "cavalry spirit." A great cavalry soldier, General Sir Hubert Gough, once defined that spirit as a combination of independence of thought, quickness in decision, and boldness in action. I would choose to add one other quality—that gaiety of spirit which the French prefer to call *élan*, or even *panache*.

As an illustration of this cavalry spirit, I have selected ten battles or engagements in which cavalry have played an important and in certain instances a decisive part. Not all these battles are well known, and in certain of them the sun went down on defeat. They serve to illustrate, however, the cavalry spirit, which has sometimes wrested victory from what seemed to be almost certain defeat, and which on other occasions has been so bold that it has become rash. The borderline between boldness and rashness will always present a problem to the commander of mobile troops, and for this very reason I have included just such a situation.

I have discharged a long-standing debt by the writing of this book. Nearly twenty years have passed since I sat on the steps of a Buddhist monastery in Central Burma and had described to me the manner in which a friend of mine had met his death while leading the last horsed charge ever to be made by British or Indian cavalry. I vowed at the time to write the story of that charge should I survive the war. Now I have done so.

I am indebted to a great many people for their help in the writing of this book—too many for me to be able to mention all of them individually. Some, however, I must mention. The first is my wife, who has been a constant source of help and encouragement. I am indebted to Alan Hodge and Peter Quennell, the editors of *History Today*, for the encouragement they have always given me in my writing and for their permission to quote from an article on cavalry which I wrote for them; Gerald Gross, who persuaded me to write this book; Fräulein Margaret Frese, who typed the manuscript; and Staff Sergeant Franklin, who did the original work for the maps; Major Brian O'Connell of the Royal Canadian Dragoons, who has found time among his many other duties to read the manuscript and advise me; and last, but by no means least, Mr. D. W. King and Brigadier John Stephenson, the Librarians of the War Office and Royal United Service Institution, whose assistance has been invaluable.

And, finally, I must thank the officers and men of the 16th/5th The Queen's Royal Lancers who through so many happy years taught me all that I know of the true meaning of "cavalry spirit," and without whom this book could never have been written.

J.D.L.

Verden/Aller
Germany
May 1960

CHARGE TO GLORY!

CHAPTER ONE

Toungoo

MARCH 21, 1942

*"The charge will always remain the thing in which it
will be the cavalryman's pride to die sword in hand."*
CAVALRY JOURNAL (1909)

IN THE late afternoon of March 20, 1942, a mounted detachment of the Burma Frontier Force rode into the bomb-shat-
tered town of Toungoo in Central Burma. At its head rode the
British commander of the detachment, Captain Arthur Sandeman of the Central India Horse.

The war had reached Toungoo at the beginning of March.
A force of Japanese bombers, flying high and in tight formation,
had struck at Toungoo airfield, the base of General Claire Chennault's American Volunteer Group. Missing the airfield, their
bombs had pitched among the closely packed wooden houses
of the town, starting huge fires, and killing and wounding
large numbers of Indian refugees who were camped on the
sidewalks or in lean-to shelters on the outskirts of Toungoo.
A few days later, while the fires were still smoldering and the

dead were still unburied, Chennault withdrew his P-40's to a less exposed base; in the absence of any Early Warning system it was the only sensible thing to do.

The British forces were about halfway, both in time and distance, in their long withdrawal from Burma into India, and the 1st Burma Division was in the process of handing over responsibility for the Central, or Sittang, sector of the Burma front to General Stilwell of the United States Army, and to the Fifth Chinese Army, which he commanded. The Burma Division was then to be switched to the Irrawaddy sector where it was to join the 17th Indian Division and form the Burma Corps under General Slim. By March 21 the division had begun its movement westward by march route and by rail, and the 200th Chinese Division was digging itself in around Toungoo. So far as anyone knew at either Stilwell's or the Burma Division headquarters, the Japanese advance guards were still thirty miles or more to the south.

The Burma Frontier Force, to which Sandeman's column belonged, had been formed in 1937 from the Burma Military Police. Both were para-military forces under civil control, and their task was "watch and ward" along the jungle-covered and mountainous frontiers of Burma. As such they were gendarmeries rather than conventional military forces, and it had certainly not been envisaged that the Burma Frontier Force would ever have to take the field against a first-class enemy like the Japanese. The Frontier Force contained both mounted troops and infantry, and included in its ranks most of the races of Burma; there were also Gurkhas, Kumaonis, Sikhs, and Punjabi Mussalmans from India, and it was from these two latter classes that the mounted branch was recruited.

The few British officers serving with the Frontier Force were on loan from the Indian army, attracted by the higher pay that the Frontier Force offered and by the opportunities for increased responsibility that service on Burma's frontiers provided. There was always the chance of taking part in some minor expedition against head-hunting tribesmen, armed with bows and poisoned arrows, and a comparatively junior officer might well find himself in charge of a huge tract of country with only his mother wit to guide him in moments of crisis. For cavalry officers the Burma Frontier Force had an additional attraction, since by 1942 it was one of the few remaining forces under British control which still retained horses; every regular and territorial cavalry regiment in both the Indian and British armies had been mechanized by the end of 1941.

When Japan invaded Indochina, and the Japanese threat to Burma loomed closer, the British started to expand their forces in Burma. There were no troops to spare from farther afield, and so Burma had to make the best use of its limited resources. The mounted squadrons of the Burma Frontier Force were organized into a reconnaissance force, and divided into independent columns of from sixty to one hundred sabers in each. The troopers rode the small but sturdy Burmese ponies, few of which exceeded 14.2 hands in height, but they made up in stamina for what they lacked in stature. Even so, it looked incongruous at times to see some burly Sikh trooper go cantering past on his diminutive mount, his heels barely clearing the ground.

Sandeman's column bivouacked the night of March 20 some miles north of Toungoo. The town itself had been a place of no particular significance before the war, and had few attractions to offer. It was situated about two hundred miles north of Rangoon, on the main road and railway to Mandalay, and was the center of an administrative district; as such it contained some brick buildings—jail, courthouse, and so on— but most of the town was made up of two-storied wooden houses, jostling together on either side of the potholed and dusty streets. Fifteen miles away to the west were the thickly wooded slopes of the Pegu Yomas, and about the same distance to the east the Karen Hills. Around the town itself the terrain was flat, consisting mainly of paddy fields, which in March were dry and very dusty. The climate was hot and rather unpleasant, and over the town there hung that once-smelled, never-forgotten stench of the 1942 campaign in Burma—a compound of cordite, dust, dried fish, smoldering timbers, excreta, and rotting bodies.

The Burmese inhabitants had taken refuge in the nearby

jungle villages, but the Chinese merchants and the Indian artisans and laborers had joined the weary hordes of refugees, which had been pressing northwards through Toungoo in a steady stream ever since January. Cholera was rife among them and was far more deadly in its effects than all the Japanese bombs; the cholera victims lay unburied because the street-cleaners and scavengers had fled. Only the pi-dogs remained, flitting furtively through the streets by day, and making the nights hideous with their howling.

Toungoo was a hive of military activity during those days in mid-March. It had a definite strategic importance since it stood astride the main north-south communications in the Central sector, and the road linking Central Burma with the Shan States started from Toungoo. North of the town was the airfield, one of the best in Burma, and some ten miles farther north was the village of Yedashe where the headquarters of the Burma Division was temporarily located. Stilwell was planning to move the forward echelon of his headquarters to Yedashe, once the British had pulled out, and he had set the 200th Chinese Division burrowing like rabbits on the southern approaches to Toungoo, hoping that the Japanese would find in it another Changsha.

But where were the Japanese? Their advance guards were in contact with the British on the Irrawaddy sector, and the 55th Division had been engaged with the British on the Central sector as recently as March 18. Thereafter the Japanese troops operating on the Central sector had vanished into thin air, and their locations were unknown. The fog of war, as impenetrable perhaps in that Burma campaign as in any other campaign in history, hung thickly everywhere, and effectively masked the operations of the quick-moving and tough Japanese infantry. Information was vital, but how was it to be obtained? Reports from refugees were wildly inaccurate, and information from Burmese sources was suspect since most of the local inhabitants were thought to be pro-Japanese. The Japanese air force ruled the skies, and even when the occasional Allied reconnaissance sortie slipped past their guard, it found nothing that gave away the Japanese dispositions.

It was for precisely this task of reconnaissance that the Burma Frontier Force columns had been organized. They could move faster on their ponies than could men on foot; they carried light machine guns on pack transport, which permitted them to meet the Japanese patrols on equal terms; and unlike the mechanized units they were not confined to the roads by the terrain. A Frontier Force column had been sent down from the north to operate on the Central sector, but unfortunately half the column, under its commander, Captain Nigel Loring of Skinner's Horse, was ambushed at night and scattered. Loring himself was taken prisoner and spent the rest of the war in Rangoon jail, where he conducted himself with the utmost gallantry.

What remained of Loring's column, under the command of Sandeman, was placed at the disposal of General Stilwell as a temporary measure. That testy but sorely tried warrior needed information badly. He was getting markedly little co-operation from the Chinese field commanders who were ostensibly under his orders, and he was receiving a succession of contradictory instructions from the Generalissimo in distant Chungking. He therefore accepted the offer of Sandeman's force with more outward enthusiasm than he usually displayed for anything British.

Stilwell's major worry was the situation to the east of Toungoo where the River Sittang winds its way, between thickly wooded banks, to the south. He believed that the Japanese would launch one of their classic encircling attacks from that direction, having first moved their troops up the Sittang in boats, while at the same time they would make their main thrust along the axis of the Rangoon-Mandalay railway. He was prepared to deal with the latter, but he would require early warning of any outflanking attack from the direction of the Sittang if he was to switch his reserves in time to counter it. Sandeman was therefore ordered to reconnoiter as far as the Sittang on March 21, and to watch that flank.

Arthur Sandeman, known throughout the Indian cavalry as "Sandy," was one of those characters thrown up from time to time who contradict the widely held impression that all pro-

fessional soldiers are cast from the same mold. Sandeman was
an individualist of individualists, with a passionate love for
horses and all that goes with horses. Despite his glasses and
his stoop, which combined to give him a somewhat unmilitary
appearance, he was a born cavalryman, and it was always his
contention that he had been born at least a century too late.
Indeed, it was not difficult to picture Sandy charging at the
head of a troop at Balaklava or scouring the Great Plains under
Custer to the strains of "Garry Owen." He was an authority on
Surtees,[1] dressed in extreme Edwardian fashion at a time when
"Teddy Boys" were still a phenomenon of the future, and
carried a silver snuffbox from which he took snuff at frequent
and earsplitting intervals.

The historian of his regiment had this to say about him:

> Sandy was another young officer of exceptional promise.
> A polo ball he decided was much too small an object for
> him to see, a pig was much nearer the requisite size, and
> in a short time he became an intrepid, and according to
> some, a reckless hog-hunter. His defence was not without
> logic. No horse, he argued, could have worse eyesight than
> that with which he was handicapped, and it was safer for
> him to allow the horse to decide where to put his feet.
> The flaw in the logic of this argument lay in the fact that
> Sandy insisted on dictating the pace—always the maxi-
> mum.
>
> For one who joined so late he was singularly unim-
> pressed with the idea of mechanization; all his ideas
> centred around an earlier period, and the spruce figure of
> Sandy, faultlessly attired, with no error in detail, in the
> costume of half a century ago, driving about cantonments
> in a horse buggy, was one that was quaint, even startling.
> It was also one that was copied by many subalterns in
> other regiments.
>
> Whether it was felt that the inception of this cult
> represented too marked a departure from the concept of

[1] Robert Smith Surtees (1805-1864), an English novelist and essayist
whose chief interests were horses and hunting.

the standard man, whether for some other reason, this slightly childish and totally harmless display earned a disproportionate amount of criticism, in the midst of which Sandy packed his bags and departed for the eastern frontier of Burma, where he commanded an independent squadron. It was thus that 1941 [1942] found him probably the last soldier in the Empire to ride into battle in a mounted attack.[2]

The stories of Sandeman's adventures hunting the Indian wild pig with spear in hand are legion.

Sandeman . . . was a most courageous chap. He was as blind as a bat and rode [after] his boar wearing powerful glasses. As he was always falling about he had a white tape tied to his glasses, and often could be seen groping about in the cover looking for them. Without the tape he had no hope of finding them. Many will remember riding with him, often behind him, with his white tape streaming behind him.[3]

There is an entry in my diary for March 21, 1942, which reads:

Our train is sitting on an embankment at Kyungon, a few miles outside Toungoo, waiting for an engine to arrive to pull us away. We have been waiting for 24 hours now and one hasn't turned up yet! The whole of Brigade headquarters and the 5/1st Punjabis are here, sitting about on the embankment, and it is uncomfortably exposed with so much enemy "air" about. Sandy Sandeman rode by with his troopers earlier this morning; they are carrying out a reconnaissance towards the Sittang, he says. Rather him than me—it's too damned hot for a quiet ride in the country! "Sandy" reckons there must be a lot of pig in the *chaungs* between here and the Sittang and was moan-

[2] Brigadier A. A. Filose, *King George V's Own Central India Horse* (William Blackwood, Edinburgh and London, 1950), pp. 121-122.
[3] Brigadier J. Gannon, *History of the Kadir Cup* (Odhams, London, 1959).

ing because he had left his hog-spears behind in Lashio.
He also told me he was riding the best polo pony in
Burma; probably true as she was a lovely little mare. He
moved off with his column about nine o'clock—about sixty
of them, and nearly all Sikhs.

We watched them go, the curb chains jingling as they went,
and the dust hanging above them in the still morning air.
Behind them there lingered the smell of leather and sweating
horses, and we were left with an unforgettable memory in a
war which was waged mostly with machines. The Guides[4] must
have looked like that, I thought, as they scouted ahead of
"Bobs"[5] on the way from Kabul to Kandahar. Then the dust
clouds merged with the shimmering heat haze, and the sound
of hoofs died away in the distance. Although we did not
know it at the time, we had been present at a unique moment
in all the long history of the British mounted arm.

Sandeman led his men out towards the airfield, and then
they moved east along the airfield's southern perimeter. Ahead
of them lay gently rolling country, intersected by deep *chaungs*
and low ridges, and observation was made difficult by the heat
haze and by the thick clumps of *lentana* bushes which dotted
the countryside. In the distance the woods lining the banks of
the Sittang showed as a dark smudge against the copper sky;
and away to the south, columns of dust showed where the
Chinese were blasting defenses out of the brick-hard soil.

On the airfield itself the Indian gunners of the 23rd Mountain Battery, Indian Artillery, were digging defenses among the
airfield buildings, but there was nothing to suggest that an attack was imminent. The Chinese regiment at Pyu, thirty miles
south of Toungoo, had not reported any contact with the
enemy, and it seemed as if a lull had settled over the battlefield after all the alarms of the past few weeks.

The Frontier Force column had covered about four or five
miles when its scouts reported that a body of troops appeared

[4] An Indian cavalry regiment, now part of the Pakistan army.
[5] Field Marshal Lord Roberts was one of the leading British soldiers of
the nineteenth century. He commanded the British Expeditionary Force
in the Second Afghan War in 1879.

to be digging trenches and erecting defenses directly to their front. The position appeared to be well within the line of the Chinese forward defenses, as marked on Sandeman's map, and he probably assumed that the troops ahead of him were Chinese. He searched the position through his field glasses but they told him nothing—to the uninitiated there was little to differentiate the Chinese soldier from the Japanese. In most essentials they looked the same, and their uniforms were almost identical. The column rode peaceably on towards them.

They were well within machine-gun range before Sandeman suspected that he might have been mistaken. Even then, as the enemy took cover behind their defenses, he still thought they might be an outpost of the Chinese 200th Division. (It was a practice among the Chinese to suspect everyone of being hostile until they were able to identify them, and only the previous day Sandeman had been held up for several hours outside Toungoo by a Chinese roadblock which kept him and his command covered while they checked the column's credentials.) He halted the column and rode on alone, calling out in English and Burmese that they were a British patrol. As he did so, fire was opened from every side; the column had ridden straight into an ambush.

Sandeman's instinctive reaction was to draw his sword, calling out at the same time to his trumpeter to sound the "Charge!" Then he set his horse's head at the enemy and galloped towards them, followed by about half his men shouting the Sikh war cry *Sat Sri Akal* as they came.

The remainder of the column, realizing the hopelessness of their situation, wheeled round and only drew rein when they clattered into the airfield buildings and told the amazed gunners of the mountain battery that there were Japanese troops only five miles away. It was as well that they did so, since it gave the gunners time to man their defenses, and to add to their laurels the stubborn defense of Toungoo airfield.

Arthur Sandeman never reached the enemy. Nor did any of the brave *sowars*[6] who rode after him "into the jaws of death." Sandeman's horse was killed under him and he died as he

[6] The Hindustani word for cavalry troopers.

would probably have chosen to die—at the head of his men, with a good horse between his thighs, and his sword drawn in his hand. With him fell several of his men, others were wounded and taken prisoner, while a few escaped to tell the tale of the last mounted charge ever to be made in all the long and glittering history of the British cavalry.

It was the end of an era.

CHAPTER TWO

The Mounted Arm

"Any cavalry officer awaiting an attack will be cashiered."

THE REGULATIONS OF FREDERICK THE GREAT

THE era of horsed cavalry goes back almost to the beginning of recorded history. For thousands of years the horse has been associated with war—"He saith among the trumpets, Ha, ha; and he smelleth the battle afar off, the thunder of the captains, and the shouting."

Yet when Job was writing about the horse as an animal of war, he was referring not so much to cavalry as we understand the term today as to the horse as a draft animal which hauled the war chariots into battle. The first recorded instance of war chariots is to be found in Exodus, chapter 14, but many years were to pass before the horsed cavalryman superseded the charioteer.

The classic definition of cavalry is that they are "horsemen trained to achieve the purpose of their commander by the combined action of men and horse." [1] However it was not until the horsemen had been provided with stirrups so they could control their mounts, and with long lances or powerful bows in order to deal with men on foot, that the mounted arm began to play a dominant part on the battlefield. Thereafter, and for nearly a thousand years, the mounted arm was the decisive one in war on land.

During the heyday of the Byzantine empire, Belisarius and his captains won many of their campaigns with forces composed entirely of cavalry, while in the thirteenth century the Mongols under Genghis Khan and Sabutai swept across Asia and as far as the Danube with a completely mounted army. At the same time in Europe, however, the horseman was growing increasingly useless on the battlefield; both rider and mount were so weighted down with armor that they could scarcely move out of a slow walk, and the smallest ditch presented an impassable obstacle. The value of cavalry was beginning to decline, and for the next five hundred years the man on foot, armed with pike and bow, was more than a match for the horseman.

As weapons and their means of delivery have been developed, soldiers have been forced to adapt their tactics to make the best use of their weapons. Certain basic requirements have nevertheless remained constant throughout history. One of these is the need for mobility. Another is the need for information about the enemy—his strength, his location, and his probable courses of action. The campaigns of Joshua were just as much affected by these requirements as were those of Eisenhower.

The development of the mounted arm has owed much to this need for reconnaissance, since the man on a horse is necessarily more mobile in most types of terrain than the man on foot. In the earliest times, moreover, warfare was a matter of cut and thrust, and victory went to the army with the best discipline, and which could use sword, spear, and club to the best effect in close combat. The men on foot fought shoulder to shoulder, and safety lay in keeping the ranks unbroken.

[1] Encyclopaedia Britannica, 11th edition.

There was little to fear from cavalry, always providing the ranks of infantry could present an unbroken face of steel. Consequently, cavalry were employed mainly on raids behind the armies, or for reconnaissance, or in pursuit once the enemy had been worsted in the hand-to-hand combat of the infantry.

The invention of gunpowder, and the arrival of the artillery arm on the battlefield, had little immediate effect on the employment of cavalry. Theoretically, the artillery should have been used to make a breach in the human wall opposite, and the cavalry should then have been launched into the gaps. In practice, however, the cavalry were employed against the enemy artillery, in an attempt to capture the guns and so prevent the artillery from destroying their own infantry. The enemy's cavalry would be deployed to protect the guns, and so there developed a series of cavalry-against-cavalry combats, while the gunners cut the traces and made off as fast as they could. The infantry were then left to carry on as before.

The first of the Great Captains of modern times to understand the true value of cavalry on the battlefield was Gustavus Adolphus of Sweden, and he owed much to principles elaborated by Prince Maurice of Nassau. Gustavus organized an army which made a virtue out of mobility, and his well-drilled and highly disciplined soldiers were able to outmaneuver the slow-moving and heterogeneous forces of the Imperialists, whose cavalry charged in loose order and with little effect against the eighteen-foot pikes and muskets of the Swedes. Since their discipline was virtually nonexistent, it was almost impossible to rally the Imperialist cavalry once it had been launched into battle. When they were at their most disorganized and confused state, Gustavus led his own cavalry against them. Riding knee to knee, in close order and three deep, the Swedish cavalry galloped through the Imperialists as a knife goes through butter.

Cromwell owed the inspiration of his "Ironsides" to the example of the Swedish King. The tactics he employed were Swedish in origin, as indeed were those of Prince Rupert on the Royalist side, but Cromwell made a particular point of keeping his cavalry under tight control. With Cromwell the

cavalry charge was not the spectacular affair that it was to become later; his horsemen came on "at a pretty round trot,"
halted when within pistol distance of the enemy ranks and
discharged their cumbersome weapons, after which they closed
with the shaken infantry and exchanged sword thrusts.

By this stage the battle had to all intents and purposes been
won, because the infantry had lost the cohesion on which,
above all, their safety depended. Breaches had been made in
the wall of steel through which the cavalry could ride, and as
the infantry recoiled to take the shock they were overwhelmed
by the weight of horse and man. The foot soldiers broke, the
battlefield then became the scene of individual combats in
which the mounted man usually possessed the advantage, and
as the unfortunate infantry took refuge in flight, the cavalry
took up their historic role of the pursuit.

Yet Cromwell was quick to realize that discipline and training were not sufficient to produce the perfect cavalryman. He
understood the vital importance of that cavalry spirit, or
panache, which has always been a characteristic of the mounted
arm. It was not for nothing that he told Hampden, as they rode
together from the field of Edgehill:

> Your troopers are most of them old decayed servingmen
> and tapsters and such kind of fellows—their troopers are
> gentlemen's sons, younger sons and persons of quality; do
> you think that the spirits of such base and mean fellows
> will ever be able to encounter gentlemen that have honour
> and courage and resolution in them? You must raise men
> of a spirit . . . that is likely to go on as far as gentlemen
> will go, or else you will be beaten still.[2]

The spirit which Cromwell succeeded in instilling into his
troopers of the New Model army did not derive from rank or
breeding, as was the case with Prince Rupert and the Royalist
cavalry, but came from deep religious conviction, victory in
battle, and confidence in their commander. Nevertheless the
cavalry of Cromwell's army seem to have possessed that same

[2] Alfred H. Burne and Peter Young, *The Great Civil War* (Eyre &
Spottiswoode, London, 1959), p. 225.

inalienable sense of superiority, as much in regard to their own infantry as towards the enemy, which has characterized the cavalry of all armies and in all ages. The other arms have never loved the cavalry for their superior airs and *panache*, but they have often envied them. "Perhaps I need not tell the reader," wrote Gleig on service relations during the Peninsular War, "that between the infantry and cavalry in the British Army a considerable jealousy exists; the former regarding the latter as little better than useless, the latter regarding the former as extremely vulgar and ungenteel." [3] It is a description by no means confined to the British army, nor to the times to which it refers.

It is important, when considering the development of the mounted arm, to bear in mind that the horse was being employed primarily as an aid to mobility. The horseman was required either to scout ahead of the armies "to see the other side of the hill," or to bring mobile weapon-power to bear on the battlefield. Cromwell, like Gustavus before him, realized that the success of shock action depended entirely on the ability of a commander to "soften up" the opposing lines of infantry before the cavalry was launched against them, and that once the charge was launched, it could only succeed if it went home as one cohesive whole. Hence his insistence on a high standard of horsemanship, believing, as he must have, that "the cavalryman's true weapon is his horse," and his practice whenever possible of charging at the trot, which enabled him to retain complete control over his men. His great opponent, Prince Rupert, who was in no way inferior to Cromwell as a cavalry leader, and who had taught his troopers to charge at the gallop like the Swedes, always failed in the last resort because he found it impossible to rally his soldiers after their first successful charge.

After Cromwell there was no great trainer of cavalry until Frederick the Great. Despite the genius of Marlborough, Turenne, and Prince Eugene, warfare became largely formalized, and success was usually dependent on the skill of a

[3] The Rev. G. R. Gleig, *Life of Arthur, First Duke of Wellington* (Longmans, London, 1862).

general in outmaneuvering his opponent and capturing some
fortification or magazine. Cavalry had still a part to play, but
as time went on their uniforms grew increasingly fancy, their
horses were increasingly overloaded, and horsemanship received
less and less attention. A regiment was the property of its
colonel and as such represented a considerable economic risk,
and it was not unnatural that he should be averse to risking
it in either peace or war. Horses rarely left their stables during winter months, their officers devoted their time more and
more to the complications of ceremonial drill, and the infantry
ousted the cavalry from the throne of the "Queen of the battlefield." Some infantrymen believe that they occupy it still.

It was left to Frederick the Great to revive the greatness
of cavalry. When he succeeded to the throne he found himself the possessor of 114 superbly drilled cavalry squadrons
whose glittering accouterments and meticulous drill would
have gladdened the heart of any sergeant major. Unfortunately,
however, their horsemanship did not live up to their appearance
on parade, and they drilled better on foot than on horseback.
Frederick said of them: "The heavy cavalry consisted . . . of
very big men, mounted on monstrous horses. These colossi
on elephants, however, could neither manoeuvre nor fight. No
parade went by without some of them falling off. The officers
had no conception of cavalry service." He went on to complain
that, "they manoeuvre with the precision of my grenadiers,
but they are as slow; and before the enemy they are no use,
and are always too late." [4] Mobility had ceased to be the
prerequisite of the horseman.

Frederick first saw his cavalry put to the test at Mollwitz in
1741, and they failed disastrously. The Austrian cavalry were
no more successful in breaking through the Prussian infantry,
but they did display much more *élan* and tactical sense than
the Prussian cavalry. It is as well to remember the stopping
effect of the musket ball at a time when it was an eight-bore
spherical ball with a charge of $1\frac{1}{4}$ ounces of powder behind it.
The well-drilled Prussian infantry, drawn up in line three deep,

[4] Lt. Col. F. N. Maude, *Cavalry: Its Past and Future* (Wm. Clowes,
London, 1903), p. 93.

could load and fire five times in a minute. The result was a discharge of thirteen bullets per yard per minute, and the eight-bore bullet could have dropped a bison in its tracks, let alone a horse. The failure of the Austrian cavalry to make much impression is therefore understandable, but it does not excuse the Prussian cavalry's failure against the less well-drilled Austrian infantry.

The disaster at Mollwitz fired Frederick with the determination to produce a mounted arm which would be decisive on the battlefield. A stream of regulations followed, all of which were designed to increase mobility, and to instill into his cavalry officers the principle of charging home at the gallop. Once cavalry were committed to the charge, it was forbidden to use firearms—"cold steel" alone was permitted—and any officer who waited to be attacked, instead of himself attacking, was to be severely punished.

Constant drilling, both in horsemanship and in the execution of drill maneuvers at the gallop, became the rule. In 1748 the King required attacks of 700 yards in all, 300 trot and 400 gallop, but by 1755 they were being carried out over 1,800 yards with the last 600 at full gallop. Frederick demanded perfection, generally riding in the attacks himself, and repeating them several times until he was satisfied. On one occasion a regiment delivered five attacks in one morning, and then had to turn out in the afternoon for two more; not surprisingly, when the King ordered a repeat the next day, the horses broke down. Even so, the martinet was seldom prepared to accept excuses. In 1754 the Bayreuth Dragoons were ordered three months' extra drill for not reaching the required standard.

Probably never before, or since, have cavalry reached such perfection on the battlefield as Frederick's cavalry did under the leadership of Seydlitz. Seydlitz was a superb cavalry commander who knew how to get the maximum use out of the instrument confided to him by the king; at Rosbach in 1757, and again at Zorndorf in 1758, the Prussian cavalry covered themselves with glory. Although much of their success was due to the inspired leadership of Seydlitz, and the ease with which the Prussian cavalry could be maneuvered even when charg-

ing at the gallop, much more was due to the care with which
Frederick mounted his men. He devoted as much attention to
the breeding of horses, and the matching of men to their
mounts, as he did to their drilling.

By Frederick's time the cavalry was beginning to evolve into
three distinct types—heavy cavalry, light cavalry, and a kind of
mounted infantryman who most approximated to the cavalry
soldier of the preceding two hundred years. The heavy cavalry
were used for shock action and were carefully selected big
men riding big horses. They were known as cuirassiers, from
the armor they wore to protect chest and back during the
cut and thrust of the charge. The light cavalry were employed
mainly for reconnaissance and were called hussars, a term
which is Hungarian in origin. In the British army the light
cavalry were known as light dragoons and first received formal
recognition in 1759. Occasions might arise when they would be
employed to charge infantry, but usually only when in the
company of heavy cavalry, or to reinforce the success of heavy
cavalry.

The third type of cavalry were called dragoons. They were
essentially soldiers who used their horses to convey them to a
suitable tactical position on the battlefield, whereupon they
usually dismounted and continued the fight on foot. They
were virtually mounted infantry, thereby foreshadowing the
role of the horsed soldier in the American Civil War and the
South African War, and were much looked down on by the
cuirassiers and hussars. "How absurd is the training of our
dragoons!" wrote Rogniat. "When mounted they are taught
that no infantry can resist the impetuosity of their charges;
when drilling on foot they are taught to consider themselves
invulnerable against cavalry. It is from these causes they are
despised by both horse and foot." [5]

Not every European army profited by the example of Frederick's cavalry. At Minden in 1759 six regiments of British infantry—"the unsurpassable six"—accompanied by two Hanoverian battalions, actually charged and routed the eighty-

[5] Field Marshal Sir Evelyn Wood, *Achievements of Cavalry* (George
Bell, London, 1897), p. 243.

three squadrons of French cavalry drawn up to receive them.
"I never thought," said Marshal Contades, the French commander, "to see a single line of infantry break through three
lines of cavalry ranked in order of battle, and tumble them
to ruin." Nor would they have done so, however great their
gallantry, had the cavalry been Prussian, and under the command of Seydlitz.

A rot set in after Seydlitz' death. Frederick was well aware
of the state of affairs, but he could no longer spare the time
to set matters right himself, and he lacked an inspired lieutenant to help him. An address which he delivered to cavalry
officers at Potsdam shows how deep the evil had gone.

> Gentlemen [he said] I am entirely dissatisfied with the
> cavalry; the regiments are completely out of hand; there
> is no accuracy, no order. The men ride like tailors; I beg
> that this may not occur again, and that each of you will
> pay more attention to his duty, particularly to the horse-
> manship.
>
> But I know how things go. The captains think only of
> making money out of their squadrons, and the lieutenants
> how to get most leave. You think I am not up to your
> dodges, but I know all, and will recapitulate them. Tomor-
> row, when you start on your march back to your garrisons,
> before you are ten miles away, the squadron commander
> will ask his sergeant-major whether any of the men live in
> the vicinity, and the sergeant-major will reply, "Yes, sir,
> there are 'Muller' and 'Meyer' who live quite close here,
> and would be glad to get furlough." "Very well, then," the
> captain will say, "we can save their pay. Send the names
> to me tonight, and they shall all have it." And so it goes
> on every march. The subalterns get leave to visit their
> friends, and the captain arrives at his garrison with half
> the squadron mounted, leading the horses of the other half,
> like a band of disreputable Cossacks.
>
> Then, when the season for riding drill comes on, the
> captain sends for the sergeant-major and says, "I have an
> appointment this morning at so-and-so; tell the first-lieu-

tenant to take the rides." So the sergeant-major goes to
the senior subaltern, and gives him the message, and the
latter says, "What! the captain will be away! then I am off
hunting; tell the second-lieutenant to take the men." And
the second-lieutenant, who is still probably in bed, says,
"What! both of them away! then I will stay where I am;
I was up till three this morning at a dance; tell the
cornet I am ill, and he must take the rides." Finally the
cornet remarks, "Look here, sergeant-major, what is the
good of my standing out there in the cold? You know all
about it much better than I do. You go and take them."
    And so it goes on, and what must be the end of it all?
What can I do with such cavalry before the enemy? I tell
you I think so much of the importance of your arm, that
I expect more from a lieutenant of cavalry than from a
major of infantry. . . . Now go; attend to your duties
better; and don't let me have to speak to you like this
again.[6]

It was indeed a far cry from the great days of Seydlitz, but
at least the Prussian cavalry were spared the even worse evils
which afflicted the British cavalry. Regiments were usually at
skeleton strength and scattered round the country in small
detachments. The 5th Royal Irish Dragoons, which had captured a set of French kettledrums at Blenheim and destroyed
the French regiment of Picardy at Ramillies, came home from
the wars only to be dispersed in troops all over southern Ireland,
where they languished for eighty years to the detriment of
their efficiency and discipline. The conditions were such that it
was virtually impossible for commanding officers to maintain
proper discipline and train their men, but there were many
officers, like Surgeon Smet of the 8th Light Dragoons, who
found the life much to their taste.

    Cavalry corps in Ireland were extremely select [wrote
    Smet] as from the very low establishment it was in the
    power of Colonels of choosing a number of young gentle-
    men of distinction who might wish to get a commission,

[6] Maude, *op. cit.*, pp. 117-118.

and who all could easily afford to add a hundred pounds a year to their [the colonels'] pay. The warrants were also purchased at a high price, often by the sons of gentlemen for as much as 500 guineas. The privates were always young men well recommended and whose connections were known. Two thirds of the officers had in general leave of absence for the greater part of the year. Many of the dragoons were on furlough, who were sometimes allowed to take their horses to their parents' houses, and generally wore their own clothes with their friends. The horses were a considerable time of the year at grass, when the proportion of the furlough men were usually greater than at other times; but the whole corps assembled at headquarters once a year and were kept together for a couple of months to perfect themselves in its evolutions preparatory to its being reviewed, after which most of the officers were again indulged in leave of absence, many of the men allowed to go on furlough, and several troops detached to out quarters. Such a service had many attractions.[7]

A pleasant enough life no doubt, but hardly soldiering. One can only wonder how such a service was able to produce its Wolfes and Wellingtons, conquer Canada, and establish British rule in India. In Austria, too, the story was the same. "Even in 1769," wrote Mack, "the cavalry could not ride, could not manage to control their horses. Not a single squadron could keep its dressing at a gallop, and before they had gone fifty yards at least ten out of forty horses in the first rank would break out to the front." [8]

Much of the trouble stemmed from a failure to comprehend the simple fact that cavalry could never exert any influence on the battlefield unless the soldiers were able to control their horses. Frederick the Great never lost sight of the paramount requirement for good horsemanship, and one of his earliest regulations laid down that "the officers must see that their

[7] W. T. Willcox, *History of the Fifth (Royal Irish) Lancers* (Arthur Doubleday, London, 1908), p. 133.
[8] Maude, *op. cit.*

men ride continually, so that each man can handle his horse by itself, turn and twist it and be completely its master."

No one who has found himself being carried away at a gallop by an apparently uncontrollable horse would choose at that moment to be encumbered by a heavy sword or lance; under such circumstances one's entire endeavor is to remain seated in the saddle and to regain control over a plunging and seemingly demented animal. Yet most cavalry troopers of the eighteenth century, however incompetent their horsemanship, were loaded down with accouterments, trussed in the tightest of uniforms, and thrown into battle with little or no hope of controlling their mounts. It is little wonder that most charges, apart from those carried out by Seydlitz and Zeiten, were made at the trot, and even so the saddles emptied rapidly.

When reading about famous cavalry charges, like those of the Royal Scots Greys at Waterloo and the Light Brigade at Balaklava, we often forget how much of the success of those charges depended on the skill of the soldiers as riders. This is particularly so when we are considering that period in history when the horse was the principal means of locomotion; men rode horses, or traveled in carts or carriages pulled by horses. And yet, although the ordinary man in those days was far more intimately acquainted with the horse than is the case today, it by no means follows that he was any better equipped to control a horse under the exceptional conditions of battle. The horsed soldier still required training, not only in his weapons but also in the handling of his principal weapon, the horse. Those cavalry leaders who understood this, and were prepared to teach their soldiers to ride correctly, usually won their battles, but they were in a minority.

Horsemastership was also neglected, and the problem of keeping horses fit was never fully mastered. Cromwell's troopers marched from Stamford to Gainsborough in two days, a distance of sixty-five miles by the route they took, and then fought two sharp actions which involved a further thirty miles across country. On another occasion his cavalry covered 250 miles in nine days, and it would be fair to assume that each horse was carrying 250 pounds; nor did the horses of those days compare in size with modern cavalry chargers, seldom exceeding 14.2 hands in height. Such feats of endurance, repeated on innumerable occasions by the cavalry of most armies, inevitably took a heavy toll of the horses, and in the later stages of a campaign the proportion of raw remounts to trained horses increased considerably. The result was decreased efficiency in battle and a decline in the importance of the mounted arm.

Nowhere is this better exemplified than in the case of the French cavalry immediately before the French Revolution. Horse breeding was neglected, the cavalry appeared only for ceremonial duties, and the officers were far more interested in the minutiae of dress than in the tactical handling of their commands. So indifferent was the French horseflesh that even as late as 1807 the dragoons of Napoleon's cavalry were mounted on 14-hand ponies, and their horsemanship was usually indifferent and frequently bad. No attention seems to have been given to the example of Frederick the Great, who had devoted as much thought to the breeding of his horses as to the training of those who were to ride them.

A lack of sufficient horses of suitable size, coupled with insufficient training in the riding school, may account for the fact that most of the cavalry charges made by Napoleon's cavalry were made at the trot. A German witness of the charge of the French heavy cavalry at Eckmühl in 1809 wrote of this action:

> Meanwhile the cuirassier divisions had followed at a trot, and met the attack of the Austrian Reserve Cavalry in so brilliant a fashion that the Infantry of Lannes' corps halted to cheer them . . . the cuirassiers laid special stress on riding boot to boot, and never moved at a faster pace than a trot.[9]

In his early days Napoleon preferred to use his cavalry more for reconnaissance and pursuit than for shock action. Most of his early battles were won by infantry. Marengo was an exception, and it was not until after Austerlitz in 1805 that the French cavalry really came into their own. The greatest artilleryman of all time then began to mass his batteries to smash

[9] Maude, *op. cit.*, p. 132.

a hole through the enemy infantry, and great masses of cavalry were held ready to charge home and complete the rout. Few other armies have contained such a brilliant number of cavalry leaders: Lasalle, Kellermann, Sainte-Croix, Colbert, and Montbrun of the Light Chasseurs. But the greatest of them all was the innkeeper's son who carved for himself a kingdom with his sword and then died before a firing squad: Joachim Murat, a Gascon of Gascons, who had formerly been in the 21st Chasseurs, who married Caroline Bonaparte, and who led one of the greatest cavalry pursuits in history, after the Battle of Jena in 1806. In twenty-four days he led his squadrons five hundred miles in pursuit of the routed Prussians, and halted only when he reached the Baltic at Lübeck. The numerous defeats of the past at the hands of the Prussian cavalry had been avenged; the French cavalry was the best in Europe.[10]

The year 1800, with the brilliant handling by Kellermann of his cavalry brigade at Marengo, saw the resurgence of the mounted arm. It was to reach its peak on the field of Mars-la-Tour in 1870, and then gradually decline as the machine gun and barbed wire came into their own, but it was during the last one hundred and fifty years of the horse's appearance on the battlefield that some of the best-known cavalry actions in history took place. The charge of the Royal Scots Greys at Waterloo has been immortalized by Lady Butler in her painting "Scotland for Ever!" The Light Brigade at Balaklava have had their gallantry inscribed in the poetry of Tennyson. The "Death Ride" of the 7th Cuirassiers and 16th Uhlans at Mars-la-Tour is one of the best-known events in German military history, just as the stand of Custer's 7th Cavalry at the Little Big Horn is one of the most cherished stories in American military history. The charge of the 21st Empress of India's Lancers at Omdurman, when the routed dervishes were driven from the field and Gordon was avenged, has been enshrined forever in our literature by the pen of Lieutenant Winston

---

[10] It is interesting to note that Field Marshal Montgomery's army group ended its advance across Germany at Lübeck. Once again the cavalry was in the van, but on that occasion it was mounted in tanks and armored cars instead of on horses.

Churchill, detached from the 4th Queen's Own Hussars, who charged with the 21st Lancers that day.

There was something about the cavalry charge which appealed to the imagination, no less to the man in the street than to the artist and the poet, and even when the value of the horse on the battlefield became suspect, there were still those who refused to look facts in the face. In this atomic age, when the shadow of the mushroom cloud haunts every thinking man and woman, it seems incredible that intelligent men could have been arguing the respective merits of sword and lance less than fifty years ago! Yet during the first decade of this century the pages of military journals were filled with precisely that argument: Should the lance replace the sword as the cavalryman's main weapon, or should both lance and sword give way to the rifle? Should the glittering cuirassiers, hussars, and lancers follow the example of the uncouth Boers of South Africa, and the scarcely less uncouth Confederate and Federal cavalry of the American Civil War, and discard the shock action of cold steel for the less glamorous but more workmanlike role of mounted riflemen?

In every army there were those who simply could not contemplate the idea of using cavalry to fight on foot. General Rosser, writing of the employment of cavalry during the Civil War, maintained that "the cavalry soldier should *never* be dismounted to fight if you expect him to ride over masses of infantry, and should be educated to believe that nothing can withstand a well-executed cavalry charge." [11] This view was endorsed by Field Marshal Sir Evelyn Wood, who formulated the doctrine "Cavalrymen should never be dismounted to fight when there is suitable ground for their employment on horseback."

There were, of course, a few heretics. Among them was Colonel G. F. R. Henderson, the professor at the British Staff College whose biography of Stonewall Jackson is one of the great military classics. He believed that "the horseman of the American war is the model of the efficient cavalryman." Henderson's detailed study of the Civil War convinced him that

[11] Wood, *op. cit.*, p. 246.

the increased firepower of infantry and artillery had reduced
the value of cavalry as a "shock arm," although he considered
that cavalry still had a valuable part to play both in reconnaissance and in pursuit. Anything that Henderson said was
heard with respect, but it was not necessarily accepted as
gospel.

It would be true to say that the cavalryman's main weapon
throughout history has been the sword—*l'arme blanche*. The
lance had its day, and there was a time when the cavalryman
first halted to fire his pistol before drawing his sword and
charging home. Yet there were few at the beginning of this century who disputed the necessity of the sword as part of the
cavalryman's equipment; however, there were those who held
the view that the sword should only be complementary to the
rifle or carbine, while others maintained that the sword should
be a cutting rather than a thrusting weapon. The British cavalry,
like most European cavalry, were taught to charge with the
point of the sword, whereas Oriental armies sharpened their
tulwars so that they would "split a hair." Sergeant Forbes-
Mitchell of the 93rd Highlanders, in his *Reminiscences of the
Great Mutiny*, recounts the story of a British cavalry regiment
in action against the Sikhs (probably the 14th Light Dragoons
at Ramnaggar):

> The Sikhs wore voluminous thick *puggries* round their
> heads, which our blunt swords were powerless to cut
> through, and each horseman had also a buffalo-hide shield
> slung on his back. They evidently knew that the British
> swords were blunt and useless, so they kept their horses
> still and met the British charge by laying flat on their
> horses' necks, with their heads protected by the thick
> turban and their backs by the shields; immediately the
> British soldiers passed through their ranks the Sikhs
> swooped round on them and struck them back-handed
> with their sharp, curved swords, in several instances cutting
> our cavalrymen in two. In one case a British officer was
> hewn in two by a back-handed stroke which cut right
> through an ammunition pouch, cleaving the pistol bullets

right through the pouch and belt, severing the officer's backbone, and cutting his heart in two from behind. It was the same in the Balaclava charge, both with the Heavy, and the Light Brigade. Their swords were too straight, and so blunt that they would not cut through the thick coats and sheepskin caps of the Russians, so that many of our men struck with the hilts at the faces of the enemy as more effective than attempting to cut with their blunt blades.[12]

It can be argued of course that the evidence of such a witness, a noncommissioned officer in the infantry, is hardly sufficient evidence on which to condemn the British cavalry sword, and it is cited here only as an example of the controversy which did exist. It must even have outlived World War I, because as late as 1937 there was a paragraph in the Mobilization Instructions of my regiment which read, "On receipt of the orders to mobilise, all swords will be sharpened"! This may seem the less surprising if one remembers that it was not all that long before 1937 that the time-honored but complicated drill movement known as "Forming square to repel cavalry" was removed from the British Drill Manual.

Second only to the sword as the cavalryman's weapon *par excellence* was the lance—indeed there were those who considered the lance to be the queen of weapons. Its origins go back into the mists of history, and it has been carried in battle by the horsemen of nearly every nation. We read in Doughty's *Arabia Deserta* of the Bedouin gallants who galloped into battle with their long lances pointing towards the enemy, and it was the Polish lancers of John Sobieski who saved Vienna from the Turk. From then onwards every lancer must either be a Pole or dress like one. Since there were not enough Poles to provide every country with its lancers, armies were compelled to raise their own, but so far as they could they dressed and equipped them on the Polish model. Napoleon had his Polish lancers, as well as a Polish marshal in Poniatowski, and they

[12] *The Cavalry Journal* (Royal United Service Institution, London), January, 1907, p. 76.

rendered him good service at Somo-Sierra in Spain, and else-where. In Germany the 19th Würtemberg Uhlans were direct descendants of Polish lancers enrolled in the Würtemberg service, and the regiment survived until 1918. Prussian uhlans and French *lanciers* charged against each other at Mars-la-Tour and Gravelotte in 1870, and in 1890 the lance was adopted as the principal weapon of the German cavalry. The British cav-alry did not adopt the lance until after the Napoleonic Wars, but in 1816 several regiments of light dragoons were converted to lancers. One of these, the 16th The Queen's Lancers, was the first British cavalry regiment to charge with the lance in battle—at Bhurtpore in India in 1825. The United States cav-alry, alone among Western armies, never really adopted the lance. The German cavalry regiments of the Reichswehr took up the lance again for a short time after World War I, but soon afterwards discarded it forevermore.

There have been few more gorgeously dressed soldiers in all the history of armies than the lancers of the nineteenth century. The lance cap was modeled on the Polish style and was even called a *chapka*, the Polish for hat. The short, double-breasted jacket of scarlet or blue was known similarly as the *ulanka*, and in the German and Austrian armies the lancer regiments were called uhlans. To the glittering uniforms, waving plumes, and splendidly caparisoned saddlecloths there was added the color of the waving lance pennants.

Lance pennants were originally small flags fastened just be-low the steel tips of the lances. They bore the coat of arms of the commander, and were intended to serve as a means of identification on the field of battle. Under Frederick the Great each squadron had a different colored pennant, and this devel-oped further until lance pennants denoted the national colors of an army, red and white for St. George of England, and black and yellow for Austria. Among the cavalry of the German em-pire the effect was particularly striking; there were the black and white pennants of the Prussian uhlans, the blue and white of the Bavarians, the green and white of the Saxons, and so on. Heraldic designs were imprinted on the national colors—a black eagle on some pennants, the prancing horse of Brunswick, and the skull and crossbones of the "Death's Head" hussar regiments. The pennants were usually swallow-tailed, like cavalry guidons, although in some armies they were square.

If there can be beauty in weapons of war, then there can be little doubt that the sword and lance win the palm. But they became obsolescent from the moment that man first invented gunpowder, although like Charles II they were "an unconscionable time in dying." Their fate was finally sealed when Hiram Maxim invented the machine gun, but there were still those who could not read the writing on the wall. In America there was more readiness to accept the fact, since by 1861 fire had already become the predominant factor in battle. Infantry correctly disposed had little to fear from sword and lance, as was proved on numerous occasions during the Civil War, and both the Confederate and Federal armies tended more and more to arm their cavalry with rifle or carbine and to employ the horseman as a mounted rifleman. The cavalry of Stuart and Sheridan, Forrest and Custer, achieved their greatest successes when carrying out the other historic roles of the mounted arm—raids far behind the enemy lines like Wilson's through Alabama and Georgia in March, 1865; pursuit; and harassing a retreating enemy as Custer harassed Lee before Appomattox.

The lessons learned by the American cavalry leaders during the Civil War were less evident at the time than they are today. European cavalrymen pointed out that the closely wooded terrain in Virginia made it almost impossible to employ cavalry in mass; at Brandy Station, scene of the most important shock action by mounted troops, the largest clear space was under eight hundred yards in extent, and the cavalry was compelled to charge in close column of squadrons; it was contended, therefore, that what applied in North America did not necessarily have the same relevance in Europe. To some extent this point of view was reinforced by the success of the German cavalry during the Franco-Prussian War.

The relative failure of the British cavalry regiments when fighting the Boers on the South African veldt and the Russian defeats during the Russo-Japanese War in no way convinced cavalrymen that the day of the horse was over. The armies that took the field in 1914 were largely dependent on the horse for their means of transportation forward of railhead, and they contained a considerable number of cavalry divisions. Even the experience of Von der Marwitz' cavalry in Belgium on August 12, 1914, when they hurled themselves in vain against barbed wire and machine guns, failed to shake the generals. Right up till the day when the war ended they still nursed the delusion that one day "the cavalry would go through." Only in Palestine did the British cavalry's success against the Turks offer some crumb of comfort for the supporters of the school of shock action.

It was in some ways a tragedy that Allenby was so successful in Palestine. That big, bluff, bullying cavalry general of the old school was the last commander to win a campaign by the bold use of horsed cavalry, but by doing so he put back the military clock by nearly twenty years and may have contributed indirectly to the defeat of the British and French armies in 1940. The British, who can lay fair claim to have invented the tank as far back as 1915, were never solidly behind their invention. There were at least as many generals who opposed the supersession of horsed cavalry by the tank as there were supporters for the school of thought propagated by Fuller and Liddell Hart. And while the British General Staff argued over the merits of their invention, the Germans took advantage of it.

It is difficult today to recall the bitter controversies which raged from 1920 to 1935 over the rival merits of horse and tank; it is no easier to understand the arguments that the supporters of the battleship employed against the advocates of air power. Not every soldier who believed profoundly that horsed cavalry still had a part to play in war was a fool, any more than every sailor who argued that the battleship could defeat the bomber was a knave. Convictions were held honestly, and they were backed up by arguments which may not have faced the facts, but which were—to the authors at least—founded on the most reasonable of premises.

The protagonists of horsed cavalry failed to comprehend the fact that the vastly increased firepower of modern weapons had deprived the old-style cavalry of their role as a fighting arm.

Horses could no longer be used to convey weapons from point to point around the battlefield; they were far too vulnerable and provided too easy a target. At best they had a role in reconnaissance, but even then they were less efficient in most types of terrain than the automobile and the airplane. They could not cover the same distance in the same time, and they were severely limited by the need for water and forage at frequent intervals. It all seems very obvious to us today, but hindsight is more common than foresight.

Not all soldiers wore blinkers, however, even though they still paid homage to tradition. General Douglas MacArthur, in his 1935 report as chief of staff of the United States army, stated his conviction that warfare of the 1914-1918 type was out of date:

> The protective power of modern weapons is so great that where these are strongly and deliberately organised for defence they practically assure invulnerability. Only through surprise action can collision with the enemy's prepared positions be avoided, and to gain surprise nothing is more important than superiority in mobility. The constant trend in the modern world is towards greater and greater speed. Any army that fails to keep in step with this trend is, far from making necessary progress towards modernization, going steadily and irrevocably backward.

The horse was just not fast enough.

The year when MacArthur wrote those words is significant. In that same year an as yet unknown German soldier had been appointed to command the 2nd Panzer Division at Würzburg, having just completed two years as chief of staff of the Armored Troops Command. His name was Heinz Guderian, and before he finally laid down his arms he had led his new-style cavalry as far west as the Channel, and as far east as the outer suburbs of Moscow. Guderian, like MacArthur, had no doubts about the future of cavalry; it was only the mount which would have to be changed. The spirit and the characteristics of the mounted arm were needed as much as ever.

There were still many who remained unconvinced by the

arguments of the exponents of armor. In 1927, the British
Defense Budget made provision for £607,000 for forage, but
only £72,000 for gasoline. Six years later the British army's order
of battle showed 20 horsed regiments in the regular army, 16
in the territorial army, and 21 in the Indian army. There were
exactly 4 regiments of tanks. When, in 1936, the Secretary of
State for War informed the House of Commons that it had
been decided to mechanize eight cavalry regiments, he felt con-
strained to apologize for such a monstrous decision. "It is," he
said, "like asking a great musical performer to throw away his
violin and to devote himself in future to the gramophone."

The horsed cavalry "lobby" was powerful and it had sentiment on its side. The horse is, after all, one of the most beautiful of God's creatures, but not even the most ardent devotee of
armor could claim the same for the tank.

Nor was this ostrich-head-in-the-sand attitude peculiar to the
British. In every army there was a reluctance to face the military facts of life, and, as Guderian makes clear, even in Germany the development of the *Panzertruppen* had to be carried
out in the teeth of the most violent opposition. Much of the
trouble stemmed from an inability to examine the problem from
first principles, and these related to the historic fact that the
cavalryman was a soldier who fights mounted in order to perform his two classic roles of reconnaissance and shock action.
Deprived of the ability to fight mounted owing to the vulner-
ability of the horse, the horseman had no longer any *raison
d'être*; he would either have to exchange his horse for a tank
or airplane or else quit the battlefield.

This thesis, proclaimed day in and day out during the inter-
war years by the supporters of the tank, was proved beyond
doubt in Poland and France during 1939 and 1940. There were
no longer any doubters, and the last British regular cavalry
regiments to be mechanized were the Royal Scots Greys and
Royal Dragoons in 1941; the United States cavalry had given
up their horses even earlier. The Allied armies which defeated
Hitler still employed some horses, but they were used mainly for
transportation or for reconnaissance in hilly terrain. General
Patton is on record as saying that there would have been a use

for horsed cavalry in certain parts of Italy, and that gallant cavalryman even went so far as to suggest that a limited number of horsed regiments should be retained in the postwar army. How much this statement was inspired by sentiment and how much by wartime experience is hard to say, but the one thing certain is that the United States Third Army could never have advanced so fast, nor so far, had it been horsed instead of tanked. (This refers, of course, to its means of conveyance and not to its physical condition.)

It is, however, a historical fact that both the German and the Russian armies employed horsed cavalry during World War II. The 1st Cavalry Division formed part of Guderian's 2nd Panzer Group during the invasion of Russia in the summer of 1941, and the horsemen succeeded in keeping up with the *Panzers*; when it was withdrawn from his command, Guderian was sorry to see it go, but eventually it went the way of all other German cavalry formations and was mechanized.[13]

The Russians were the only army to employ cavalry on a large scale. There were thirty-five cavalry divisions in the Red army in 1942, and two cavalry corps played an important part in the counteroffensive to free Moscow in December, 1941. Later, in November, 1942, the ring round the German Sixth Army outside Stalingrad was closed by Soviet cavalrymen, and there were three cavalry corps involved in the final Russian advance into Germany. Russia is probably one of the few countries where horsed cavalry still has a part to play in war, but then only when the state of the ground is such that wheels and tracks cannot turn because of the mud or intense cold.

[13] In 1943 the Germans raised several squadrons of cavalry to operate in the rear areas against Russian partisans, and eventually the equivalent of nearly two cavalry divisions were in existence for this purpose. It is interesting to note that the officers, noncommissioned officers, and troopers of these regiments were hand-picked—and one of the qualifications required was sympathy with the "resistance movement" against Hitler! Finally, after the plot against Hitler had failed, many of the more senior officers fell victims to Himmler and the Gestapo, while the more junior officers were scattered with their squadrons between Russia and Italy. One of them finally surrendered with his squadron to the British 78th Division in Austria in 1945; an interesting example of a cavalry officer who began and ended World War II with horses, although in between he had also served with tanks.

The only horses remaining in most armies today are retained for either ceremonial purposes or pack transport. The glittering squadrons of the Life Guards and The Blues, which escort Queen Elizabeth to the opening of Parliament, are all that remain of the horsed squadrons which once lent so much color to the British army. Dragoon guards, dragoons, hussars, and lancers now drive into battle in tanks or armored cars, their sabretaches replaced by sadly prosaic map cases, and their waving plumes and gold lace by greasy overalls and berets. The same is true of France, the United States, Germany, and almost everywhere else. There is still horsed cavalry in the Turkish army, probably in the Chinese, and possibly in the Russian; but to all intents and purposes the horse has left the battlefield. All of us who love the horse cannot but rejoice that this is the case.

Perhaps the disappearance of the horse from the battlefield marks more than just the end of an era; it may even mark the time when man began his headlong slide down the slope to self-destruction. Filth, disease, cruelty, and suffering have always been inseparable from war, but never has this been so universally true as today. War in all its horror now embraces combatant and noncombatant alike. It was no more pleasant to die from a sword or lance thrust than from a bomb or nuclear radiation, but killing was more selective in the past. Custer's men who fell at the Little Big Horn died barbarously, but at least their women and children were spared. The same is no longer true.

Such glamour as ever existed on the battlefield has completely disappeared, as has much of the chivalry which once helped to redeem the harshness of war. That code of chivalry came down to us from medieval times, and it owed much to the code of warfare which the Arabs brought with them out of the desert, and which the Crusaders copied. By that code, which until only a few years ago still bound the Bedouins of central Arabia in their tribal wars, war was considered to be the most honorable pursuit open to men, but women, children, and the stranger within the tent were sacrosanct. Any man who laid hands on them, even by accident and in the heat of combat, was an outcast. It was a noble code, but it has no relevance in total war.

Men first began to fight mounted far back in the mists of antiquity. They drove chariots and rode elephants, and then they improved their horsemanship and fought from horseback. For thousands of years they scouted ahead of armies, raided far behind the enemy's lines, pursued the routed, or charged to capture the guns. They rode in loose order in individual combat, or knee to knee in all the irresistible might of the controlled charge. When trained and led by a cavalry leader of genius, like Cromwell or Seydlitz or Murat, they wheeled about the battlefield in lines of magnificent precision; or when less well trained they came on "at a pretty round trot" in close squadron columns.

There was something about the cavalryman which is difficult to put into words, but the French have translated it best as *panache*; it means the boundless self-confidence, the gaiety and swagger, and, above all, the comradeship, which is fostered by the horse. Cavalrymen have always thought themselves a breed apart, and it was not for nothing that the English cavalry during the Peninsular War used to assert that the main purpose of cavalry was to give tone to what otherwise would be simply a vulgar brawl. The horse has gone, but the spirit has survived in the armored cavalrymen of today. Long may it remain!

The years which lie between Napoleon's victory at Marengo in June, 1800, and the great days in 1918 when Allenby's troopers went thundering across the Plain of Esdraelon in pursuit of the Turks saw the last, splendid flowering of horsed cavalry. Some of their exploits are told in the pages which follow, but they are only a few among the many. For them all, told and untold, great and small, the trumpets have sounded in Valhalla.

CHAPTER THREE

Marengo

June 14, 1800

"A moi la peine: aux illustres le profit."

FRANÇOIS-ETIENNE KELLERMANN—count, then marquis, and finally duke—was a little, nimble man, dark-complexioned and with a cast in one eye which gave him a furtive, sly look. He was also the finest leader of heavy cavalry who ever drew saber in the service of Napoleon Bonaparte, and if Marengo was Napoleon's "Crowning Mercy," it was to Kellermann that he was indebted for snatching victory from defeat. On that blazing June day in 1800, when all seemed lost for France, Kellermann's brilliant charge saved the day, altered the course of history, and cleared the way for the former Citizen Bonaparte to crown himself as emperor of the French.

Kellermann was the son of an old hussar officer who deserted Louis XVI to throw in his lot with the Revolution, and who, according to Goethe, changed the history of Europe by holding firm at Valmy. There, in 1792, the ragged and ill-disciplined soldiers of France held the passes of the Argonne against the armies of Prussia and Austria; much to everyone's surprise, and despite the Prussian cannonade, the *sans-culottes* stood their ground. France was saved thereby for *liberté, fraternité, et egalité*, and also, incidentally, for the Terror. When Napoleon created eighteen marshals of France in 1804, the elder Kellermann received his baton and was made Duke of Valmy. His son succeeded him in the title, but a marshal's baton always eluded him. Napoleon's favors were only grudgingly given to the man who had saved the day at Marengo.

For Napoleon was never disposed to share his triumphs, and Marengo least of any of them. "I am, and always will be, for the French much more the man of Marengo than that of Jena and Friedland," he said on his return from Tilsit; and when he lay dying on St. Helena they covered the body of the greatest of all Great Captains with the shabby blue overcoat he had worn at Marengo. It was a battle that could never be shared with anyone.

In no other period in history has genuine military talent enjoyed such opportunities as those which existed under Napoleon. The sons of masons, peasants, innkeepers, and barrel-coopers rose to become marshals, princes, and dukes, and all that they achieved was due to their swords and the military genius of their master. When such opportunities existed for those without influence, how much greater must have been the opportunities for professional soldiers and for the sons of professional soldiers, such as Kellermann. That he never rose to the highest rank was owing more to faults in his own character than to any lack of military ability.

He was born in 1770 and by the age of fifteen he had acquired a commission in his father's regiment, the Hussars Colonel-General. Not long afterwards the French Revolution burst upon a horrified Europe, but young Kellermann did not follow the example of so many of his contemporaries and serve his apprenticeship in the Revolutionary Wars. Instead he exerted his influence to obtain the appointment of additional military attaché in the young republic across the Atlantic, and

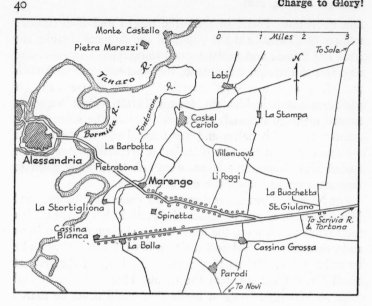

for three inglorious years he vegetated in Washington. There, step by step, he rose in the military hierarchy without hearing a shot fired in anger, until by 1793 he had attained the rank of lieutenant colonel of infantry. His battalion, which he had never seen, formed part of the Army of the Alps, and the general in chief was his father, the victor of Valmy. Kellermann was twenty-three.

This was the moment when he judged it advisable to return to France and join his father's staff as aide-de-camp. His timing was bad. France was racked with fear and intrigue, Robespierre and Saint-Just were in control of the Committee of Public Safety, and the margin between suspicion and the guillotine was narrow indeed. The elder Kellermann only narrowly escaped with his head, but he was sent to prison as a traitor to the regime. His son hastily resigned his commission and sought to prove his loyalty by enlisting as a private soldier in a newly raised regiment of hussars.

By 1795 France was sickened of the Terror, and Robespierre was devoured by the monster he had created. The survivors

emerged from obscurity, blinking in the daylight and congrat-
ulating themselves on their deliverance, as the Germans did
after Himmler. Two of the lucky ones were Kellermann and his
son; the elder went to command the Army of the Alps, and
the younger, restored to his rank of lieutenant colonel, resumed
his appointment as aide-de-camp to his father. It had been
touch and go, but they had survived.

The year of the Army of Italy was 1796—the year of the
flowering of Napoleon's genius, the year of Arcole, of Mantua,
and of Lodi. Young Kellermann took part in the Italian campaign as chief of staff of the cavalry division, and in the following year he displayed such gallantry at the passage of the Piave
and Tagliamento that he was selected to escort the captured
Austrian standards to Paris. Perhaps he was lucky to have been
on detached duty at a time when Napoleon was planning the
expedition to Egypt—luck is one of the most important factors
in war and it cannot be measured beforehand. At all events
Kellermann did not accompany Napoleon to the Pyramids but
remained in Italy, where he fell ill with *"une violente neural-
gie."* He was now a brigadier general and just twenty-nine.

Napoleon was in Egypt. His aim was the elimination of British influence in the East, and only sea power thwarted him.
His hopes were blown to pieces by Nelson's guns at Abukir
Bay. Thenceforward he was master of Egypt but a prisoner of
his ambition, and while he lingered in Cairo conditions went
from bad to worse in Paris. While the politicians squabbled and
intrigued, the armies of Austria and Russia advanced towards
the frontiers of France. As was to happen again in 1870 and
1940, a curious *malaise* had afflicted the most gifted, talented,
and cultured of all the races of Europe.

Napoleon deserted his army in August, 1799, slipped through
the British blockade, and returned to Paris. There, on the 18th
Brumaire,[1] he overthrew the Directory, replaced it by the Con-
sulate, and had himself named first consul. Mirabeau's proph-
ecy was fulfilled and the Deputies were thrown out by bayonets;
they were followed by a military dictatorship as harsh as any
that Europe was to see until Hitler's brown shirts goose-stepped

[1] November 9, 1799.

through the streets of Berlin and the world was once again sent marching to the drums.

It is not true that all soldiers are nonpolitical animals, and we have no need to go back so far in history as Napoleon to find the proof of this. Yet it is probably true to say that soldiers as a breed are reluctant to intervene in politics so long as they have confidence in their political masters; it is only when intrigue and wirepulling get beyond all bearing that the soldiers step in and take a hand in politics. By their action they may save the nation, but in doing so they sow the seeds for their own destruction, for loyalty is the most cardinal of all the military virtues. Napoleon's coup of the 18th Brumaire has had repercussions which have not been without their effect over a century and a half later.

During that winter of 1799 the task seemed clear enough. Less than three years previously France had been supreme, her frontiers secure, and northern Italy was a French satrapy. All this and more had been cast aside by the futilities of the politicians. Austria had regained her mastery in Italy, and her armies were advancing up the Danube towards the Rhine. Nelson's fleet cruised off the coasts and hamstrung all trade, while far away in Russia a colossus was stirring. A French army under Masséna was besieged in Genoa, unable to break out to landward through the Austrians, and denied relief by water because the Royal Navy under Admiral Keith commanded the Ligurian Sea.

Almost the first task of Napoleon as first consul was to assemble an army to relieve Masséna. It was vital that no inkling of this intention should reach the Austrians, and so the force was named the Army of the Reserve. Dijon was its headquarters, and as part of the cover plan, Berthier was nominated as the commander although the driving force came from Napoleon himself. Kellermann was appointed to command a brigade of heavy cavalry in this Army of the Reserve.

Meanwhile conditions went from bad to worse in Genoa. Masséna knew of Napoleon's intention to relieve the garrison, but the blockade was total and was causing great suffering to the civilian population. All dogs and cats were killed and eaten within the first few weeks of the siege, and soon rats were being sold at prices that only the very rich could afford to pay. Nettles were worth their weight in gold, and sparrows made a fortune for those clever enough to snare them. For most of the population, soldiers and civilians alike, the daily ration was a handful of flour mixed with starch, sawdust, and linseed. Disease was rife and there was rioting in the streets. April went by, and then May, and each dawn Masséna mounted to the ramparts and looked anxiously towards the Ligurian Hills, through which the relieving columns must debouch. They never came.

On June 6, 1800, Masséna could do no more. He surrendered. The city had been defended so gallantly that the French were granted unusually honorable terms; they were permitted to march out with all the honors of war, retaining their arms and baggage. Masséna and his army lived to fight another day, but even so, Napoleon never really forgave him for surrendering. Only a few more days and Genoa could have been relieved.

The Army of the Reserve had left its cantonments in May, and by forced march had entered the north Italian plain by way of the St. Bernard Pass. By June 6, the day that Masséna surrendered, the French were marching across the Plain of Lombardy on their way from Milan to Genoa. In one brilliant strategic stroke Napoleon had severed the long lines of communication between the Austrians and Vienna and had turned the tables on the Austrian army which was besieging Genoa. It was now the turn of the Austrians to be cut off from all reinforcements and from their arsenals. The Alps had been crossed on May 20, and Milan had been captured on June 2, but it was too late to save Genoa.

Napoleon was thirty-one and Kellermann was a year younger. Baron Melas, the Austrian commander in chief, was seventy. There were only two alternatives open to him; either he could give battle on the open Plain of Lombardy or he could retreat on Genoa and rely on the Royal Navy to take him off by sea. His mind was made up for him by the defeat of one wing of his army at Montebello by Lannes, and by the loss of his fortress at Piacenza to Murat's cavalry. He decided to fall back on Genoa. Napoleon followed him.

Neither Napoleon nor Melas used their cavalry properly and neither had the remotest idea of the other's intentions. By June 13 the Austrians were flooding through the fortress town of Alessandria on their way to the passes through the Ligurian Hills, and Napoleon's advance guards, thirsty, weary, and caked with dust, were less than ten miles behind them. Napoleon was convinced that the Austrians were in full retreat, and because of this conception he flung out his divisions to cut off the escape routes through the hills.

Napoleon described a battle as "a dramatic action, which has its beginning, its middle, and its end." There is no better way of describing Marengo. In the beginning, the Austrians surprised the French, who had expected to occupy Alessandria without a fight. In the middle of the battle, victory lay within the Austrians' grasp and the French were in full retreat; the narrow gap which separates a disciplined withdrawal from panic flight was quickly narrowing, and all but the most stouthearted among the French were looking fearfully over their shoulders. And at the end, Napoleon slept on the battlefield, as was his custom, and the Austrians sent plenipotentiaries to ask for terms of surrender. It had been a dramatic action, in which Kellermann's cavalry had rung down the curtain; but for them, the boot might well have been on the other leg.

Marengo is a typical north Italian village. Scattered farmhouses are set among the vineyards and mulberry trees, and for miles around, the countryside lies as flat as any billiard table, intersected by the rivers draining down from the Alps and the Apennines into the River Po. Three miles from Marengo the ancient walled city of Alessandria rises above the vines, and in the distance are the Ligurian Hills. The day of the battle was June 14, and the year was 1800. It was as hot as a hot June day can be, and there was all too little shade.

On the night of June 13 the narrow streets of Alessandria were jammed with the carriages, carts, and gun teams of the Austrian army. Every house and inn had been requisitioned by the officers, and outside the city walls the troops were bivouacked round the campfires. Melas had collected his senior officers together, and there were interminable discussions about the next move; some counseled retreat, and others attack.

Napoleon needed no council of war to determine his course of action, but he failed to order a reconnaissance of the Austrian position. Convinced that the Austrians intended to retreat on Genoa, Napoleon was obsessed by the need to cut their line of withdrawal. He therefore detached part of his army under Desaix, his favorite companion-at-arms, who had escaped from Egypt to join him, and ordered him to make a wide outflanking march to seize Novi astride the Austrian escape route. At the same time Napoleon strung out the rest of his army in a wide arc and advanced in a southwesterly direction towards the Ligurian Hills. He made little or no attempt to reconnoiter with his cavalry, and appeared to have formed his plan on the preconceived idea that Melas would always choose retreat in preference to battle.

This impression was strengthened by two incidents on June 13. In the first of these an Italian peasant was brought to the French headquarters at eleven o'clock; he informed the First Consul that the Austrians were preparing to march from Alessandria to Genoa and that their cavalry had already left. The second incident was the easy occupation of Marengo by the leading French division under Victor. Victor had no difficulty in driving the Austrians out of Marengo, and he followed them up to the east bank of the River Bormida, which flows between Marengo and Alessandria. The French were halted on the Bormida by the fire of the Austrian artillery, which was positioned on the far bank, and any idea of forcing a crossing was prevented by a violent rainstorm which dampened the powder and made the primitive muskets of those days useless.

Nothing happened during the night of June 13 to cause Napoleon to alter his mind about the enemy's intentions. There were fewer bivouac fires than usual outside Alessandria, and the noise of troops standing to arms outside the walls was taken to indicate an Austrian withdrawal under the cover of darkness. Napoleon at once sent an officer galloping after Desaix to urge that officer to hasten his outflanking movement. Desaix, however, had been delayed by the heavy rain; the River Scrivia rose to its banks, compelling Napoleon to spend the night of the 13th nearer to Marengo than he had originally intended, and Desaix was forced to halt until the weather cleared and the river went down. As a result the day dawned on June 14 with both Napoleon and Desaix nearer to Marengo than had been planned. The fates of empires may depend on such trivial and natural occurrences as sudden rainstorms.

Contrary to all expectations the Austrians attacked. At 6:00 A.M. on June 14 they marched out from Alessandria, crossed the Bormida, and attacked the leading French division, which was bivouacked round Marengo. The Austrian army totaled around thirty thousand men, of which seven thousand were cavalry. They had over one hundred guns. Baron Melas was a brave and experienced commander, but greatly handicapped by his age; over seventy himself, three of his senior generals were sixty years or more. The contrast with the French was significant: the average age of Napoleon and his subordinate commanders being thirty-two, while the oldest of them, Victor, was only thirty-four. The advantage of youth lay with the French, and this was even more important then than it is today; generals in the Napoleonic era were expected to spend long hours on horseback, galloping from one side of a battlefield to the other, and the strain became unendurable unless a man was young and fit. However, the French were not without their own problems. Quite apart from the fact that Napoleon's misjudgment of the situation had caused him to disperse his army at a time when he should have been concentrating every man at the decisive point, there was also a grave shortage of artillery and cavalry. Napoleon had only twenty guns at Marengo and his cavalry were outnumbered by nearly three to one. The great artilleryman who always preached the virtue of concentration fought the most vital battle of his career with too few guns, his troops scattered, and his cavalry reconnaissance so sketchy that he had little or no information about the movements and location of his enemy.

Marengo ought to have been a victory for the Austrians by midday on June 14. The fates decreed otherwise, and for two reasons. The first of these was due to the Austrians' failure to study the terrain, and the second was due to Kellermann's handling of his cavalry brigade. When the French infantry were forced to withdraw, it was Kellermann who covered that withdrawal and prevented the Austrians from following up and overrunning the French.

Between Marengo and Alessandria are two obstacles—the Bormida River and the Fontanone Brook. The Bormida was deep and wide enough to require bridging, while the Fontanone was a sluggish stream flowing between high banks. Both of these obstacles restricted maneuver, and both would have to be bridged before the guns and wagon train could come forward. Infantry could scramble through the Fontanone, but they would be vulnerable while doing so, and cavalry would find it difficult to cross. Despite all this, Melas decided to force a passage across both the water obstacles, and then recapture Marengo. Once this had been accomplished, Marengo would be utilized as a strong point on which the Austrian infantry could pivot before rolling up the French flank. The Austrian superiority in cavalry and guns was such that Melas believed the French would be driven back in flight towards Milan.

By nine o'clock much of this optimism seemed to be well founded. The Austrians under O'Reilly had recaptured Marengo, and Victor's troops were hanging on grimly in the vineyards east of the village. The battlefield was shrouded in dense black smoke from the guns and muskets, and it was difficult to distinguish friend from foe, particularly because the vines were in full leaf and provided excellent cover.

If one is to understand the tactics of those days, it is important to remember that the infantryman's weapon was the muzzle-loading musket of limited range and extremely indifferent accuracy. It was difficult to load, and after frequent use it fouled to such an extent that the cartridges could not be driven home.[2] It is not surprising that the infantry often preferred the bayonet to the bullet. The troops were trained to

---

[2] A French officer who fought at Marengo said that by midday the muskets were so clogged that the soldiers were compelled to urinate in the barrels to free them of the deposit of gunpowder.

maneuver in very close formation, shoulder to shoulder and making little use of ground, and they were constantly being exhorted to "Close up! Close up!" as their ranks were torn open by bullet and shell. It was a form of tactics dictated partly by the inefficient weapons of the time, partly by tradition, and partly because of the inability of conscript armies to operate in loose formation. It demanded rigid discipline and resulted in serious casualties.

Marengo had changed hands several times by midday, but Victor's division was now exhausted and could do no more. The day was appallingly hot and the men were caked with dust, while more and more Austrians seemed to be pouring across the Fontanone and into the shattered village. A withdrawal was ordered, and the weary French began to retire towards the village of San Giuliano, three miles to the east of Marengo. This was the opportunity for which the Austrian cavalry had been waiting, and Pilatti's cavalry brigade trotted forward and then crossed the Fontanone in single file. Some little time elapsed before this maneuver could be completed, and then Pilatti deployed into line preparatory to charging the retreating French infantry.

Kellermann's cavalry brigade were drawn up to the south of Marengo and were covering Victor's left flank. There were some eight hundred sabers all told, divided among the 2nd, 6th, and 20th Cavalry. The 8th Dragoons (328 sabers) were also temporarily placed under Kellermann's command, and he was discussing the critical situation with the Dragoons' commanding officer when Pilatti's cavalry began to appear up the bank of the Fontanone. The 8th Dragoons immediately charged them but were halted by Austrian artillery fire before they could get to close quarters; they fell back in some disorder but were rallied by Kellermann. Placing himself at their head, he led them forward at a steady trot until they were within fifty yards of the Austrian cavalry. He then ordered his trumpeter to sound the "Charge," and the 8th Dragoons crashed into the flank of Pilatti's disorganized and bewildered brigade. The Austrians could not go forward, and were forced back down the steep sides of the Fontanone until they landed, a confused, kicking, and

struggling mass of men and horses, in the brook itself. Kellermann captured over one hundred horses in this action and effectively destroyed the Emperor's and Karaczay's dragoons of the
Imperial Austrian army.

This charge brought a welcome respite to the French infantry,
who were at the end of their tether. Victor's division was on the
brink of collapse, and the supporting division under Lannes was
in little better order. The weight of the Austrian artillery was
beginning to tell, and if only Melas could have brought more
of his guns forward across the Bormida he would have destroyed
the French. Yet, incredible though it may seem, the man who
counted Marengo among his most glorious victories seems to
have been unaware of the critical situation until comparatively
late in the battle. Napoleon failed to realize that Melas was
fighting anything else but a rear-guard action, and it was not
until eleven o'clock, by which time Victor's division was beginning to disintegrate, that he sent an officer galloping off in the
tracks of Desaix with urgent orders for that General to retrace
his steps back to Marengo.

Could Desaix reach the battlefield in time? Napoleon had
no idea how far he had marched on the way to Novi, but the
chances were that he had gone too far to be able to reach the
battlefield before darkness fell. There was little else left with
which to influence the battle, and the only reserve was Bessières'
Consular Guard. These picked veterans, in their bearskin caps,
were sent marching steadily down the road towards Marengo
in an attempt to cover the withdrawal of Victor and Lannes.
They made a brave sight with their superb drill and flying
colors, but they were no more proof against the deadly Austrian artillery than the more humble regiments of the line.

Once again it was Kellermann who came to the rescue of the
exhausted infantry, many of whom had fired their last cartridge
and were reduced to holding off the Austrian cavalry by throwing stones at them. Rapidly deploying his brigade to form a
screen between the advancing Austrians and the retreating
French, Kellermann retired his squadrons by alternate troops,
and thereby prevented the Austrians from capturing a single
French prisoner. The wounded were given stirrup leathers to

hang onto, and Kellermann was to be found wherever there was the greatest danger. His energy was phenomenal as he galloped from troop to troop, exhorting, threatening, and praising, and he escaped death by a miracle. The Austrians were following up the French with twenty artillery pieces which halted from time to time and poured canister shot into the wavering ranks ahead of them. It would be merely a matter of time before the iron discipline gave way, and the French infantry became a disorganized rabble.

At two o'clock in the afternoon the battle seemed lost. According to the Official Bulletin, "the enemy was advancing all along the line, over a hundred guns were firing case shot. The roads were crowded with fugitives, wounded, and abandoned materials." Half Kellermann's brigade were lying dead and wounded beside their horses, and the Austrian cavalry were roaming the battlefield. At one time the 72nd Infantry were surrounded by a sea of cavalry, charging the French regiment from front and rear simultaneously, but the rear ranks faced about and beat off the horsemen. This was the moment when Murat rode up to Napoleon and counseled retreat. "General," he said, "it is time for us to retire; there is the Austrian cavalry turning our flank."

Fifteen years later, almost to the day, another great soldier saw his infantry being subjected to a similar bombardment. "Hard pounding this, gentlemen," observed Wellington at Waterloo, "but we will see who can pound the longest." On that day Wellington's indomitable will kept his hard-tried troops in action until Blücher came up and the Allies could close in for the kill. At Marengo, only Napoleon's will power sustained his reeling, exhausted, and powder-blackened infantry until Desaix could come to his aid. Meanwhile his elderly opponent had had enough. He had been in the saddle since midnight, two horses had been killed under him, and he had been slightly wounded. The heat, the strain of responsibility, and sheer physical fatigue had become insupportable. Turning to his chief of staff, Melas told him, "It is now an accomplished thing . . . they are retiring at all points. . . . I am quite worn out, for I have been in the saddle since midnight, and must get back to

Alessandria to rest." [3] Melas thereupon quitted the battlefield, and rode back to Alessandria a contented man, leaving General Zach to complete the French rout. That night Count Radetzky galloped out of Alessandria bearing the dispatch of victory to the Emperor in Vienna.

A lull settled over the battlefield. The Austrians were reorganizing for the final assault, and the French fell back behind San Giuliano. Kellermann's depleted brigade still covered the French withdrawal, but the Consular Guard had been severely handled by the Austrians. There was still no sign of Desaix, and ammunition was running short. Most of the French guns had been lost, and some of them were now being used against the French by Austrian gunners.

The Austrian infantry were issued more ammunition, put into proper formations, and led forward by officers confident that the battle was theirs. So confident were they that they scarcely bothered to take proper precautions. They began their advance with bands playing as if on a peacetime route march, laughing and joking as they came forward, and brushing aside contemptuously the feeble attempts of the French skirmishers to delay them. Wallis' brigade led the advance, and behind were nine more battalions, covered on the left flank by twelve squadrons of cavalry. In the rear was a cavalry corps of two thousand sabers whose task it would be to complete the destruction of the French after the Austrian infantry had been able to close with the bayonet.

It was four o'clock in the afternoon of June 14. Then, out of the smoke, appeared Desaix, his charger caked with sweat, with the information that his leading division was thirty minutes' march behind him. There is a story that Napoleon greeted him with the words, "Well, Desaix, what do you think?" "Think?" replied Desaix. "Why, that the battle is completely lost, but it is only four o'clock, and there is time to win another. To win, however, we must use artillery before we attack. To forgo its use will cause us another defeat." The story may be apocryphal but it is certain that Napoleon's first action after Desaix's ar-

[3] G. A. Furse, *Marengo & Hohenlinden* (Wm. Clowes, London, 1903), p. 385.

rival was to order Marmont to collect together every available
piece of artillery. There were ten already on the battlefield, and
another eight came up with Desaix's leading division. They
were few enough to confront the massed artillery of the Austrians.

The French took heart from the arrival of Desaix, and not
least among those who did so was Napoleon himself. He rode
out to greet the first of Desaix's divisions as it approached the
battlefield. "We have gone back far enough," he said. "You
know that my custom is always to sleep on the battlefield."
The division was immediately deployed on the outskirts of
San Giuliano, covering the shaken remnants of Victor's and
Lannes' divisions and blocking the road from Marengo. Marmont's battery was mounted on the right of the road, and
Kellermann's brigade was positioned to the right rear, just
behind the infantry brigade which Desaix was leading forward
in person.

All this took time to accomplish, and a determined attack
by the Austrians at this stage would have driven the French
from the field. The Austrians, however, contented themselves
with bombarding the French; their infantry made no attempt
to interfere with the moves of the French, and the opening
cannonade of Marmont's battery took them by surprise. The
leading battalion of Wallis' brigade fell back, and Desaix at
once led forward the 9th Light Infantry to charge the Austrians.
Almost immediately he was shot through the heart—almost certainly by an accidental shot from one of his own men. The
regiment he had been leading outpaced the supporting artillery,
and Marmont lost sight of them in the thick, black smoke
which drifted across the battlefield. As he struggled to get his
guns forward, he suddenly saw a French regiment falling back.

> All at once [he said] I saw in front of me and to the left
> the 30th Half-Brigade in disorder and in flight. . . . I
> perceived, fifty paces from the 30th, in the midst of a
> mass of thick smoke and dust, a mass in good order. At
> first I thought them French, but soon detected that this
> was the head of a deep column of Austrian grenadiers.[4]

[4] *Ibid.*, p. 396.

This was the vital moment in the battle. Marmont was probably mistaken in his identification of the French regiment; almost certainly they must have been the 9th Light Infantry falling back in disorder after Desaix's death. But what is significant is the distance at which battles were fought—fifty paces! The Austrians were Latterman's Grenadiers, led on by General Zach himself, and they were confident of victory. Shouting and cheering, the grenadiers pressed forward, their officers beckoning them on with their swords as the kettledrums rattled out the step. The French line was recoiling, the entire Austrian army was heaving forward like a battering-ram, and there was very little to stop them. Marmont's few guns were still firing, and the Consular Guard was formed up behind them to protect Napoleon and his personal staff. Desaix was dead, and the battle he had expected to win seemed lost.

Kellermann's cavalry brigade had advanced on the right of Desaix's infantry, when Desaix had led the 9th Light Infantry forward, and had been halted just outside the range of the Austrians' muskets. The cavalrymen were hidden from view by the vines, and Kellermann had ridden to a flank to watch the progress of Desaix's attack. He saw the 9th Light Infantry begin to waver, and then Latterman's Grenadiers appeared through the smoke. They halted, fired a volley, and then rushed forward to deliver the *coup de grâce* with their bayonets. As they did so, Kellermann wheeled the 2nd and 20th Cavalry into column of troops, and without a moment's hesitation led them against the Austrian infantry. The full shock of charging cavalry took the Austrians in the flank at a moment when their muskets were empty and when they were advancing at the double.

The two regiments of cavalry, with Kellermann at their head, rode right through the Austrian column. Three battalions of grenadiers, the entire brigade of Wallis, were trampled over, sabered, and broken. General Zach, who was riding forward with the grenadiers, was taken prisoner, and two Austrian standards were captured. The 2nd Cavalry lost seven of the eleven officers who had ridden in the charge, but they had saved the day for France. With Melas back in Alessandria resting after his labors, and Zach a prisoner, the Austrians were without a commander at the critical moment in the battle.

Kellermann led his brigade back through the Austrians, and he was re-forming them on the flank when Lichtenstein's cavalry regiment came galloping up to the assistance of the Austrian advance guard. There were only two hundred men left in Kellermann's brigade, but he deployed them into line and led them at the gallop to meet the Austrian cavalry. The Austrians were ridden down and fell back in disorder, carrying away as they did so the infantry coming up behind them. The Austrian center was in the act of deploying when the mass of their own cavalry crashed through them, causing utter confusion.

One of the most remarkable features of Kellermann's handling of his cavalry brigade was his control over his men. All too often cavalry charges disintegrated into futile skirmishes on the outskirts of the battlefield; the troopers would be carried away by the excitement of the charge, they would lose control over their horses, and entire squadrons would disappear over the horizon. It often took hours to collect them together, and there was ample opportunity for the cowards and poltroons among them to stay away from danger. The standard of horsemanship was indifferent, to say the least, and the pace had to be kept down to the trot if saddles were not to be emptied. Yet despite this, and the fact that the French horses were smaller and lighter than those of the Austrian cavalry regiments, Kellermann was able to lead three charges in quick succession, and still at the end have his brigade completely under control.

A lesser soldier might have contented himself with following up the routed Austrian cavalry. Instead, Kellermann galloped back to where Napoleon was waiting, surrounded by the mounted portion of his Consular Guard, and asked that they should be placed under his command. As soon as this was granted he led the Consular Guard, in company with what remained of his own dragoons and hussars, against the reserve regiments of the Austrian cavalry. Cutting and thrusting, mad with the exhilaration which comes from success, the French smashed their way through the Austrians. Panic, which will destroy the finest army if ever it takes hold, seized the Austrians. Until that moment they had fought with great bravery and determination, but now they were leaderless and confused. The pall of black smoke which hung over the battlefield, the sudden reversal in their fortunes, and the fear-crazed cavalry troopers who came blundering past with the French cavalry in hot pursuit, all combined to break the Austrian morale. They poured back towards Marengo, running down the road up which they had marched only an hour or so previously with bands playing and hearts high, and as they ran they threw away anything which might impede their flight—muskets and bayonets, ammunition pouches and their tight tunics, and in some cases even their boots. The wake of a retreating army is like the seashore after a storm.

Marengo was back in French hands before darkness fell. The bridges across the Bormida were choked by abandoned artillery pieces, wagons, carts, and dead horses; only the left wing of the Austrian army under General Ott preserved any semblance of discipline or cohesion. The Austrians had lost nearly all their guns, of which more than twenty were later recovered from the bed of the Bormida, and they were hurriedly throwing up defenses round Alessandria. Their cavalry was scattered, and riderless horses roamed the countryside.

The French were back in the positions they had been occupying when the Austrians had first attacked at daybreak, but the battle had cost them nearly seven thousand casualties. The Austrians had lost as many, and in addition three thousand three hundred of their officers and soldiers were prisoners, among them no less than seven generals! Both armies were utterly exhausted, and as the sun went down and darkness settled over the battlefield, someone brought Napoleon the story of Desaix's death: Desaix, of whom Napoleon said later, "By this stroke I was deprived of the man I esteemed most worthy of being my lieutenant."

Next day the Count of Neuppberg rode up to Napoleon's headquarters. He came from Melas under a flag of truce, and requested a forty-eight-hour armistice. This was agreed on con-

dition that the Austrians withdrew their remaining troops
from the left bank of the Bormida, and sometime later that
day Melas agreed to evacuate Genoa, Piedmont, and the greater
portion of Lombardy; in return he was allowed to march his
army behind the River Mincio with the honors of war. Napoleon was disposed to be generous since he knew how near
he had been to defeat; "In one day," he said, "we have recovered Italy." But the French might just as easily have lost
the battle.

Long after dark on the day of Marengo the main room of
the inn at San Giuliano was crowded with staff officers, con-
gratulating Napoleon on the victory and commiserating with
him on the death of Desaix. "Little Kellermann made a lucky
charge," Napoleon said to Bourrienne, his aide-de-camp. "He
did it just at the right moment. We are much indebted to
him. You see what trifling circumstances decide these affairs."
Then, turning to Bessières, he congratulated him warmly on
the conduct of the Consular Guard, implying that the Consular
Guard had played a decisive part in the battle.

Kellermann was furious at having to share the glory with
Bessières. "I am glad you are pleased, Consul," he said coldly,
"for this will put the crown on your head." Then he stamped
off angrily to rejoin his brigade in their bivouacs. They at least
knew the true worth of their commander, even if Napoleon
was not disposed to recognize the crucial part Kellermann had
played in the battle. He did in fact promote Kellermann to
general three weeks later, but even this brief delay seemed
intolerable to the eager recipient. Moreover, in the Official
Bulletin, Kellermann's share in the victory was slurred over
if not deliberately minimized. "It was I who placed the crown
on that man's head," wrote Kellermann to a friend in Paris,
and the letter was shown to the First Consul. It was not calculated to endear Kellermann to a rising, but not yet risen, master.
It may even have cost Kellermann his lifelong ambition, the
baton of a marshal of France.

For a soldier of his talents his subsequent career was not
particularly outstanding. He commanded cavalry divisions in
Germany and Spain, always with distinction, and on occasions

with brilliance, as was the case at Alba de Tormes when he defeated thirty thousand Spaniards with only three thousand cavalry of his advance guard. But his reputation for ruthlessness, venality, and graft was even too much for his by no means squeamish colleagues. He behaved with such complete disregard for the interests of the people he was supposed to be governing in northern Spain that Napoleon was forced to recall him in 1811. His conduct undoubtedly merited the most severe punishment and the confiscation of all his ill-gotten wealth, but Kellermann's was the kind of mentality which always regards itself as more sinned against than sinning. He sought an interview with the Emperor, but was left in no doubt that a lesser man would have been stripped of all his honors and sentenced to imprisonment. "General Kellermann," said Napoleon at the end of the interview, "whenever your name is brought up before me, I can remember nothing but Marengo."

There must have been something particularly unlikable about Kellermann. His marriage is a case in point. Soon after Marengo he fell in love with an Italian lady who was separated from her husband, and the couple decided to take advantage of French law, which permitted divorce by mutual consent. The French ambassador at Milan was induced to declare the former marriage annulled on the flimsy pretext that the lady, living in territory occupied by French armies, was thereby subject to the laws of France. Eighteen years later Kellermann succeeded in persuading the French courts to declare his marriage null and void, on the grounds that his wife had all along been subject to Italian law, and that therefore her divorce could never have been legal.

Kellermann commanded the 3rd Corps of Cavalry (cuirassiers) at Waterloo. The Bourbons had loaded him with honors, but he deserted them without a qualm on Napoleon's return from Elba. At Quatre Bras he was ordered by Ney to charge the British infantry; "the fate of France," he was told, "is in your hands." Placing himself at the head of his men, he charged headlong and caught one British battalion in the act of changing formation, scattered it, and penetrated another square. Then, at the critical moment, he was brought down, and his

soldiers panicked. They turned tail and fled, leaving Kellermann to make his escape on foot, bareheaded and gripping
the manes of two horses. Two days later he again led his
cavalry as they shattered themselves against the iron walls of
the British squares. Barely a third of the French cuirassiers
left the field. It was a long way from Marengo, and all the
glory had departed. Kellermann never drew his sword again,
although he lived on until 1835.

It is for Marengo that he will always be remembered. "A
minute earlier, or three minutes later, and the charge could
not have succeeded, but the timing was perfect, and North
Italy was recovered in that moment for the French Republic." [5]
There are some who will say that the whole affair was a matter
of luck. Luck for Napoleon that Melas left the field when he
did, and that the flooding of the Scrivia delayed Desaix's march
to Novi and left him within marching distance of the battlefield at the critical moment. Luck for Kellermann that he
chose to charge at the moment when the Austrian grenadiers
had fired their muskets and were surging forward, unprepared
to form square and hold off the cavalry by fire. There will
always be an element of luck in war, and without his fair
share of luck no general can hope to win a battle. But it was
not only luck that induced Kellermann to order his trumpeter
to sound the "Charge" when everything else seemed lost. It
was that quickness of perception which is the hallmark of
the born leader of mounted troops, and the indomitable
courage which inspires soldiers to follow their commander without regard for the odds against them.

A greater soldier than Kellermann claimed the credit for the
victory, but to Kellermann and his troopers belongs the true
glory of Marengo. It was a great day for the cavalry.

[5] A. G. Macdonnell, *Napoleon and His Marshals* (Macmillan, London,
1934), p. 77.

CHAPTER FOUR

Garcia Hernandez

J U L Y 23, 1812

"La charge la plus audacieuse de la guerre d'Espagne."
GENERAL FOY

THE British have always tried to avoid the hazards of a land campaign in Europe. Indeed, it might be said of them that Raleigh's celebrated dictum on the advantages of sea power has been accepted more as an article of faith than as a pronouncement on strategy, and its truth has been proved by the unfortunate outcome of so many of their expeditions on the Continent. They have not forgotten the numerous occasions on which the Royal Navy has been called upon to rescue their army from what has seemed certain destruction, and as recently as 1942 a destroyer captain was heard to remark that his acquaintance with the army was limited to hauling them off hostile beaches in the teeth of enemy fire. These lessons of history probably account for the navy's superior attitude, which is best described in the words of Nelson to Lord St. Vincent:

59

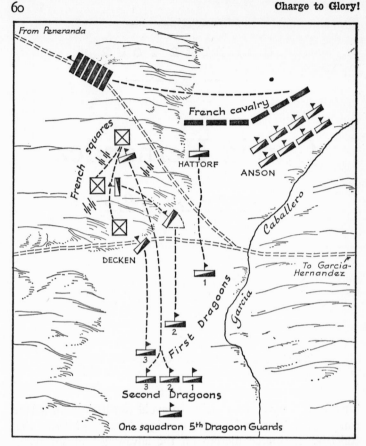

"The Army is, as usual, well dressed and powdered . . . but, as you know, great exertions belong exclusively to the Navy." [1]

It is hardly surprising that British strategy should be founded on command of the seas. For hundreds of years their strategic thinking has been conditioned by sea power, and it was this as much as anything else that underlay the differences between the British and American chiefs of staff in World War II, and between Lloyd George and his generals in World War I. "Find

---

[1] The United States Navy's views on soldiers do not differ materially from those of Nelson, only Fleet Admiral Ernest King would probably have expressed himself a good deal more violently—and vitriolically.

another way round," or "Strike at the soft underbelly," implored the advocates of sea power. "Strike the enemy where he is strongest but in an area where his defeat will be mortal," argued the supporters of the Direct Approach school.[2]

Despite their reluctance to involve themselves in Europe, the British have often been compelled to do so by force of circumstances, and this occurred quite frequently during the hundred years when the king of England was also elector of Hanover. When Britain went to war with France in 1803 almost the first action of Napoleon was to invade Hanover. This produced a furious outburst from the British, who claimed that George III had declared war only in his capacity as king of England and not as elector of Hanover, and they argued that therefore Hanover was not at war with France. Such niceties of diplomacy were lost on Napoleon, who, blandly ignoring the furious *démarches* from the Court at St. James's, ordered General Mortier to disarm the Hanoverian army, requisition every horse in the Electorate, and squeeze as much gold as he possibly could out of the wretched inhabitants. By this policy he succeeded in alienating the Hanoverians against the French in just as effective a manner as Himmler's S.S. set Russians against Germans in World War II. The Hanoverians cared no more for George III than any tenant farmer cares for his absentee landlord, and with a modicum of skill Napoleon might have succeeded in winning them over to his side. As it was, the plundering and the posturing of Mortier's soldiery roused the placid Hanoverians to detest everything French; all they asked for was an opportunity to strike a blow against them.

Reports of this rising discontent reached the Duke of York in London. As commander in chief of the British army he was grappling with the perennial problem of his high office—how to induce sufficient of his fellow countrymen to fill the ranks of a regular army which was small enough in all con-

[2] The strategists are still arguing whether the development of nuclear fission and intercontinental ballistic missiles has rendered all previous arguments academic. At the moment, however, the navy seems to be winning—as it always will.

science. The Duke of York's sordid private life, which did not differ markedly from the private lives of his numerous brothers, coupled with his incompetent performance as a commander in the field, has tended to obscure his real worth as a military administrator. He served the British army extremely well, and not least among his services was his decision to take advantage of the anti-French feeling in Hanover to form a battalion or two of foreigners to serve alongside the British army in the fight against the common enemy. This proposal was subsequently extended to include cavalry, artillery, and infantry, and on December 19, 1803, the Duke of Cambridge[3] received a letter from the War Office:

> SIR,
>
> In pursuance of the King's commands, communicated to me by his royal highness the commander-in-chief, I have the honour to acquaint your royal highness that his majesty has directed the independent levies of baron Decken and major Halkett to be discontinued, and has been pleased to order that the men raised under the letters of service granted to those officers shall be formed into a legion to be composed of foreigners, not exceeding five thousand men, which his majesty is pleased to authorize to be raised by your royal highness, upon the conditions hereafter specified.[4]

The conditions were that each recruit was to be enlisted whenever possible for ten years, that the upper age limit was forty, and that no Frenchmen, Italians, or Spaniards were to be enlisted under any circumstances. Every other nationality in Europe was acceptable, and the minimum height was to be five feet three inches—"except for young healthy lads likely to grow," who could be enlisted an inch or two shorter. The Isle of Wight was to be the depot for the infantry, while the

---

[3] Another of George III's many sons. His interests lay mainly in Hanover where he acted as viceroy for his father; it was in this capacity that he was nominated colonel in chief of the King's German Legion.

[4] Ludlow Beamish, *History of the King's German Legion* (Thomas & William Boone, London, 1832), Vol. I, p. 350.

cavalry and horse artillery were to be assembled at Weymouth in Dorset.

A steady trickle of loyal Hanoverians had been crossing the North Sea to take service under their king, and as soon as official authorization was received a widespread recruiting campaign was launched in Hanover. The French reacted by prescribing the death penalty for anyone caught recruiting Germans "for the English service," and several such sentences were carried out. Yet despite the intimidation, the trickle became a flood and the Hanoverian army was virtually reconstituted in England by February, 1804, less than six months after it had laid down its arms to General Mortier. Its new title was the King's German Legion.

The cavalry regiments of the Legion eventually consisted of the 1st, 2nd, and 3rd Hussars, and the 1st and 2nd Dragoons. Their uniforms were the same as those worn by the British hussar and dragoon regiments, and that of the 1st Dragoons found particular favor with George III, who wore it on frequent occasions. The King seems to have gone out of his way to visit his German regiments; he was a serious-minded monarch, until his mind deserted him forever, and it may be that he found the serious-minded German officers more to his taste than the wild and skylarking British. Their sober attitude towards cavalry soldiering must have contrasted forcibly with the high-spirited amateurishness of the British cavalry officer, of whom General Excelmann[5] said after Waterloo:

> Your horses are the finest in the world and your men ride better than any Continental soldier; with such material the English cavalry ought to have done more than has ever been accomplished by them on the field of battle. The great deficiency is in your officers . . . the British cavalry officer seems to be impressed by the conviction that he can dash or ride after everything; as if the art of war were precisely the same as that of fox-hunting.[6]

[5] Remy Excelmann was one of Napoleon's finest cavalry leaders.
[6] *The Reminiscences and Recollections of Captain R. H. Gronow* (Smith, Elder, London, 1862), p. 109.

The truth of the matter lay in the fact that the aristocratic young sprigs who officered the dashing British regiments cared little for the humdrum business of soldiering. All they asked for was a thoroughbred horse, a glamorous uniform, and the same opportunity to cut a dash on the battlefield as they were accustomed to find in the hunting field. Their most bitter critic could not accuse them of lack of courage, but the majority of them were utterly lacking in discipline. The Germans, who took their profession so seriously, set a standard that all too few British cavalry officers could bother to emulate.

The first task of the King's German Legion was intended to be the liberation of Hanover. Britain had joined with Austria and Prussia in a coalition against Napoleon, and an expeditionary force sailed from Ramsgate in January, 1806, with the object of joining forces with the Austrians and Prussians. Lord Cathcart, who commanded the expedition, had eighteen thousand men under his command, and of these more than six thousand were provided by the King's German Legion. The German troops had set sail with all the high hopes of returning exiles, but they were dogged with the bad luck which always attended the Legion whenever it embarked on the sea. On almost every occasion their transports were scattered by gales, vessels were sunk or driven onto hostile shores, and their horses were killed by exposure or by the conditions under which they were expected to exist. These conditions were so rudimentary that it is surprising that any horses ever survived any voyage.

Horse transports were constructed to carry between eighteen and forty horses. The animals were huddled into the hold, their heads facing inwards, and with small upright posts fixed between each horse. This device was intended to prevent the wretched animals from lying down, and their chests and haunches were covered with sheepskins to save them from being skinned alive as they were tossed backwards and forwards by rough seas. The hold was packed as tightly as possible to restrict all movement and was ventilated by means of sacks which hung down into the main hatchway from the deck. If the weather was in the slightest degree warm the horses were nearly suffocated or were driven mad by lack of air, while in heavy seas they were thrown around like ninepins. At the end of the voyage they were either dumped into the sea and left to swim or wade ashore, or they were slung overboard into flat-bottomed barges. Their condition after a sea journey was such that they were rarely fit to perform even the shortest patrol, and the wastage was enormous.

The first voyage of the cavalry of the King's German Legion set the pattern for the others which came later, for it almost ended in disaster. Half the dragoon regiment was forced back to England by contrary winds; at one stage the transports were blown under the guns of Calais, and the French were just setting out to board the ships when a fortunate shift in the wind allowed the British vessels to slip away. The hussar regiment was driven onto the coast of Holland, and the other half of the dragoons arrived at the mouth of the Elbe in a state of complete exhaustion.

Worse was to follow. While Cathcart had been embarking his troops, Napoleon had won his brilliant victory over the Austrians at Austerlitz. Austria and Prussia had capitulated and Napoleon was now the undisputed master of Europe. Although Austerlitz had been won before the British expeditionary force set sail, the news did not reach England until after Cathcart was on the high seas. When he landed at Bremen he had no prospect of support from Britain's former allies, and he took the sensible decision to return to England.

The effect of this on the morale of the King's German Legion was disastrous; it was as if the Free French had been landed in Normandy on D Day only to be sent back to England again a few days later. The Germans had sailed in the expectation that they would liberate Hanover and be reunited with their families. Many of their families had arrived to join them at the market town of Verden on the Aller, which had been chosen as headquarters of the Legion, and now after all they had endured they were expected to get back on their transports and return to England, leaving behind their wives and children to the tender mercies of the French. It is not surprising that desertions were numerous, and the citizens of Verden and Bremen made matters worse by spreading rumors that the

British intended to employ the Legion in the Cannibal Islands, from where few could expect to return. It says a great deal for the discipline of the Legion that most of the soldiers remained true to their allegiance and sailed for Ireland in the returning transports from the Elbe.

The first casualty by fire that the Legion was to suffer occurred in Ireland. Several of the German regiments were sent there on their return from the Elbe, and they found the inhabitants much friendlier than the English. Perhaps the Irish preferred a German to an English garrison, but there can be no doubt that the Legion's marriage rate soared. The local Irish militia were jealous of the Germans' success with Irish girls, and fierce fighting broke out in the streets of Tullamore; it did not end until a private of the King's German Legion had been killed and one officer seriously wounded. Further trouble was averted by the dispatch of part of the Legion on the expedition to Sicily, and the remainder sailed the following spring for Denmark.

The Legion passed most of 1807 campaigning round the periphery of Napoleon's empire, and in building up its strength until it amounted to a complete division, with its own artillery, engineers, and staff. Since Germans were not permitted to attend the Royal Military Academy at Woolwich, where the British trained their artillery and engineer cadets, the Legion set up its own officer-training establishment, which was reputed to be far superior to the British equivalent. But, when all was said and done, the Germans were exiles, and their chances of returning to Hanover seemed remote indeed. The eagles of France were being carried in triumph through every capital in Europe and the "old mustaches" of Napoleon appeared invincible.

There are certain dates in history which mankind should write in letters of gold. Such a date is June 22, 1941—the day when Hitler unleashed his *Panzers* into the vastnesses of Russia, and Nazism began its slide into chaos. Another date of equal significance is October 18, 1807. That was the day when Junot crossed the Pyrenees with his Corps of Observation of the Gironde. He bore with him the civilizing mission of Napoleonic

France, supported on bayonets and cemented by gunpowder, and as his soldiers took the road to San Sebastian, past the sullen and unfriendly Spaniards, they may have felt the first twinges of the "Spanish Ulcer" which was to gnaw at French vitals until it destroyed them. The *Grande Armée*, the most powerful fighting instrument that the world had seen since Rome, was entering Spain and it would be bled white before it left the detestable Peninsula.

Junot's men entered Lisbon six weeks after their crossing of the Pyrenees, and by then they were beginning to wonder whether war in such terrain justified itself. Two-thirds of the army had fallen by the wayside, through disease, knives in the darkness, the appalling climate, and the worse terrain. Their morale had been lowered by the gloomy valleys through which they had marched and the sour-faced peasants who had watched them go by. Their guns had crashed down the precipices, the horses stank from the sores raised by the sodden saddlery, and the unending rain made the gunpowder as useless as wet sand. The French soldiers, accustomed to campaigning in sunny Lombardy or amid the green fields of Westphalia and Bavaria, were out of their element in the most backbreaking terrain in western Europe, and they hated the climate. They were to remain out of their element until Wellington succeeded in driving them back across the Pyrenees, but that was not to happen for another six years.

Few wars in history have been waged with such relentless ferocity as Napoleon's war with the Spaniards. It is true that between the British and French there existed a good deal of grudging respect, by no means unlike the relationship between Rommel's Afrika Corps and the British Eighth Army, but the Spanish and Portuguese peasants had no use for such conventions. Their hatred for the French was all-embracing, everlasting, and knew no limits. For them the only good Frenchman was a dead one, and in order to encompass such a death no treachery could be sufficiently vile, no crime sufficiently criminal. A miller, whose mill had been burned down by a French cavalry patrol, bided his time until one day a wounded French soldier sought his assistance. After lulling the soldier's apprehensions, the miller waited till he was asleep and then tied him up with a rope. Then he collected together his friends and they cast the wounded man into the millstream with the fairly reasonable hope that he would be swept into the mill wheel and mangled horribly to death. Unfortunately for them, and their entertainment, the wounded man could swim, and struggled desperately to reach the bank, whereupon the blood-crazy onlookers stoned him to death in the water. A soldier of the King's German Legion who was compelled to witness this performance was horrified, but that was the kind of war it was.

On July 31, 1808, the Legion sailed from England to take part in the war. They had already been on the transports since May 10. The British had fitted out an expedition under Sir John Moore to go to the assistance of the King of Sweden, but the enterprise had been an abortive one. The British and Swedes failed to agree on a plan of campaign, and after six weeks of tiresome negotiations the expedition had returned to England. Officers and men had managed to alleviate the tedium of shipboard by catching lobsters and exploring the creeks and inlets round Gothenburg, but no such diversions were open to the horses. They had to stand flank to flank in the stifling holds, tormented by flies, and enduring miseries whenever any sort of a sea was running. After seventeen weeks of this unnatural existence they were thrown into the sea off the mouth of the River Mondego in Portugal and were expected to swim ashore through heavy surf and rising seas. Forty of them had been shot for glanders, brought on by their confinement on board the transports, and the remainder were hopelessly lame and unfit for service. Later, when it turned to continuous rain, the feet of the horses had been so affected by the conditions on the transports that many lost their hoofs altogether.

Napoleon had sent his army marching into Spain because his ambition knew no bounds; he also knew that Bourbons ruled in Spain and that Bourbons had recently ruled in France. It might be safer all round if the throne of Spain were occupied by one of his own nominees, brother Joseph for example, but he did not immediately declare war. On the contrary, he maintained that Junot's army had entered Spain to defend her against the odious British, and to coerce the Portuguese, whose attachment to their ancient alliance with Britain, and their disregard for Napoleon's restriction on trade with Britain, provided every good reason for their extermination.

The British landed an army in the Peninsula for rather different reasons. In part they felt bound to honor their treaty with Portugal, but the main reason for their descent lay in the fact that a campaign in Spain would permit them to make the maximum use of their sea power. Their command of the seas, the consequences of which were always lost on the landsman Napoleon, would permit them to "take as much, or as little of the warre as they felt inclined." The ultimate success of their undertaking was due as much to the Royal Navy as it was to a self-sufficient and reserved Anglo-Irish aristocrat[7] who "rode a knowing-looking thorough-bred horse, and wore a grey overcoat, Hessian boots and a large cocked hat." [8] Sir Arthur Wellesley, better known as the Duke of Wellington, first achieved distinction as a general on the plains of India, about as far from the sea as it was possible to get, and yet no British general in history has had a better appreciation of the advantages of sea power. It is because of this that one of the greatest historians of the British army has seen fit to describe Wellington as "Neptune's General." [9]

Junot's army had been in Portugal for over six months before the Spanish rose in a *levée en masse* against the hated French. The rising began on May 25, 1808, and by then there were well over 100,000 French soldiers scattered in large and small garrisons throughout the Peninsula. A brilliant collection of officers

---

[7] The Anglo-Irish have produced an astonishing galaxy of military leaders for Britain. In World War II no less than four field marshals came from this stock—Alexander, Alanbrooke, Dill, and Montgomery—and in World War I their contribution was no less important.

[8] *The Reminiscences and Recollections of Captain R. H. Gronow*, p. 4.

[9] In his trilogy on the Napoleonic Wars, *The Years of Endurance, The Years of Victory*, and *The Age of Elegance*, Sir Arthur Bryant succeeded in recapturing the spirit of the British army in a way that only Sir John Fortescue has managed to do before him.

had come hurrying down from France to join them, scenting
from afar the fresh opportunities for glory, loot, and the
marshal's baton that every French officer could hear rattling
in his knapsack. To Barcelona, Seville, Madrid, and Lisbon
came the glittering figures who were the constellations round
Napoleon's sun—Moncey and Bessières, Kellermann of the
heavy cavalry and Lasalle of the light, Grouchy, who waited till
1815 to receive the coveted baton, and Lefebvre-Desnouettes
whose subsequent capture is claimed by the British 10th Hussars and the 3rd Hussars of the Legion.[10] They flocked to
join an army which was detested by every man, woman, and
child in Spain—an army which had swept all before it from the
coasts of Calabria to the frozen marches of Poland but which by
the summer of 1808 was already beginning to show signs of
strain. At Baylen nearly seventeen thousand French troops were
surrendered by General Dupont to a pack of tatterdemalion
Spaniards, and on August 21 on the coast of Portugal the full
effects of British musketry were experienced by Junot's veterans
for the first time. By Napoleon's standards the Battle of

[10] General Lefebvre-Desnouettes was captured in a cavalry action at
Benavente on December 29, 1808, during Moore's retreat to Corunna.
The capture is claimed by the 10th Hussars but there can be little doubt
that the Frenchman was first taken by Private Bergmann of the King's
German Legion. Lefebvre-Desnouettes fired his pistol at Bergmann, missed,
and then offered him his sword. He demanded to be taken to General
Charles Stewart, the commander of the British cavalry brigade, and it was
while Bergmann was inquiring Stewart's whereabouts that a soldier of the
10th Hussars came up and led the Frenchman away. The capture is the
scene of a well-known painting, depicted with more than a little artist's
license. Lefebvre-Desnouettes, who was something of a character, later
broke his parole and succeeded in escaping back to France from England
in 1811.
    The King's German Legion was later to be involved in another famous
capture. This took place at Waterloo when General Cambronne, riding
at the head of a brigade of the Imperial Guard, had his horse shot from
under him. Halkett, commanding a brigade of the Legion, dashed forward
and threatened to cut Cambronne down if he did not surrender. This
Cambronne did, regardless of the fact that "La garde meurt, mais ne se
rende pas," but as Halkett was escorting him back to the British lines his
horse was wounded and fell. While he was on the ground struggling to
disentangle himself, Cambronne walked coolly back towards his own lines,
but Halkett managed to bring his horse back onto its legs, overtook the
Frenchman, and thrusting his hand into the General's aiguillette, he dragged
him off at a canter to captivity.

Vimeiro was a trumpery affair, but it had nevertheless been a French defeat. Junot took his army home thankfully by sea, but he left the British in Portugal.

When the news of Baylen and Vimeiro reached Paris, Napoleon was speechless with fury. Soon the really great field commanders of the *Grande Armée* went posting down the *pavée* on their way to take over command in Spain. Summoned without ceremony from their comfortable *Schlosses* and palaces in occupied Europe, the marshals were bustled down to the Peninsula to work their old magic. Across the bridge at Hendaye rattled the traveling-carriages of Masséna, Marmont, Soult, Lannes, and Ney, and soon they would be joined by the greatest soldier of them all. For Napoleon learned in the fall of 1808 that a British army had dared to leave the security provided by its ships and was already marching through Salamanca on the way to Madrid. At last the British had given him the opportunity he had been waiting for, and the Emperor set out for Spain to direct the operations in person.

The British force which had caused such blood pressure in Paris was about thirty-five thousand strong and was commanded by General Sir John Moore. Moore, after returning from the abortive expedition to Sweden, had sailed for Vigo Bay on July 31, 1808, but before he got there Wellesley had defeated Junot at Vimeiro. Moore's force had then been switched to Portugal, after which it was dispatched into Spain in the hopes that its appearance there would encourage the Spaniards. Moore had six thousand men of the King's German Legion in his army, and the 3rd Hussars of the Legion headed his advance guard. They reported a sad lack of enthusiasm on the part of the Spaniards, and a marked reluctance to do anything save offer their scraggy chickens at exorbitant prices and lock up their daughters whenever the cavalry appeared. Moore eventually succeeded in reaching Madrid, but by then he had learned the folly of trusting to the promises of the Spanish guerrillas. He was also aware that Napoleon had set every French division in Spain marching against him, and that his long and tenuous communications with the sea were in grave danger of being cut. On the night of December 23, 1808,

Moore came to the conclusion that it was either withdrawal or defeat, and the retreat to Corunna began.

The weather was terrible, the terrain heartbreaking, and discipline broke down under the strain to which the troops were subjected. The French were close behind.

> Many a man [wrote an officer of the Legion] who for four days and as many nights had never been refreshed by one half-hour's sleep, became so indifferent to life, that at the close of a long day of exhausting duty he has thought within himself, and even secretly hoped, that the foreboding might be realized—"Tomorrow I shall, probably, be no more"! [11]

Yet in the end the British reached the ships, so patiently waiting for them, and were able to embark, although they buried their commander beneath the ramparts of Corunna before they did so. As was to happen again to a British army, at Dunkirk, Moore's army had been saved by the Royal Navy and a near-miracle. At Dunkirk the near-miracle was Hitler's incredible order forbidding the *Panzer* divisions to close for the kill, and at Corunna it was Napoleon's decision to hand over the final stages of the pursuit to Soult and to return, himself, to Paris. He believed victory was within his grasp and that Soult would be capable of finishing the business for him, but Soult failed to destroy Moore's army, and the British escaped to fight another day. Had the Emperor been there it could never have happened.

Napoleon never again went back to Spain, and as a result he consistently underestimated the "Sepoy General" [12] who harried and harassed his marshals up and down the barren valleys and stony crags of the Peninsula. Whenever he felt the pace was growing too hot for him, Wellington knew that he could withdraw back to the sea, where the Royal Navy could always be relied upon to be waiting. Sea power, good

[11] Beamish, *op. cit.*, Vol. I, p. 175.
[12] The Duke of Wellington, having learned his soldiering in India, was often contemptuously referred to by Napoleon as a "Sepoy General": *sipahi* in Hindustani means "soldier."

generalship, and the superb fighting qualities of the army he trained so well, all combined to make Wellington the most formidable of all Napoleon's adversaries—and yet the surprising thing is that Napoleon could never see it.

Four years of hard campaigning in Spain and Portugal produced the finest army that Britain had ever possessed up till that time. Its morale was superb and its confidence in its commander supreme. With the scarlet-coated regiments of the line and the green-jacketed rifles marched the Portuguese under Beresford, and the Spaniards under Alva; but the most durable and dependable of all the allied contingents were the horse, foot, and artillery of the King's German Legion under Baron Victor Von Alten. Behind them were the victories won at Vimeiro, Torres Vedras, Fuentes d'Onor, Albuhera, and Bussaco, and ahead were victories even greater. It was an army in which gaiety and resourcefulness, marksmanship and tough living, counted for far more than pipe clay and the barrack square. The nearest the British have ever come to its equivalent was the "Desert army" which jousted back and forth across the sands of Libya.[13] By the spring of 1812 this splendid Peninsula army had captured the two fortresses which guard the way from Portugal into Spain at Ciudad Rodrigo and Badajoz, and the time had come at last for it to turn its back on the sea and march towards the Pyrenees.

Two of France's finest soldiers were lying in wait for it. Soult was in the south in Andalusia, while Marmont was in Léon with the so-called Army of Portugal. Together they could muster nearly twice as many men as Wellington's 75,000, while as many again were holding Catalonia, Aragon, Valencia, and Castille. But they were all tied down by the Spanish insurgents they affected to despise so much, and after leaving Hill in Estremadura to mask Soult, and sending a seaborne force to harry eastern Spain, Wellington turned north across the Douro. He intended to destroy Marmont before any of

[13] Wellington, who cared little for the sit of a button or the other niceties of uniform, would have relished the story of the cavalry officer in the western desert in 1941 who accepted the surrender of an Italian fort when dressed only in a Panama hat (with the old Etonian ribbon round the brim), a pair of crumpled shorts, and suede desert boots.

his brother marshals could come to his assistance. On June 13 the leading scouts of Von Alten's cavalry brigade forded the Agueda on the Portuguese frontier and drove in Marmont's vedettes towards Salamanca. It was just eleven days before the *Grande Armée* crossed the Nieman and Napoleon's "Russian Adventure" began.

The cavalry of the King's German Legion were Wellington's usual choice to lead the vanguard. They tended to be a little more cautious than the British, and less inclined to go "hollahing-off" in pursuit of some French outpost. The Germans had other uses as well. During the maneuvering before the Battle of Fuentes d'Onor in 1811, the British were marching through a narrow defile when Wellington decided to halt the head of the column. However, the road was so packed with troops that no staff officer could force his way through to the front, and a colonel in the King's German Legion volunteered his services to halt the column. This officer was remarkable for his powerful word of command, and exerting his talents to the fullest extent, he bellowed forth, "The army is to halt by Lord Wellington's order." The message got through, which is more than can be said for many radio messages on the modern battlefield, but the poor colonel was so overcome by his effort that he had to be removed to hospital. It was the only time during the entire campaign that he was absent from duty—"for making too much noise!"

For nearly six weeks Marmont and Wellington played cat-and-mouse with each other across the rolling hills of Léon. The two armies marched and countermarched, with each General's intention perfectly clear to the other. Marmont was endeavoring to place his army across Wellington's communications with Portugal and make him fight to regain them. Wellington was waiting until Marmont was caught off balance; then, and only then, would the cautious Wellington risk the weapon he had forged with such patience and with such skill. In the meantime he would cover his communications and keep Marmont guessing.

The moment that Wellington had been waiting for arrived between two and three o'clock in the afternoon of July 22.

Ever since dawn the two armies had been marching parallel
with each other, the British covering Salamanca, five miles
away to the northwest, and the French striving to outflank the
British to the westward and cut the highway from Salamanca
to Ciudad Rodrigo. Only a low ridge separated the marching
divisions, and for most of the time they were within gunshot
of each other. The French were slightly quicker marchers than
the British, and it looked as if they would reach the highway
before the British could prevent them. Then, reasoned Marmont, Wellington must either stand and fight or be forced to
retreat through the mountains of northern Portugal. Either
way he reckoned that he had Wellington exactly where he
wanted him.

Some of Wellington's officers thought that Marmont might
well be right. Just after 1:00 P.M. a German hussar went galloping off to Salamanca from the headquarters of Baron Von
Alten's cavalry brigade. Earlier that morning the Baron had
been seriously wounded in the thigh while reconnoitering the
French positions. He had been carried back to Salamanca, but
before leaving his headquarters he had impressed on his aide-de-
camp that he would rather die than fall into the hands of the
French. If, therefore, there was any possibility of a British
defeat, he was to be informed at once, so that he could mount
his horse and die in the saddle. The orderly who came galloping
into Salamanca brought a pessimistic message from the aide-de-
camp, and although the Baron had only just left the operating
table, he mounted his horse and rode off down the Ciudad
Rodrigo road. Another messenger caught up with him, saying
that Wellington had attacked and the battle was going in
his favor, and the General subsequently returned to his sick-
bed. His breeches by then were so full of blood from his wound
that they looked like the cherry-colored overalls of the 11th
Hussars.

Wellington waited to strike at Salamanca until he saw the
gap between the leading French division and those following
behind it begin to widen. This was the moment; his army was
concentrated and under his hand, while Marmont's was strung
out in a wide arc with the gaps between divisions rapidly

widening. He threw the 3rd Division against the French advance guard, cut it to pieces, and almost simultaneously launched the rest of his army to take the French in the flank. In less than half an hour the battle was won and Marmont's army was reeling back in defeat. The British infantry mowed down the French with their deadly musketry, and Wellington clinched the victory by hurling Le Marchant's heavy cavalry brigade against the shattered French. The 5th Dragoon Guards and the 4th and 5th Dragoons rode down Macune's infantry division, and then burst through Brennier's division beyond. To add to the confusion the grass was set on fire by burning gunpowder, thick smoke drifted across the battlefield, and the seriously wounded were in danger of being burned to death. Marmont was wounded by a cannon ball early in the action and only just managed to avoid capture. He left behind in Wellington's hands two eagles, six colors, twenty guns, and seven thousand prisoners.

Eight miles to the southeast of the battlefield was the bridge across the River Tormes. The fort at Alba de Tormes commanded the bridge and it was garrisoned by some of Wellington's Spanish troops. Reasoning that this escape route was blocked, Wellington sent his Light Division with Ponsonby's cavalry to hold the ford at Huerta, away to the northeast. The Tormes was a formidable obstacle for all but unencumbered cavalry and infantry, and it seemed that the retreating French must be trapped. But the Spanish commander at Alba de Tormes abandoned his post without orders, and the disorganized French poured across the bridge without hindrance. Their withdrawal was covered by the division of General Foy which alone had retained its discipline and formation, and Spanish incompetence had deprived Wellington of complete victory.

The 1st and 2nd Dragoons of the King's German Legion had been held in reserve over on the left flank during the battle. As night fell on July 22 they went into bivouac beside the village of Pelebravo, but shortly after midnight were roused by a galloper clattering through the streets and inquiring for the lodgings of Major General Von Bock, who commanded the dragoon brigade. The galloper brought orders that the dragoons were to pursue the retreating French as soon as it was light. They were saddled up before dawn on July 23 and reached the Tormes about ninety minutes later. There they joined forces with Anson's brigade of light cavalry and waited for the infantry of the 1st and Light Divisions to catch up with them. At eight o'clock they forded the Tormes at Babilafuente and spurred on after the French.

The delay at the ford had given the French time to deploy two of Foy's regiments to cover their withdrawal. This was taking them along the narrow and marshy valley of the Garcia Caballero, a tributary of the Tormes, by way of the rough and stony track leading through Garcia Hernandez to Peneranda. The banks of the stream were steep, and the ground was hopelessly rough for the proper employment of cavalry. For much of the way the track led through a defile and it was impossible to see very far ahead. The rolling nature of the terrain provided excellent positions for infantry, and the horses were tired after their forced marching since dawn. Anson's light cavalry led the advance with Von Bock's dragoons following close behind them. Farther back were the weary British infantry, stumbling and falling over the broken ground as they tried to keep up with the trotting cavalry.

After about three miles the valley widened into a stony plain, crossed by the road running from Garcia Hernandez and flanked by rolling and stone-covered hills. As Anson's cavalry breasted the rise leading out of the valley they suddenly came upon the French rear guard deployed in front of them. To the left there were several battalions of infantry drawn up in square formation on the hills. Beyond the infantry and out in the plain were some squadrons of enemy cavalry. It was these squadrons which first attracted Wellington's attention; he was unable to see the French infantry from his position. Lieutenant Colonel May was immediately sent galloping forward with an order to Von Bock to charge the enemy cavalry with his dragoons, and May came up with Von Bock as his brigade was galloping through the defile. Von Bock, who was very shortsighted, could not see the French. "Perhaps

you will be good enough to show us the enemy," he said to
May, and the Englishman therefore found himself riding in
the front rank of the leading German squadron. He was
wounded later in the action, remarking afterwards, "This is
what I get for leading Germans!"

Under normal conditions Von Bock would have wheeled his
squadrons into line before charging, but the valley was so
narrow that his leading three squadrons were compelled to
advance echeloned back from the front. Every dragoon's attention was riveted on the French cavalry ahead of him, but the
Frenchmen did not wait to receive the charge, and wheeled
away to a flank. As they did so the leading squadron of the 1st
Dragoons was taken in enfilade by the fire of the French
infantry drawn up on the heights to their left.

The left squadron of the regiment was echeloned back some
two or three hundred yards to the left rear of the leading
squadron, and the first intimation it received of the presence of
French infantry was the sudden burst of musketry and the
thick black smoke drifting down from the heights. Captain
Von der Decken, commanding the left squadron, could see
the effect of this fire on the leading squadron, and he knew
that he must run the gauntlet of the same death-dealing
musketry. He at once decided to charge the nearest French
square, although the ground favored infantry more than cavalry and despite the fact that there was no artillery available
to redress the balance and clear a passage for his sabers.
Wheeling his squadron into line, he led it headlong against
the French, who greeted him with volley after volley. The
dragoons enveloped two sides of the square but could not
break into it. The two front ranks of the infantry were kneeling, and behind them were four more ranks standing. Fluttering over the center of the square were the bullet-torn colors,
and out in front were the lightly equipped skirmishers picking
off the leading dragoons. Von der Decken was one of the first
of his squadron to fall.

In face of such a wall of musketry and steel, it seemed that
the wave of horsemen must break and fall back, but at the

crucial moment a shot killed one of the dragoon horses and it fell with its rider on top of the French ranks. The opening was made and with a wild yell the dragoons urged their terrified and snorting horses into the gap. It was like the flood which follows the bursting of a dam. The infantry disappeared under the onrush of slashing, yelling, thrusting horsemen, the confusion made a thousand times worse by the plunging and kicking of the fear-maddened horses. By the time the dragoons were finished the entire battalion had either been cut down or taken as prisoners, and where the square had once stood lay the disemboweled carcasses of nearly forty horses.

Meanwhile the third squadron of the 1st Dragoons under Captain Von Reitzeuslen had followed Von der Decken's example and charged the second French square. This was drawn up on the edge of the heights and it was even better placed to drive back cavalry. But its morale was shaken by the fate of the other battalion. The cohesion essential if infantry was to withstand the shock action of cavalry was ruined by a number of soldiers who broke the ranks and took to their heels. The dragoons smashed their way into the gaps left by the fugitives and sabered their way through to the other side of the square; then, rallying as one man to the trumpet call, they rode back the way they had come and completed the rout.

A few unwounded French officers hastily rallied the survivors and attempted to form a third square. This in its turn was charged and destroyed by the two squadrons of the 2nd Dragoons which had been following behind their sister regiment. Foy's rear guard had ceased to exist as an effective fighting force, and all who remained alive and untaken were withdrawn to some rising ground near the Peneranda road. The King's German Legion followed them, but by now their horses had been virtually ridden into the ground. The French held them off with the courage that is lent by despair, picking up the stones which littered the ground and hurling them at the legs of the heaving and staggering horses. Wellington then sent orders for the dragoons to retire, and they made their way slowly back to the rear through the cheering ranks of the

British infantry. They left behind them in the valley of Garcia Hernandez fifty-two dead dragoons and sixty-seven dead horses; their wounded totaled slightly more.

The charge of the 1st and 2nd Dragoons of the King's German Legion at Garcia Hernandez was probably the most brilliant cavalry action of the whole Peninsular War; it was certainly one of the few occasions in history when cavalry has succeeded in charging and breaking infantry squares drawn up on ground favorable to the infantry. Everything seemed to be in the infantry's favor, and it was for this reason that General Foy described the action as *"la charge la plus audacieuse de la guerre d'Espagne."* The likelihood is that Wellington agreed with him. Never lavish with his praise, in his dispatch on the battle he wrote:

> I have never witnessed a more gallant charge than was made upon the enemy's infantry by the heavy brigade of the King's German Legion under major-general von Bock, which was completely successful, and the whole body of infantry, consisting of three battalions of the enemy's first division, were made prisoners.[14]

There were other evidences of his admiration. Two days' rest on the field was ordered for Von Bock's men, and the heavy brigade of the Legion was ordered to provide Wellington with a personal guard. Three weeks later, on Wellington's recommendation, the following order was received from the War Office in London:

> In consideration of the King's German Legion having so frequently distinguished themselves against the enemy, and particularly upon the occasion of the late victory obtained near Salamanca, His Royal Highness the Prince Regent is pleased, in the name and on behalf of His Majesty, to command that the officers, who are now serving with temporary rank in the several regiments of that

[14] Beamish, *op. cit.*, Vol. II, p. 86.

corps, shall have permanent rank in the British army from the date of their respective commissions.[15]

Garcia Hernandez was undoubtedly the most distinguished single victory that the King's German Legion was to win under British command. It was not the end of their services, however, and they continued to fight brilliantly under Wellington until the last Frenchmen had been driven out of Spain. They were with him at Waterloo, and it was the infantry of the Legion who held La Haye Sainte against the ponderous might of the French cuirassiers. When the Legion reverted to the service of Hanover after Napoleon's departure to St. Helena, they took with them the battle honors they had won under British command—"Peninsula," "Barosa," "El Bodon," "Sicily," "Garcia Hernandez," and "Waterloo." [16] These honors they were allowed to retain when the Hanoverian army was incorporated into the Prussian army in 1866, and a visitor to the museum at Celle, the former seat of the electors of Hanover, will see the names blazoned on the helmet plates of dragoon, artilleryman, and infantryman, and on the faded colors.

The hussar and dragoon regiments of the Legion ended their days as regiments of the Imperial German army. The 1st and 2nd Dragoons became the 13th and 14th Uhlans, and two of the hussar regiments were renumbered as the 15th Hussars and the 9th Dragoons. The tradition of the 13th Uhlans was carried forward into the post-1918 German Reichswehr by the 1st squadron of the 13th (Prussian) Cavalry Regiment, but this

[15] *Ibid.* Temporary officers, who in war have had occasion to reflect on the impermanence of their rank and the permanence of death, will probably be able to judge the delight with which the officers of the King's German Legion greeted this announcement.

[16] An additional honor won when under British control was "Göhrde." This commemorates a victory won on September 16, 1813, by an Allied army over the French commanded by General Pecheur. The Allied commander was General Wallmoden whose father had commanded the Hanoverian army at the time of its surrender to the French in 1803. The younger Wallmoden was an international soldier who makes even the NATO commanders of today sound almost national. He managed to serve in the Austrian, Russian, and British armies at one time or another.

tradition, like so many other things, died with Hitler. A lot had happened since the first recruits slipped across the sea from Hanover to enlist under King George III in the 1st Dragoons at Weymouth.

Battle honors won under Wellington are no longer commemorated in the new German army, but a statue of a mounted lancer of the 14th Uhlans still stands under the limes beside the cathedral at Verden. That statue reminds us of a tradition of bravery and discipline which overcame seemingly impossible odds at Garcia Hernandez, and it seems strangely appropriate that it should have been erected beside the quiet-flowing Aller in the town where the King's German Legion established its headquarters during its short-lived return to Hanover in 1806, and where today a British garrison is serving beside the German army in defense of the same ideals. *Tapfer und treu* (Brave and True) was the motto inscribed on the guidon that was carried into action by the 1st Dragoons at Garcia Hernandez, and it is not a bad motto for any alliance.

Perhaps, in these days of the North Atlantic Treaty Organization, that statue of the German uhlan at Verden is something of a symbol for us all.

CHAPTER FIVE

Aliwal

JANUARY 28, 1846

"H.M. *16th Lancers on this occasion have added to their former reputation acquired in various fields of battle in Asia by routing the enemy's cavalry in every direction.*"

SIR HENRY HARDING,
GOVERNOR GENERAL OF INDIA (1846)

ON JUNE 12, 1822, four troops of the 16th (The Queen's) Lancers embarked on board the East India Company's *General Hewitt* at Tilbury. Two days later the regimental headquarters and the four remaining troops embarked on the *Marchioness of Ely*. The 16th were sailing for India on a journey which was to take them six months. It was not until December 30 that the two halves of the regiment were joined together at Fort William, Calcutta.

Twenty-four years later, on August 14, 1846, the regiment marched once more aboard the transports to return to their own country; they had been a long time away from the green fields of England.

During those years in India they had marched with Comber-

83

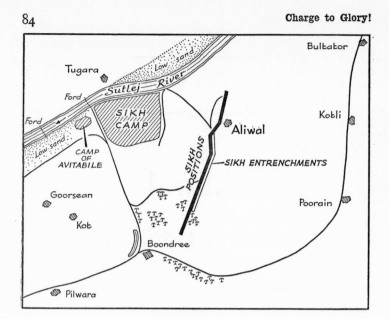

mere[1] to Bhurtpore, where they were the first British cavalry regiment to charge with the lance in battle, and with Keane to Kandahar, Ghazni, and Kabul in Afghanistan. In that campaign against the Afghans the 16th Lancers had covered 2,405 miles in thirteen months—one of the longest of all cavalry marches. They had added six more battle honors to the nine already blazoned on their drum banners, and at Aliwal they had ridden in one of the most famous cavalry charges in British history—a charge which they still commemorate today, although the horse has long ago given way to the tank, and lances no longer have a part to play on the modern battlefield.

[1] Lord Combermere, who commanded the expedition against the Rajah of Bhurtpore, had been lieutenant colonel of the 16th in 1805. He was reputed to be a remarkably stupid man. The story goes that the British Cabinet, seeking a general to command an expedition to capture Rangoon, consulted the Duke of Wellington. "Send Lord Combermere," said the Duke. "But, Your Grace," protested the Prime Minister, "we thought you had always considered Lord Combermere to be a fool." "So he is," said the great man, "and a damned fool, but he can take Rangoon."

In 1943 Field Marshal Wavell, then commander in chief in India, repeated this story in a memorandum to his deputy chief of staff, adding—"Where can we find a Lord Combermere?"

The 16th Lancers had been raised in 1759 as light dragoons and their first colonel was Burgoyne. He has gone down into history as the man who surrendered at Saratoga, and like many another unsuccessful general is remembered better for his solitary failure than for his many successes, although in his day he was thought to be a particularly brilliant officer. His attitude towards his men was certainly far in advance of his times, and one of his first instructions in the 16th Light Dragoons laid down that "English soldiers are to be treated as thinking beings." He was also a gifted playwright with a turn for literature, and it must surely have been his pen which drafted the first recruiting poster for his regiment:

> You will be mounted on the finest horses in the world [promised Burgoyne] with superb clothing and the richest accoutrements. Your pay and privileges are equal to two guineas a week, you are everywhere respected, your society is courted, you are admired by the fair, which, together with the chance of getting switched by a buxom widow or of brushing a rich heiress, renders the situation truly enviable and desirable. Young men out of employment or uncomfortable—"there is a tide in the affairs of men which taken at the flood leads on to fortune"—nick it instantly and enlist.

Whether it was the pay that drew them or the hopes of switching a widow or brushing an heiress, the 16th never lacked for recruits. We do not know, however, how they felt when they discovered that after deduction their pay amounted only to 1s. 2d. a week, nor was there much opportunity to meet either rich heiresses or buxom widows in the barren valleys and impoverished villages of Portugal, where they were sent on the 16th's first campaign.

Burgoyne was but a memory by the time the 16th embarked for India. The regiment had distinguished itself in Spain and at Waterloo, and in 1816 was the first British cavalry regiment to be converted from light dragoons to lancers. It was a typical example of a cavalry regiment of its day. The officers were nearly all younger sons of the aristocracy and landed gentry, while the troopers came mostly from the yeomen farmers of England and Ireland. They thought themselves enormously superior to their comrades in the line or artillery, and prided themselves that their colonel, when addressing the regiment, always referred to them as, "Gentlemen of the Lancers." Such condescension would have been unheard of in the infantry!

It cost their officers a great deal of money to serve their country,[2] and the speed at which an officer mounted the promotion ladder depended largely on the length of his pocket, since rank had to be purchased. The colonelcy of the 16th Lancers was valued at £14,000, and before a captain could obtain his troop he would have to find nearly £5,000. Even the humble cornet (or second lieutenant) had to pay £450 before he was allowed to don the scarlet jacket of the 16th Lancers. Uniforms were expensive and constantly being altered to suit the whim of commanding officers, and there was no such thing as paid furlough back to England. One was either wealthy enough to pay the cost of a passage on an East Indiaman or one had sufficient influence to wangle a passage on official duty. If one was unlucky or dependent on one's pay, one remained overseas until the regiment returned to England—or until cholera or some other tropical disease intervened to make the whole problem academic.

The 16th considered themselves an exclusive regiment, but as cavalry regiments went they were not extravagant. Ever

---

[2] A letter from the War Office to the mother of a prospective officer (taken from an article by Lt. Col. B. G. Baker in *The Cavalry Journal*, July, 1936, p. 410) runs as follows:

Horse Guards
May 29th, 1845.

Madam,

I will thank you to let me know whether you would be desirous that your son should be appointed to the Cavalry, either at home or in India, in preference to the Infantry. You are probably aware that the Cavalry service is more expensive, and that an officer entering it requires more for his equipment and ordinary yearly expenses than an Infantry officer. The Duke of Wellington begs you will consider this inquiry strictly confidential.

I have the honour to be, Madam,
Your most obedient,
Fitzroy Somerset.

since George III had conferred on them the title of "The Queen's" in honor of his consort, Queen Charlotte, the 16th Lancers prided themselves on a particular loyalty to the queens of England [3] and this was to get them into trouble with George IV. That stout and simpering monarch, who detested his queen, Caroline, considered any manifestation of loyalty towards her as synonymous with disloyalty to himself. It was always believed in the regiment that they were sent to India because the officers drank the health of Queen Caroline in the mess. When the King heard of it he ordered the regiment overseas immediately, and from such an order there could be no appeal.

It is doubtful whether anyone in the regiment worried much about it. Life in the army in those days was very much a family affair. The men were all long-service regulars, and the regiment was their home; in it they had found a refuge from the kicks and ha'pence of civilian life, and although service conditions were rugged and hard, the comradeship and *esprit de corps* made up for a good deal. They were intensely proud of their regiment and quite convinced of its superiority over any other regiment in the army. On the whole their relations with the officers were good, and probably better than in most regiments. There were the horses, dashing uniforms, plenty of beer, and the occasional battle; what more could a man want?

Besides, the life of an English trooper in India was infinitely more comfortable than in the gloomy garrison towns of England. In India every soldier had his own servant, who waited on him hand and foot, whether in the field or in cantonments. He lay in bed in the morning while he was shaved, and the air above him was cooled by a *punkah* pulled backwards and forwards by yet another servant. Although nominally he was expected to care for his own horse, there were always sufficient native grooms available to make such an exertion unnecessary, and if grass had to be cut for fodder there were grasscutters to do so at the princely wage of eight shillings a month. When the 16th Lancers marched on their first campaign in India, one officer wrote in his diary:

[3] The colonel in chief of the regiment today is Queen Elizabeth II.

I can quite understand now how Xerxes and Darius had such multitudes with them when they took the field. Each fighting man with us has more than one follower, and a large bazaar accompanies the camp besides. We carry the men's tents on elephants, and each elephant has two men; four water carriers to each troop; a cook to every sixteen men; every horse has a man to cut grass for it; the men have six camels and two men per troop to carry their beds. Then come the grain grinders, tailors, bakers, butchers, calasseys, or men for pitching tents, and many others. . . . I should say that for 560 officers and men we must have 5,600 followers. . . . I have in my own service 40 men, 10 camels, and a hackery, five horses and two ponies, this for a mere captain! [4]

In the land of the blind the one-eyed man is king, and in India the humble cavalry trooper and infantry private were men of substance. It was a different story in their own land, where the trade of soldier was suspect, and where even the Duke of Wellington, their commander in chief, had once referred to his soldiers as "scum." It is true that the Indian climate was likely to kill one sooner or later, but that was because of the soldier's way of life and the unhygienic conditions. Drink was responsible for far more deaths than the sun, and the cholera killed far more certainly and swiftly than any bullet.

Nor was the soldier unduly worried by the absence of female companionship of his own kind. The Evangelical Revival, which in England was to turn one of the best-hearted and least-inhibited people in Europe into a race of prigs and hypocrites, had yet to reach India. "Necessity is the mother of invention and the father of the Eurasian," said the cynics, and it was entirely true of India. Many officers kept Indian mistresses, and by doing so learned a great deal more of the language and customs of the country than was to be the case later. The same was true of the soldier. Thorn, writing of those who catered for

[4] Col. Henry Graham, *History of the 16th, The Queen's, Light Dragoons (Lancers)* (George Simpson, Devizes, 1912), p. 85.

the army's luxuries, describes a military camp where "female quacks practice cupping, sell drugs, and profess to cure disorders by charms. Nearly allied to these are the jugglers, shewing their dexterity by numerous arts of deception; and to complete the motley assembly, groups of dancing girls have their allotted station in the bazaar." [5]

Above all there was liquor. Drink was the incurable vice of the British soldier. The officers drank port and claret, not the most suitable of beverages when the thermometer stood at over 100 degrees in the shade, while the soldier drank anything, from vinegary beer to the filthiest of country spirits. Not surprisingly he lowered his resistance to disease, and on regimental holidays and Christmas he virtually ran amuck. In his diary of eighteen years in India with the 16th Lancers, Captain Luard tells the story of a soldier in Baron Osten's troop, who, "as the men were mounting their horses, without any apparent cause drew his pistol and blew his brains out. This is the fourth or fifth instance of suicide that has occurred in the regiment since it has been stationed in Cawnpore." [6]

Far from home and living under conditions very different from life in England, the British in India adapted the conventions to suit themselves.

> I left Cawnpore on October 5th [wrote Captain Luard] to celebrate the nuptials of the British Resident at the court of the King of Oude, and Mrs R—, who he is taking to Lucknow and to whom he is immediately to be married; the widow about nine months ago saw her husband murdered in her presence. Her husband-to-be within a shorter period had become a widower, and was so inconsolable until he met Mrs R— that good natured people supposed his heart would break. [7]

They must have been a remarkable people who built the British empire in India. Quietly, and without noticeable com-

[5] *The Diary of an Officer of the 16th (Queen's) Lancers, June 16, 1822, to June 16, 1840* (Thacker, Spink, Calcutta, 1894, for private circulation only).
[6] *Ibid.*
[7] *Ibid.*

plaint, they endured the heat, the flies, and the disease. For every two children born to them, they buried at least one, and often both. Their graves and their memorials are to be found in almost every Indian town from Peshawar to the Coromandel coast, yet they never seem to have lost their sense of humor.

> Mrs M— is sufficiently *embonpoint* to weigh fifteen stone; all her cloaks had got wet, so she borrowed the Resident's dressing gown. How she got into it I cannot imagine, as the Resident is at most a nine stone man. I am sure there must have been a space of two feet across her bosom uncovered. In this dress she was reclining on a couch with H— standing by her side, who ever and anon plied her with a round of beef. I told Mrs M— she was playing at hide and seek; she laughed and said I was pert.[8]

Practical jokes were considered the quintessence of humor, and horseplay of the roughest description was indulged in by officers and soldiers alike. Luard describes an evening after dinner in mess when some of the subalterns turned out a cat, which they voted to be wild, and hunted it with hounds right through the camp until it took refuge beneath the dining table of Colonel L., "the very stiffest of all Adjutant Generals." One can imagine the feelings of the peppery and gallant colonel, enjoying his port with his dinner guests, when a mob of howling subalterns burst in with their hounds and killed the cat under his dinner table.

Officers and men, wives and children, they all had to be tough if they were to survive. General Thackwell, who was colonel of the 16th for some years, was so severely wounded in the arm that it had to be amputated at the shoulder; five weeks later he was back on drill parade. During September, 1833, the 16th Lancers had 364 of their 580 men in hospital, and out of forty-eight men suffering from cholera, forty-two died.[9] It is hardly surprising that Captain Luard, depressed by the numer-

---

[8] *Ibid.*
[9] Outside one barracks in India was a notice board on which was inscribed—"Cook House. Latrines. Wash House." The same building served for all of these!

ous funerals of that month, applied for leave of absence in the
Hills, and he notes in his diary that he was supplied with a
certificate, "stating that I have been suffering under dyspepsia,
atrophy, and a general attenuation of the system for the last
two years." [10] In the circumstances it is astonishing that he was
not worse.

Little or no concession was made to the differences in climate. The 16th rode to battle in the same uniform they would
have worn at Aldershot, in lance caps modeled on the Polish
pattern, and with 15½-inch horsehair plumes hanging down from
the caps. Their tight-fitting jackets were scarlet—the only lancer
regiment to wear scarlet—and ever since, the regiment has been
nicknamed the "Scarlet Lancers," or "The Scarlets." One colonel was so keen on this regimental ruddiness (so to speak) that
he did his best to enlist only red-haired men, and mount them
only on chestnut horses.

They wore tight blue trousers, with double gold stripes,
strapped under the instep, and their shoulders were protected
from enemy sword cuts by a flat brass chain strap. Officers wore
epaulettes and a profusion of gold lace, and there were as many
orders of dress as there are days in the week: full dress, half-
dress, mess dress, dress for table, for foot parade, for drawing
room, and for Court functions. The cost of it all by present-day
standards was well over £500.

Officers and men carried swords, about thirty-six inches in
length and with slightly curved blades. Only the soldiers, however, carried lances, and these were nine or ten feet long, with
red-and-white pennants fastened just below the points. An
incredible quantity of kit was carried.

> Every variety of article was heaped on the saddle,
> which was a heavy wooden-treed concern. . . . This mis-
> cellaneous assortment of rattle-traps seemed to have been
> designed on the principle of the White Knight's mouse-
> trap; the things were not likely to be wanted, but still they
> might be. They included a so-called "lassoo equipment,"
> picket peg, head and heel ropes, and heavy iron shackles

[10] *The Diary of an Officer of the 16th (Queen's) Lancers.*

in addition to the steel collar chain, and a "pioneer equipment." The consequence was that a lancer in full marching
order weighed an average of 23 stone, and a packed saddle
required two men to lift it on to a horse's back. The rattle
of a man in marching order at the trot was audible half
a mile off, and a marching order parade left the ground
strewn with odds and ends that were sufficient to fill a
cart.[11]

So much for the British *light* cavalry in the first half of Victoria's reign!

The horses were a mixture of Arabs, countrybreds, and Walers
imported from Australia. Many of them were stallions, which
added some excitement to the ordinary mounted parade. One
colonel rode on parade to see his regimental sergeant major,
mounted on a mare, being chased off parade by a stallion. The
colonel drew his sword and went in pursuit, meaning to cut
down the stallion, whereupon it turned on the colonel and
mounted his mare in full view of the whole regiment. The next
morning an order went out that all stallions in that regiment
would be gelded in future.

The winter of 1845 found the 16th Lancers stationed at
Meerut, at that time the principal military garrison in northern
India. It was reputed to be one of the pleasantest stations in
the country. There was the race course, as well as the club
where the bands played after church on Sunday mornings, and
where the subalterns made love to their senior officers' wives
on Saturday nights; there were balls and banquets, and shoot-
ing parties out after the black buck, partridges, and wild pig.
A typical Anglo-Indian society of the time amused themselves
in Meerut in a typical Anglo-Indian manner, regulating their
social intercourse by the most rigid protocol, but adopting a
fairly tolerant attitude towards those who strayed from the
strictly moral path.

A considerable gulf existed socially between the officers serving in India with British regiments, usually referred to as H.M.
regiments, and those who officered the native regiments of the

[11] Graham, *op. cit.*

East India Company; and the gulf was even wider between the military and the civilians. Lifelong enmities could begin through some trivial error in precedence—by seating the wife of a major below the wife of a captain at a dinner table, or by presenting a captain in some irregular native cavalry regiment to the general ahead of a captain in one of H.M. regiments. There was a great deal of gaiety and a vast amount of pettiness and snobbery, but it is as well to remember that this state of affairs was by no means confined to the British in India.

There was not much for the soldiers to do, apart from constant drilling and cleaning their kits. Field training, as we understand it today, consisted mainly of drill movements performed to trumpet calls. For most of the year all work finished by midday, and the soldiers drowsed away the burning afternoons in their high-ceilinged and darkened barrack huts, lulled to sleep by the ceaseless swish of the *punkahs*. A few of the men had European wives, but more of them had married Eurasian and Indian women. Organized games played little part in their lives, but the bachelors among them cultivated their gardens behind the barracks or kept racing pigeons and fighting cocks. At night there was always the "Wet Canteen" and the endless reminiscences about the battles they had fought; and how "The Scarlets" had shown the rest of the army the way; and there was always the horse to link together officer and man —the race meetings; the gymkhanas and the mad, exhilarating gallops after wild pig, with a spear in one's hand, and the flying hoofs drumming the ground like a salvo of field guns.

Life by our standards was boring, but one seldom finds anything in soldiers' reminiscences to show that they found it so. It was rugged and tough, and the discipline was Draconian, but the men seem to have been happy enough. Few of them took any leave; there was nowhere for them to go, and in any case the regiment was their home. Even fewer aspired to be officers.[12] They say that "old soldiers never die," and the fact

[12] The 16th Lancers were, however, the only cavalry regiment in the British army to produce a trooper who rose through every grade in rank until he became a field marshal and chief of the Imperial General Staff. This was Sir William Robertson, who joined the 16th Lancers as a trooper in 1877 and who served for eleven years in the ranks of the regiment. Sir

is hardly surprising when one considers what the soldier had
to endure in order to become old! Yet, despite everything, he
seems to have been happy, and became even more so when the
regiment was ordered out on a campaign—as happened to the
16th Lancers early in December, 1845.

They were to form part of the army which was being collected under General Sir Hugh Gough to fight the Sikhs who
were threatening to invade the East India Company's territory
in northern India. The Sikhs were undoubtedly the most formidable adversaries that the British were to encounter throughout their rule of nearly two hundred years in India. Sikhism is
essentially a warrior religion, and the Sikhs, whose home is in
the Punjab in northwestern India, can be loosely described as
the Protestants of the Hindu religion. They are forbidden to
worship idols, to cut their hair, or to smoke tobacco, and they
combine strict religious observance with almost fanatical bravery. They can also be extremely cruel, as was the case in 1947
during the partition of India.

The Sikh domain in 1845 comprised nearly all of what we
now know as West Pakistan. This empire had been built up
very largely by Maharajah Runjeet Singh, a man of genius, with
only one eye, a highly developed taste for debauchery, and a
complete lack of any form of scruple. His power depended on
a well-paid and well-trained army which he was careful to keep
under control; it had been trained by Italian and French soldiers of fortune, and Runjeet Singh ensured its loyalty by grant-
ing the soldier the most privileged position in his realm. The
most effective of these troops were the Aieen battalions, drilled
and often commanded by Europeans, and there was also a particularly well-equipped force of artillery.

With the aid of this army, tireless intrigue, and outright
treachery whenever it suited his ends, Runjeet Singh enlarged
the Sikh empire until it stretched from the Khyber Pass in the

William Robertson's son, General Sir Brian Robertson, was British high
commissioner in Germany after World War II, and he very nearly succeeded in emulating his father's feat of filling the highest appointment
in the British army. Sir Brian did in fact become adjutant general before
he retired—the second highest appointment in the British army.

northwest to the banks of the River Sutlej in the southwest, and from Kashmir in the north to Bawalpur in the south. "The Lion of the Punjab," as Runjeet was known to his soldiers, knew only one limit to his ambitions; he was determined never to involve himself in war with the powerful East India Company, whose boundary marched with his own along the Sutlej. This determination was dictated solely by self-interest; Runjeet had no more reason than any other Indian potentate to love the British.

Runjeet died in 1839, soon after the British had begun their disastrous campaign in Afghanistan, and the government of the Punjab lapsed rapidly into anarchy. There was no strong man to follow him, and a succession of palace revolutions failed to produce anyone fit to take Runjeet's place on the *gadi* (throne). The pay of the troops fell into arrears, and the inevitable mutinies followed; the streets of Lahore, the capital, were thronged with blustering, belligerent, and fanatical soldiers offering their swords to the highest bidder. The French and Italian officers packed up their presentation swords and jewels, sold their estates for gold, bade farewell to their harems of mistresses, and then set sail for home. Their own financial future was assured, and they had no wish to jeopardize it by involving themselves in Sikh quarrels.

The collapse of the rule of law and order in the Punjab was watched uneasily by the British. They were well aware of the fighting potential of the Sikh army, and equally well aware that the recent war against the Afghans had done nothing to enhance the prestige of British arms. At the same time they were anxious to avoid embroiling themselves with the Sikhs, because wars cost money. The East India Company was essentially a trading corporation with a duty to its shareholders, and extremely awkward questions had been asked about the cost of the Afghan war. It would be even more awkward if the Afghanistan operations were to be followed by a campaign against the Sikhs.

On the other hand there could be no doubt that the Sikhs were growing more and more bellicose. The soldiers were clamoring to be led against the detested British, and the unfortunate citizens of Lahore were beginning to think that a war with the British would in some ways be preferable to the continued existence in their midst of the swaggering and intolerable soldiery. Sir Henry Harding, the British governor general of India, who was himself a soldier, believed that he would be compelled to fight the Sikhs sooner or later. The alternative would be to hand back to the Sikhs a huge block of territory between Delhi and the Sutlej; there were large numbers of Sikhs living in this region, and the war party in Lahore was clamoring for the army to cross the Sutlej and liberate their co-religionists.

In order to deter the anticipated Sikh invasion, the British began to strengthen their garrisons north of Delhi, and by November, 1845, the largest army that the British had yet assembled in India was concentrating around Ferozepore on the Sutlej. There were over thirty thousand men collected under Gough, of which over a third were British troops, which was an unusually high proportion. In December this force was attacked by the Sikhs, who crossed the Sutlej in the middle of the month, and at the battles of Moodkee and Ferozeshah the British learned the nature of their adversary. In three days of battle they lost nearly a quarter of their strength, and the losses fell the most heavily on the white regiments, which were virtually irreplaceable. The Sikh losses were even heavier, but they had reinforcements close at hand.

The 16th Lancers formed part of the Meerut Division, and they did not arrive on the Sutlej until New Year's Day, 1846. Their first task was to bury the dead who had fallen at Moodkee and Ferozeshah.

> On our arrival at the camp ground the stench was horrible [wrote a noncommissioned officer]. A great many were buried within a few yards of our tents. As soon as we had pitched our camp we walked out on the field of battle to view the place and for miles around we could see the dead lying in all directions. At Ferozeshah, about three miles from our tents, the dead were lying in heaps. The 3rd Light Dragoons made great havoc among the enemy but have

lost the best half of their regiment . . . in one place we could see many of the 3rd and Sikhs lying together; they must have fought hand-to-hand after their horses were shot.[13]

They were not left as gravediggers for long. The battles had been inconclusive, and it was clear to Sir Hugh Gough, not one of the British army's more brilliant generals, that he could not afford any more heavy casualties. If he were to drive the Sikhs back again across the Sutlej, he would require the heavy artillery which was being dragged by elephants and yoke after yoke of oxen up the Grand Trunk road from Delhi arsenal. This line of communication ran through the garrison town of Ludhiana, seventy miles to the east of the Sutlej, and was now being menaced by roving bands of Sikhs who were terrorizing the countryside. Partly to secure his communications and partly to destroy the village of Dhurmcote near Ludhiana, which the marauding Sikhs were using as their supply base, Gough sent a force under Major General Sir Harry Smith to clear the country round Ludhiana.

Sir Harry Smith was subsequently to become one of the heroes of mid-Victorian Britain. He had fought in Spain with the rifles under Wellington, and had rescued a beautiful fifteen-year-old Spanish girl who was in imminent danger of being raped after the siege of Badajoz. "To look at her was to love her," wrote an officer about Juanita de los Dolores de Leon, but while he was looking on and loving, Harry Smith stepped in to woo her and to win her. From then onwards she accompanied him on all the campaigning in Spain, and later followed the drum with him all over the world. When, many years later, Smith became governor of the Cape Province in South Africa, Juanita Smith gave her name to a town in Natal, which became the Ladysmith of Boer War fame.

Smith marched with his force on January 17, 1846, but shortly afterwards news reached Gough that the Sikh marauders in the Ludhiana region were in considerable strength. Gough wanted no more Pyrrhic victories like Moodkee and Ferozeshah,

[13] Graham, *op. cit.*, p. 104.

so he sent the 16th Lancers and two troops of horse artillery
hurrying after Smith as reinforcements. At the same time he
ordered one of his precious British infantry regiments, H.M.
53rd Foot, to march to join Smith's force.

The winter climate of the Punjab is amongst the finest in
the world. Cold nights are succeeded by gloriously sunny days,
and the absence of rain makes for perfect campaigning weather.
The 16th Lancers, however, were unable to enjoy the climate.
They were forced to march at a killing pace to catch up with
Smith, and the ground was deep in sand. The horses threw up
a thick cloud of dust which choked their riders and produced
an agonizing thirst, and any lancer who unbuttoned a tunic to
get some relief, or who drank from his water bottle without
permission, was certain of being reprimanded and punished.

Far behind the column toiled the baggage train. In those
days it was the custom for regiments to take with them to battle
all the regimental plate, some of it of great value, besides all
the officers' and men's bedding, equipment, and stores. With
the baggage went also the sick and the wounded; they were
carried in doolies—covered palanquins offering some protection
from the sun—which were so jolted and shaken by the dooly-
bearers, four men to each, that the unfortunate inmates must
often have wished they were dead.

The 16th caught up with Smith on January 20, and found
that they were to be brigaded with the two native cavalry regiments under the command of Brigadier General Charles Cureton. Cureton was a 16th Lancer officer and enormously popular
in the regiment, although he never commanded the 16th. He
had joined the regiment in 1819 after a remarkable career which
had begun in 1806 in the militia. In his youth Cureton had
been as wild as a hawk and had incurred considerable debts.
Soon after being gazetted lieutenant, he disappeared, and his
clothes were found wrapped up in a bundle on the beach. It
was assumed that he had drowned himself rather than enter a
debtors' prison, but it later transpired that he had disguised
himself as a sailor and sailed for London. There he enlisted in
the 14th Light Dragoons under the name of Roberts, fought
throughout the Peninsular War in the ranks, had his skull frac-

tured by a saber cut at Fuentes d'Onor, and in 1814 was given
a commission in the 14th Light Dragoons for gallantry in the
field. He then reverted to his own name, and five years later
transferred to the 16th Lancers. He later achieved great distinction as a cavalry commander in India, and was eventually
killed at Ramnagar in 1848. Both of his sons were cavalrymen,
and both rose to the rank of general before they retired.

The 16th were given only two hours to rest their horses and
were then ordered to lead the advance of Smith's force to Ludhiana. The horses plodded on, fetlock-deep in sand, from
midnight to dawn, and as the sun came up, the leading scouts
reported that the Sikhs were holding the fort of Buddiwal. This
fort stood on rising ground some six miles west of Ludhiana,
and commanded the route which Smith's force would have to
take. It was too strong to be attacked, and Smith therefore
decided to try to work his way round it.

Ludhiana was six miles away across a featureless plain. There
was virtually no cover, the ground was inches deep in dust and
sand, and the day turned out to be unusually hot for the time
of year. The going was hard enough on the horses, but the
heavily laden infantry found it appalling. Any man who fell
out was cut down immediately by the Sikh horsemen who
hovered round the flanks, and many of the 31st and 53rd Foot
had good reason to be grateful to the 16th Lancers that day.
The troopers mounted many of the exhausted infantry on their
horses, or allowed them to hang on to their stirrup leathers.
Even so more than four hundred men were lost during the day,
although some of them were stragglers who managed to make
their way into Ludhiana the following night.

During the night of the 21st all that was left of the baggage
train straggled into Ludhiana. It had been attacked on numerous occasions throughout the day, and despite the gallantry
of the escort provided by the 53rd Foot, most of the sick and
wounded had been butchered, and the greater part of the baggage plundered. The 16th Lancers had lost all their regimental
plate, and Cureton was so angry when he heard of the loss
that he placed the unfortunate subaltern in charge of the regimental baggage under arrest. He promised that he would court-

martial him at the first opportunity, but that opportunity never came. Seven days later the subaltern broke his arrest to ride with the lancers at Aliwal and he never returned from the battlefield. Only one piece of the plate was ever recovered.[14]

Smith was extremely lucky to have got away with it so lightly. He had been outnumbered nearly ten to one, and he had driven his men so hard during the march that they were almost at the end of their tether. Tight red jackets, thick blue serge trousers, heavy packs, and extra bandoleers of ammunition are not the ideal clothing and equipment for marching twenty miles through soft sand under a blazing sun. Smith's infantry were in a state of collapse by the time they reached Ludhiana, and had the Sikhs been in the least degree enterprising they would have driven in the rear guard of the 16th Lancers and put the entire force to the sword. As it was, they contented themselves with harassing the British with long-range artillery and musketry fire, and cutting down any stragglers.

Two days later the Sikhs evacuated their positions round the fort at Buddiwal and withdrew towards the Sutlej. Harry Smith lost no time in following them, and early in the morning of January 28 his leading scouts made contact with the enemy near the village of Aliwal, a few miles east of the Sutlej.

> We came in sight of them about 6 A.M. [wrote Corporal Cowtan of the 16th] and formed into line. At this moment the view of the two armies was beautiful indeed—a fine, open, grassy plain, and the enemy in line out of their entrenchments ready to commence; the river in their rear, and in the distance the snowy range of the Himalayas with the sun just rising over their tops.[15]

The Sikh force under *Sirdar* Runjore Singh[16] was drawn up along a ridge of high ground which connected the two villages

---

[14] Many years later a silver-gilt cup was found in a pawnshop in York and on it was engraved the crest of the 16th Lancers. There was no other inscription, but it has always been supposed that the cup formed part of the plate lost during the march to Ludhiana, probably picked up by a camp follower, and subsequently pawned in England.

[15] Graham, *op. cit.*, p. 112.

[16] Every Sikh adds Singh—meaning Lion—to his name.

of Aliwal and Boondree. Both these villages were typical mud-brick villages of the Punjab—a maze of narrow, dusty lanes, blank-walled courtyards, and stinking middens. Dusty orchards and thin groves of trees provided the only splashes of color in a predominantly dun landscape, and the mists of early morning swirled round the houses and mingled with the bitter blue smoke from the cow-dung fires. The ground was damp from the dew, and the smells of India were everywhere—spices and dung, incense and jasmine, and hot, wet earth.

There were about forty thousand Sikhs manning the entrenchments between Aliwal and Boondree, and supporting them were sixty-seven pieces of artillery. Aliwal itself had been fortified, and the Sikh position looked down across a gently sloping plain which stretched for two miles to the low ridge along which Sir Harry Smith's leading infantry were just beginning to deploy into battle formation. Leading Smith's advance were the 16th Lancers, and behind them came the three infantry brigades; all told, Smith had about ten thousand men, of which four regiments were British.[17] The native cavalry regiments were watching the flanks, and Aliwal is memorable for being the first occasion on which the British employed Gurkhas in battle. There were two Gurkha infantry regiments present at Aliwal.

Fearing lest the Sikhs should withdraw across the Sutlej without giving battle, Sir Harry Smith ordered the 31st Foot to advance and take Aliwal village. The regiment stepped off with colors flying and drums beating, "emulous for the front" as Fortescue[18] was to write of them later, but they received a terrific hammering from the Sikh artillery as they marched obliquely across the plain before forming line to storm Aliwal village. Despite their casualties and the loss of many of their officers, the 31st took Aliwal, and the entire Sikh position was then in danger of being turned.

Runjore Singh knew that his main danger lay in the British placing themselves between his own troops and the river; if

---

[17] H.M. 16th Lancers, 31st, 50th, and 53rd Foot.
[18] Sir John Fortescue, *History of the British Army* (Macmillan, London, 1927), Vol. XII.

this were to happen, his line of withdrawal would be cut. He decided therefore that he must drive the British out of Aliwal, and as a first step he threw all his cavalry against the right wing of the advancing British. As soon as this mass of horsemen appeared across the ridge from Boondree, Sir Harry Smith ordered one squadron of the 16th Lancers, and a native squadron of the 3rd Light Cavalry to charge the enemy. The 3rd hesitated, reluctant to cross sabers with the redoubtable Sikhs, so the 16th Lancers squadron galloped off without them.

The charge of Captain Bere's squadron of the 16th Lancers set the pattern for the many other charges that the regiment was to carry out during the day. The Sikh horses were far too light to stand up to the heavy British chargers, and the Sikhs were terrified of coming to grips with the lancers, against whose additional reach their own curved swords were virtually useless. The Sikh cavalry took to their heels and thereafter played little part in the battle, although they continued to hover around the outskirts, and they cut down without mercy any wounded or stragglers making their way to the rear.

But it was a far different story with the Sikh artillery and infantry. The former were exceptionally well served by their gunners, and the guns were so sited on the ridge between Aliwal and Boondree that they could sweep all the plain below them. The Sikh infantry were equally well trained and handled. Their favorite fighting formation was more an equilateral triangle than a square; if one side of the triangle was pierced, the other two sides faced inwards and fired indiscriminately, usually killing as many of their own side as of the enemy; there could be no hope for any man who was wounded or whose horse fell within the sides of the triangle. He was cut to pieces instantly, unless he was lucky enough to be killed by a musket shot.

As Bere's squadron, after their successful dash against the Sikh cavalry, came cantering back to rejoin the rest of the regiment, they found their path blocked by a Sikh infantry regiment. Bere led his squadron straight at the Sikhs, who stood their ground and greeted him with a volley. Luckily for the lancers the Sikhs had opened fire at extreme range, and before they could fire again the British cavalry went through the Sikh ranks like an avalanche, spearing and sabering as they crashed their way over and through the infantry. It was all over in a matter of seconds, and the Sikh infantry took to their heels. This spirited action gained Bere a mention in dispatches and a nasty wound in the face, but he survived to tell the tale.

Corporal Cowtan rode with Captain Bere's squadron in the charge, and in a letter home a few days later he described his part in the action:

> The enemy soon commenced a heavy fire upon the whole line which was advancing upon them. This lasted about an hour, when my squadron was ordered to charge. We cheered and moved on like a flash of lightning, clearing everything before us, guns, cavalry, and infantry. At the first charge I dismounted two cavalry men, and on retiring we passed through a square of infantry, and I left three men on the ground killed or wounded. One fellow was taking deliberate aim at me when I put my horse at him, and just in time, for his priming blackened my face.
>
> Sergeant Brown was riding next to me and cleaving everyone down before him with his sword when his horse was shot under him, and before he reached the ground he received no less than a dozen sabre cuts which, of course, killed him. The killed and wounded in my squadron alone was 42, and after the first charge self-preservation was the grand thing, and the love of life made us look sharp, and their great numbers required all our vigilance. Our lances seemed to paralyse them altogether, and you may be sure we did not give them time to recover themselves.[19]

The charge of Bere's squadron had relieved the pressure on the 31st Foot, who were still holding Aliwal village, but the Sikh artillery was giving the British right wing a tremendous pounding. Two squadrons of the 16th Lancers were covering that flank, and were drawn up on the crest of the ridge and in full view of the enemy. The Sikhs then brought up a battery of guns, and after them came a battalion of infantry. It seemed

---

[19] Graham, *op. cit.*, pp. 111-112.

to the waiting British as if the Sikhs were about to attack under cover of the guns, and Sir Harry Smith at once sent a galloper to order the 16th Lancers to charge and capture the guns.

In front of the waiting squadrons was the officer who that
day was acting as commanding officer of the 16th Lancers. He
was Major Rowland Smyth, a remarkable Irishman and a *beau
sabreur* of *beau sabreurs*. Smyth stood well over six feet, had the
Irishman's eye for a good horse, and enjoyed equally hunting,
gambling, fighting, and making love. As wild as a hawk, he had
been involved in one of the last duels to be fought in Britain
which ended fatally. An unfortunate Mr. O'Grady, a Dublin
civilian, was accused by Smyth of striking him with a whip
while Smyth was driving past O'Grady in a cabriolet. O'Grady
denied any such intention, but Smyth thereupon pulled him off
his horse and horsewhipped him in public. O'Grady had no
alternative than to call out Smyth, and they met the next morning in Phoenix Park. O'Grady was killed and Smyth was tried
for manslaughter, sentenced to a year's imprisonment, and
granted a year's leave by a kindly commander in chief while he
served his sentence! He eventually retired as a general, so his
earlier acquaintanceship with a cell in one of Her Majesty's
prisons does not seem to have affected his career unduly.

As soon as he received the orders to advance, Smyth ordered
his trumpeter to sound the "Trot." Then, as the two hundred
troopers moved forward with perfect dressing, Smyth turned in
his saddle and shouted:

"Now, 16th, I am going to give the word to charge. Three
cheers for the Queen!"

Seven or eight hundred yards in front of the advancing lancers were the guns, firing as fast as the bearded gunners could
load and prime. Smyth led his men straight at them, and the
Sikhs threw themselves flat on the ground to avoid the lances.
In the middle of all this confusion the Sikh infantry appeared
suddenly out of the smoke and dust, and Smyth was confronted
with a wall of swords and bayonets less than sixty yards away.

There was only one thing to do, but it needed a good horse
to do it. Putting his horse at the line of Sikhs in front of him,
Smyth clapped in his spurs and took his fences as a fox hunter

should—only in this case the fences consisted of men standing or kneeling, three deep, and facing outwards with their swords, spears, and bayonets. Over the first line, straight through the center of the square, and out over the far side went Major Rowland Smyth, and behind him came the wildly cheering "Scarlet Lancers."

Sergeant Gould rode in that charge and described it as follows:

> Down we swept on the guns. Very soon they were in our possession. A more exciting job followed. We had to charge a square of infantry. At them we went, the bullets flying round like a hailstorm. Right in front of us was a big sergeant, Harry Newsome. He was mounted on a grey charger, and with a shout of, "Hullo, boys, here goes for death or a commission," forced his horse right over the front rank of kneeling men, bristling with bayonets. As Newsome dashed forward he leant over and grasped one of the enemy's standards, but fell from his horse pierced by nineteen bayonet wounds.
>
> Into the gap made by Newsome we dashed, but they made fearful havoc among us. When we got out the other side of the square our troop had lost both lieutenants, the cornet, troop sergeant-major, and two sergeants. I was the only sergeant left. Some of the men shouted, "Bill, you've got command, they're all down."
>
> Back we went through the disorganised square, the Sikhs peppering us in all directions. One of the men had both arms frightfully slashed by a Sikh, who was down under his horse's feet and who made an upward cut at him. We retired to our own line. As we passed the general, he shouted, "Well done 16th. You have covered yourselves with glory."
>
> Then, noticing that no officers were with C Troop, Sir H. Smith enquired, "Where are your officers?" "All down," I replied. "Then," said the general, "go and join the left wing under Captain Bere." [20]

[20] Graham, *op. cit.*, p. 111.

Smyth emerged from the melee with a very severe bayonet wound. The bayonet had penetrated his body just below the waist, and had then broken off and remained in the wound. Although he was covered in blood and reeling in the saddle, Major Smyth led his men in a return charge through the Sikh infantry, and it was only after this that he allowed himself to be taken back to the rear. He was in great pain, the bayonet having pushed part of his tunic and sword belt into his stomach, but even so he refused to permit his wound to be dressed until the rest of his men had received attention. Six weeks later he was back in the saddle, and seemingly none the worse, for he lived on for another thirty years, to die at a ripe old age.

The Sikhs had fought with great bravery, but they began to give way after the 16th Lancers' charge. The British infantry fought their way into Boondree, and Sir Harry Smith was then able to bring his own artillery forward to the ridge from where formerly the Sikh artillery had been pounding him. A confused mass of Sikhs were falling back to the river, hemmed in on the flanks by Cureton's cavalry, and swept by the grape and canister which was poured into their ranks at virtually point-blank range. Men, elephants, horses, camels, all were struggling to get back to the river, and as they waded into the shallows, Cureton's cavalry came thundering down against them.

Time and again the 16th Lancers and the two native cavalry regiments charged home against the shattered remnants of Runjore Singh's army, until all cohesion left it. The only course left open was flight, and a bruised and bleeding rabble fled into the Sutlej and struggled across to the far side. Behind them they left their camp, all their artillery, and three thousand dead. Moodkee and Ferozeshah had been avenged.

The British losses were relatively light except among the 16th Lancers. They had lost eight officers and one hundred twenty-three men killed or wounded, as well as one hundred eighty-five horses killed, wounded, or missing. Veterans who had fought at Waterloo were loud in their praises of the Sikhs that day, maintaining that they had fought just as bravely as the French had done under Bonaparte.

By the end of the day, men and horses were completely exhausted; many of the horses could hardly stand from fatigue, and others lay down quietly and died from exhaustion. The body of Lance Corporal Mowbray, the best lancer and swordsman in the regiment, was found with his lance splintered and his sword broken, surrounded by a circle of seven dead Sikhs; in another part of the battlefield a lancer was found in a horizontal position, sitting erect on his horse with his sword arm raised in the act of striking. He and his horse had been shot through the heart and must have died instantaneously and both at the same moment.

Many were the stories told round the campfires that night, but one of the luckiest men was a trooper in Captain Bere's squadron. The story of his escape from what must have seemed certain death is worth the retelling:

> The squadron to which I belonged was ordered to charge a square of Sikh infantry. We went at them, and on coming within 40 yards they gave us a volley, a ball from which struck the chain of my lance-cap just over the left cheekbone. They then threw away their muskets, and taking their large shields, came at us sword in hand.

> I delivered a point at one fellow, but could not reach him, and was about settling a second when a blow from a sabre from behind severed my arm just above the wrist, and my hand, grasping the lance, fell to the ground.

> Not being able to make my horse break the ranks, I slipped my feet out of the stirrups and endeavoured to throw myself off. In doing this my sword belt caught the cantle of the saddle, but fortunately the belt broke, and I found myself on the ground.

> On getting up to make my way to the rear I was met by a Sikh who, seeing my helpless condition, placed his musket within a yard of my head. Just at that moment I lifted my left arm as if to strike him, and fell forward to the ground. He fired, and his charge burnt a portion of the hair off the back of my head, the ball entering my left shoulder.

> I lay for some moments, expecting the cowardly rascal

to finish me with his bayonet, but while he was re-loading an artilleryman came up and gave him the contents of his pistol, but this only wounding him, he dismounted and ran him through with his sword. After this I got up, and grasping the stump of my right arm again made for the rear.

I had not gone far before I found myself in front of a troop of artillery, who were only waiting for our squadron to get out of the way before opening fire on the retreating enemy. I managed to get between two of the guns, and then bolted as fast as I could. I walked on about a mile, and met with a doctor, who applied a tourniquet to my arm and gave me a glass of brandy and water and directed me to the field hospital, where, on arriving in a very exhausted condition it was found necessary to amputate my arm just below the elbow.[21]

The unfortunate man eventually recovered, and a grateful country returned him to civilian life with a pension of £13 a year!

Although the charge of the 16th Lancers at Aliwal is a forgotten episode today, in its time it captured the imagination of Victorian England. Sir Harry Smith became known as "the hero of Aliwal," and as is often the English way, the highest possible honor was paid him—large numbers of public houses were named after him! For a time, until the charge of the Light Brigade at Balaklava drove it out of the public's memory, the charge of the 16th Lancers at Aliwal was the talk and the pride of the country. It had certainly been a major contribution to the defeat of the Sikhs and prevented the Battle of Aliwal ending in the same bloody stalemate as had previously been the case at Moodkee and Ferozeshah.

England today has forgotten Aliwal—there have been other and sterner battles to fight—but the 16th Lancers have never forgotten. In 1922, they were amalgamated with the 5th Lancers, and they are known today as the 16th/5th The Queen's Royal Lancers. Their horses have long since vanished and their

[21] Graham, *op. cit.*, p. 113.

steeds today are tanks. No longer do they ride to battle with the red-and-white pennants fluttering bravely below the lance points, and the only lances left are the three which stand outside the regiment's headquarters.

Examine these lance pennants and it will be seen that they are carefully crimped. This commemorates a regimental custom which began the day after Aliwal when the regiment was assembled on parade, and it was noticed that the lance pennants were so encrusted with dried blood that they appeared to be starched and crimped. Ever since that day the 16th Lancers have crimped their lance pennants, and by so doing the regiment honors those who went before them and who fell at Aliwal.

It is a tradition well worth preserving.

CHAPTER SIX

Brandy Station

June 9, 1863

If you want to smell hell
If you want to have fun
If you want to catch the devil
Jine the cavalry!
MARCHING SONG OF GENERAL "JEB" STUART

WHEN South Carolina seceded from the Union in December, 1860, there were only five regular cavalry regiments in the United States army, and of these, two had been in existence for less than five years. The two senior regiments, the 1st and 2nd Dragoons, raised in 1833 and 1836 respectively, had already seen much service against the Indians and in Mexico. The Mounted Rifles, first raised in 1846 to guard the Oregon Trail, had joined General Zachary Taylor in Mexico during the autumn of that year. In March, 1855, conditions along the Indian frontier were such that Congress had authorized the formation of two more regiments, the 1st and 2nd Cavalry,[1] but even so, this was a small enough force with which to maintain watch and ward along a frontier which was being pushed steadily westward in the face of determined and growing resistance from the Indians. Yet from this tiny nucleus of regulars there grew a cavalry force that on the Union side totaled eighty thousand horsemen by the end of the war, while the Confederate cavalry at their peak could muster about half that number.

The cavalry tradition of the United States army dates from the Revolutionary War when Congress first authorized the formation of four regiments of dragoons, all of which subsequently faded away, until by 1784 none of them were left. Prominent among the cavalry leaders of those early days was "Light-Horse Harry" Lee, the father of General Robert E. Lee. Henry Lee had originally served in the British army; he commanded a detachment of the 16th Light Dragoons during that regiment's first campaign in Portugal, when they distinguished themselves against the Spaniards at Villa Velha in 1762. Lee's conduct on that occasion was specially commended, and it was a queer twist of fate that led to his capture near Trenton in December, 1776, by a detachment of the regiment he had led with such gallantry in Portugal fourteen years previously. It may have been of some consolation to him that Burgoyne, his commander of Portugal days, had also fallen victim to the fortunes of war at Saratoga, but twelve months' captivity must have been particularly irksome for a man as active and as hot-tempered as "Light-Horse Harry" Lee.[2]

After many vicissitudes, cavalry was formally incorporated into the United States army in 1833 when the 1st Dragoons

[1] OLD NAME	DATE OF ORIGIN	NEW NAME
1st Dragoons	1833	1st Cavalry
2nd Dragoons	1836	2nd Cavalry
Mounted Rifles	1846	3rd Cavalry
1st Cavalry	1855	4th Cavalry
2nd Cavalry	1855	5th Cavalry
3rd Cavalry	1861	6th Cavalry

[2] Among the duels he fought was one against Washington's aide-de-camp, Colonel John Laurens.

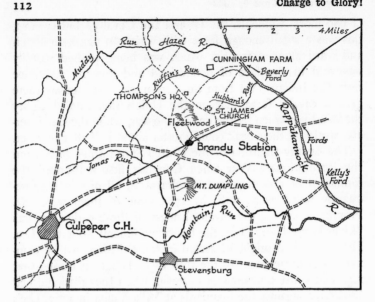

were organized; the regiment numbered among its officers a young West Pointer named Jefferson Davis. Three years later the 2nd Dragoons were raised for service against the Seminole Indians in Florida. In their early days the 2nd Dragoons won themselves a reputation for hard riding, hard drinking, and a marked disregard for military punctilio. At one period, two of their companies were trained as lancers, an experiment which was soon abandoned, but in August, 1842, the regiment was reduced to unprintable fury by the news that they were to be turned into a regiment of infantry. Their sentiments were the same as those of Charles Lee, no relation of "Light-Horse Harry" but who had served with him in the 16th Light Dragoons, when he decided to leave the British army to serve the czar of Russia: "I am to have command of Cossacks and Wallachians, a kind of people I have a good opinion of. I am determined not to serve in the Line—one might just as well be a churchwarden!"

Congress relented and gave the 2nd Dragoons back their horses in 1844. Four years later the two dragoon regiments found themselves dispersed in isolated posts all along the Indian frontier—in Texas, New Mexico, California, Kansas, Minnesota, Arizona, and Oregon. It was a vast area to be guarded by only twenty companies of understrength cavalry and was in many ways comparable with the British experience in India, where vast provinces were subdued by a mere handful of white soldiers.

Increasing commitments had led to the formation of the Mounted Rifles in 1846. They won immortal fame at the famous storming of Chapultepec Castle in Mexico, and were greeted next day by General Winfield Scott with the words, "Brave Rifles! Veterans! You have been baptized in fire and blood and have come out steel." Scott's words were subsequently taken as the regimental motto, and have been preserved as such by the 3rd Cavalry to this day. A mounted rifleman who lost an arm at Chapultepec was the redoubtable William W. Loring. The loss of a limb does not appear to have checked his ardor, for he later commanded the Mounted Rifles along the Oregon Trail, rose to become a major general in the Confederate army, and later offered his sword to the khedive of Egypt. He retired from the khedivial service, full of honors and with the rank of pasha, to end his days in the Union he had fought so hard to disrupt. Another character of those early days of the United States cavalry was Jerome Napoleon Bonaparte, a West Pointer and a great-nephew of Napoleon, who joined the Mounted Rifles in 1852 and blooded his sword on the Indian frontier. He later joined the French army, fought in Algeria, the Crimea, and the Franco-Prussian War, escorted the Empress Eugenie to exile in England, and then, like Loring, returned to the United States, where he died in 1893.

Jefferson Davis was secretary of war when the 1st and 2nd Cavalry were authorized in 1855, and he was later accused of packing the two new regiments with his favorite officers, nearly all of whom went over subsequently to the Confederacy—the 2nd Cavalry even being nicknamed "Jeff Davis' Own." It is more likely however that cavalry service appealed more to the southerners than it did to the northerners, and there was certainly a preponderance of southern sympathizers in the regular cavalry. Joseph E. Johnston and J. E. B. Stuart both served in

the 1st Cavalry, while the lieutenant colonel of the 2nd Cavalry
was no less a man than Robert E. Lee. Earl van Dorn, John B.
Hood, and Fitzhugh Lee were officers in the 2nd Cavalry, and
all three rose to high rank in the Confederate army. On the
other side of the fence, George B. McClellan, who later commanded the Army of the Potomac, was a captain in the 1st
Cavalry, and among his other claims to fame is that of having
introduced into the United States cavalry a type of saddle
which remained standard equipment, with certain modifica-
tions, until horsed cavalry was abolished in 1942.

The War Between the States was to revolutionize cavalry
tactics, although outside America this fact took a long time to
sink in; but even before American took up arms to fight American there were marked differences between the cavalry regiments of European armies and those of the United States. The
heavy cavalry tradition was never adopted in the United States,
while shock action with sword and lance was always regarded
with some suspicion. *L'arme blanche* played little part in cavalry tactics, sabers often being discarded as a useless encum-
brance in Indian fighting, and horses tended to be used much
more as a means of mobility rather than for their employment
as a battering-ram during the charge. In view of the success the
British cavalry had with the lance in India and Africa, it is
interesting to speculate whether the United States cavalry would
have benefited by the adoption of the lance for their wars
against the Indians, but it can only be speculation. The American trooper disliked the lance and used his saber only in the
last resort. Dragoons were equipped with carbines, sabers, and
pistols; the Mounted Rifles had rifles and Colt revolvers but
no sabers; the Cavalry had sabers, carbines, and Colts.

Uniforms in general followed the fashions set on the other
side of the Atlantic, although the extravagant uniforms of European cavalry regiments never found favor in Washington—
American cavalry officers preferring to show their individuality
by wearing their hair overlong and by cultivating the most
ferocious whiskers (prohibited in all except cavalry regiments).
Dragoons wore orange trimmings on their short blue jackets,
mounted riflemen wore green, and the cavalry wore yellow.

Dragoons and rifles wore the "Albert Hat," a kind of shako with orange or green pompons, and the 1st and 2nd Cavalry sported a black slouch hat, pinned up on the right side and decorated with black ostrich feathers. This article of headwear was much despised by the older-established regiments, but it would seem to have been particularly well suited to the heavily bearded and whiskered faces of the period. Military hats have a habit of adjusting themselves to current conditions. An Eisenhower or a Patton, with clean-shaven face, would look as ridiculous in a black slouch hat today as would "Jeb" Stuart in a helmet liner or a combat cap.

When the South took up arms against the North, the five regular cavalry regiments were scattered throughout the length and breadth of the United States. For the most part they were in isolated posts, days' and perhaps even weeks' march from the nearest large town, sufficient unto themselves, and united by pride of regiment and the experience of dangers shared in common. The officers for the most part were southerners, or had assimilated southern sympathies, while the enlisted men represented a fair cross section of a nation which had still to establish a true national consciousness. Both officers and men were tough, self-reliant, and battle seasoned by their numerous encounters with raiding Indians and the gangs of outlaws who had made the frontier their happy hunting ground. It was seldom that a colonel found himself with the whole of his command concentrated in one place: "During my army service," said one of the leading Confederate generals, "I learned all about commanding fifty United States dragoons and forgot everything else." Basically the training was good, but it taught nothing of the power of massed artillery, nor, for that matter, of the problem of maneuvering large numbers of men and horses.

Yet it was learned soon enough. There is surely nothing more remarkable in the remarkable American character than the ability of seemingly inexperienced regular officers to rise to great responsibilities. In the Civil War one need only consider the cases of Stonewall Jackson, who had had just four years' service in the artillery before he resigned to take up teaching duties

for ten years at the Virginia Military Institute, and of Robert
E. Lee, who had seldom commanded as many as a thousand
men before he was called upon to lead a great army.[3] Much
the same was true in World War I and again in World War
II, when we saw a junior lieutenant colonel, untried in battle,
rise in the short space of three years to command the most
hazardous and greatest invasion that has ever been launched
across the narrow seas to liberate a continent from its chains.

Armies which expand from small foundations, however sound
the groundwork, must necessarily experience many growing pains
before at long last they reach maturity. One-fifth of the West
Point graduates left the United States army on secession and
threw in their lot with the Confederacy; they comprised a high
proportion of cavalry officers and many of them rose rapidly
to high rank. Four of the full colonels of regular cavalry regiments were southerners, and the proportion was almost equally
marked among the more junior officers. They immediately set
about raising the Confederate cavalry from among a population accustomed from earliest childhood to riding and hunting.
The whole philosophy of the South was bound up with horses,
and those who flocked to enlist brought their horses with them.
The human material was superb, the horses the same, and the
spirit was as high as ever it had been when medieval knights
rode out to break a lance for Christendom. Fortunately, however, for the Union, those Confederate troopers shared one
other characteristic with the knights of old—a contemptuous
disregard for any form of discipline. It was a characteristic
which was to cost them dear in the long run.

Disorder and confusion prevailed throughout the United
States cavalry during 1861. The 2nd Cavalry in Texas were
almost denuded of their officers, who took many of the enlisted
men with them to serve the Confederacy; those who remained
at duty managed to make their way back to New York by sea,
but they were only a pale remnant of what had once been a
proud and experienced regiment—"the best mounted regiment

[3] Patrick Ronayne Cleburne, who rose to command a Confederate division, had begun his military education in the British army—where he had
risen to the rank of corporal in the 41st Foot.

the country had ever seen." [4] Farther afield, in posts scattered
all along the frontier from Wyoming to the Mexican border,
southerners and their sympathizers rode out along the trails
leading to the Confederacy, while those left behind were torn
between offering their swords to the Union or remaining at
their place of duty to defend the territory so recently won from
the Indians. Captain Alfred Pleasanton of the 2nd Dragoons
rode from Utah to Washington in the autumn of 1861, taking with him the detachment he commanded, and other detachments followed his example. But in some instances the
regular cavalry stayed at their posts along the frontier and did
their duty as they saw it.[5]

At the time when Alfred Pleasanton was riding at the head
of his dragoons on the long march back to Washington, James
Ewell Brown Stuart was busy working on the Cavalry Corps of
the Army of Northern Virginia to shape it for war. Jeb Stuart
had gone from West Point to the Mounted Rifles in 1854, and
three years later had been desperately wounded while serving
with the 1st Cavalry against the Cheyennes in Kansas. A superb
horseman and leader of men, Jeb Stuart became one of the
great soldiers of the Confederacy, and in many ways he epito-
mizes all that is meant by the expression "a born cavalry leader."
Handsome, and a great dandy, he had an instinctive eye for
ground and the ability to inspire men to achieve the impossible. For the first two years of the war he ran rings round the
slow-moving generals of the Union, raiding far behind their
lines, and once capturing the baggage and correspondence of the
commanding general of the Army of the Potomac. There was a

[4] John K. Herr and Edward Wallace, *The Story of the U.S. Cavalry*
(Little, Brown, Boston, 1953), p. 76.

[5] The dilemma facing so many United States cavalrymen during those
early months of 1861 has had a modern parallel in the break-up of the
British-controlled Indian army in 1947. Regiments in which Hindus and
Mohammedans had served together amicably for over one hundred years
were split asunder, part cleaving to India and part to Pakistan. Officers
who had been educated at the same military academy, and who had
shared the same perils in battle, now found themselves on opposite sides
of the fence, and even feverishly preparing to fight each other over
Kashmir. Fortunately, wiser counsels prevailed and Indian cavalrymen
were not called upon to fight their erstwhile comrades in the cavalry
regiments of Pakistan.

great deal of the cavalier in Stuart's make-up and he would have found little difficulty in fitting himself into the ranks of those cavalrymen who charged under Prince Rupert against Cromwell at Marston Moor. Robert E. Lee described him as his "ideal of a soldier," and the Confederates lost their finest cavalry soldier when he was killed by a chance bullet at Yellow Tavern in May, 1864. The Michigan cavalry sergeant who shot the *beau sabreur* of the Confederacy was under the command of a youthful West Pointer named Custer, who in later years consciously or unconsciously modeled himself on Stuart: and yet, for all his bravery and *panache*, Custer was never in the same class as Stuart as a cavalry soldier.

Stuart was not the only great cavalry commander on the Confederate side. Nathan Bedford Forrest began at the age of forty as a trooper, and ended the war as a lieutenant general; in that time he led some of the most remarkable cavalry raids of the war—"gitting thar fustest with the mostest"—and proving himself to be a master of cavalry tactics. He once captured a Federal gunboat on the Cumberland River, his troopers firing from the banks into the gunboat's portholes, and it is said that he had twenty-nine horses shot from under him. On one occasion, when badly wounded in the foot, he led his troops from a horse-drawn buggy. Morgan, Mosby, Wade Hampton, Fighting Joe Wheeler, and a whole tribe of Lees also distinguished themselves as cavalry soldiers in the Confederate army. Mosby particularly earned the dislike of the Federals for his daring raids behind their lines, but he survived the war to return to his law practice, became a Republican and friend of President Grant, served his country for many years as consul in Hong Kong, and died in his bed—an end which few would ever have prescribed for Mosby of "Mosby's Rangers." However, Stuart and Forrest remain in a class apart. They were the Murats of the Confederacy.

The Federal cavalry was much slower in getting into its stride, and for the first two years of the war it was definitely outclassed by the mounted arm of the Confederacy. This delay can be explained partly by the lack of suitable cavalry recruits among the urban population of the North and partly by the suspicion with which the earlier Federal commanders regarded their cavalry. They used their mounted troops for futile outpost duties, escorts, and orderlies, and considered that cavalry would be useless against the new weapons coming into the field. McClellan was a cavalryman and understood the value of an arm which he described as the antennae of an army, but he did not last long enough to put his theories to the test. Philip St. George Cooke, late of the 1st Dragoons and in his day America's most distinguished "Indian fighter," fought on the side of the Federals, even though his daughter had married Jeb Stuart. Cooke was at Gaines Mill in June, 1862, when a charge by the 5th Cavalry checked the Confederate advance, but the troopers later withdrew and carried away a large part of the Federal infantry during their somewhat hasty retreat. The conduct of the cavalry at Gaines Mill resulted later in an acrimonious dispute between Cooke and Fitz-John Porter, the Federal commander, the former contending that the charge of the 5th Cavalry had been instrumental in saving the latter from defeat, while Porter attributed the loss of more than twenty-two of his guns to the panic flight of the cavalry. The rights and wrongs of this action will be argued until the end of time, but it may be significant that Cooke never appeared again as a field commander.

In 1863 the fortunes of the Federal cavalry took a turn for the better when Benjamin H. Grierson led his Illinois Cavalry on the first successful raid into Mississippi and Louisiana. Soon Grierson was being emulated by such men as Custer, Wesley Merritt, Judson Kilpatrick, James Wilson, and Ranald Mackenzie. They were all very young—most of them had still been at West Point when the war started—but they were astonishingly brave, and they made it abundantly clear that the ability to conduct mobile operations was by no means confined to the horse-riding squirearchy of the South. They were helped by the recruits flowing in from the Northwest, where horses were as much a part of everyday life as they were in the South, and by the meteoric rise of a pugnacious little Irishman named Sheridan. Philip Sheridan, who was an infantryman by training, emerged from the ruck of the Army of the Potomac to take

command of its Cavalry Corps in 1864, and the Federals
then knew that they possessed a cavalry leader who had no
need to fear comparison with either Forrest or Stuart.

He was a stocky, lugubrious little man, taciturn and unin-
spiring on first acquaintance, but he became transformed in
battle, rousing his men to the wildest pitch of enthusiasm, and
displaying a tactical ability which at times verged on genius.
He never lost a battle, and unlike so many of the Federal
cavalry generals, he knew how to nurse his horses. The wastage
of horses in the Federal cavalry was remarkable—nearly
300,000 horses in the first two years of the war—and much
of this was due to poor horsemastership; the supply of horses
was virtually inexhaustible, however, even at the rate of re-
placement of 150 horses per day, which was Sheridan's requirement during the Shenandoah Valley campaign, whereas
the South had increasing difficulty in supplying its cavalry
with remounts.

Sheridan was in his early thirties when he was appointed to
command the Cavalry Corps of the Army of the Potomac;
Jeb Stuart was only thirty-one when he fell in action. Wesley
Merritt, George Custer, and Ranald Mackenzie had been
brevetted major generals before their twenty-fifth birthdays,
and James Wilson was twenty-seven when promoted to fill
the appointment of divisional commander. The *Grande Armée*
in its greatest days had a similar galaxy of youthful and dashing cavalry leaders—Murat was still in his thirties when he led
the pursuit after Jena—but few other wars in history have
offered such opportunities to the natural cavalry leader as did
the American Civil War. The opportunities were seized with
both hands.

Cavalry tactics had, however, to be adapted to suit the
special conditions of the theater of war and the American
temperament. The terrain did not favor the employment of
cavalry in mass, wheeling and charging in great lines of squadrons as Murat had done at Austerlitz and as the Prussians were
to do at Mars-la-Tour, nor was the training of the American
trooper aimed at teaching him to maneuver knee to knee at
high speed. Both the Confederate and Federal cavalry were

perfectly capable of charging infantry and artillery, and did
so on many occasions, but they invariably adapted their tactics
to the ground. The horse was used principally for speed and
mobility, and the rifle and revolver were preferred to the saber.
The ground usually compelled the cavalry to fight dismounted,
and the American trooper never had any hesitation about taking on the infantryman in his own element. This ability to
fight either mounted or on foot conferred considerable strategi-
cal and tactical independence on both the Confederate and
Federal cavalry, and may account for Henderson's verdict that
"the horseman of the American war is the model of the efficient
cavalryman." [6] Henderson did, however, qualify this statement
by pointing out that on neither side were large masses of
mounted men used to charge and outmaneuver an equivalent
body of cavalry, as happened frequently during the Franco-
Prussian War; and in Henderson's view the American trooper
lacked the training and discipline required for the performance
of such an operation.

The true genius of the American cavalryman was displayed
in the raids which were carried out deep into the enemy rear
areas. Large bodies of cavalry, accompanied by horse artillery
and stripped of anything which might hinder their mobility,
operated for weeks on end far behind the enemy lines, dis-
rupting communications, interrupting supplies and reinforcements, and confusing the enemy high command. General John
Morgan of Kentucky, the "rebel raider," used to ride as much
as one thousand miles during his raids, and his last raid in
June, 1863, ranged as far north as the Ohio-Pennsylvania
border. Forrest was another master of the deep penetration
operation, while on the Federal side there was James Wilson's
great raid into Alabama in March, 1865. Wilson set out from
Tennessee with 14,000 men, and in thirty days they had ridden
nearly six hundred miles, captured three important cities, and
taken six thousand prisoners and 156 guns. A detachment from
Wilson's raiding army captured Jefferson Davis at Irwinville
in Georgia, after the Confederate President's flight from Rich-

[6] Col. G. F. R. Henderson, *The Science of War* (Longmans, London,
1913), p. 57.

mond, and Wilson had the distinction of matching himself against the redoubtable Forrest and emerging the victor; although it is only just to Forrest to make it clear that those were the twilight days of the Confederacy, with everything— most notably ammunition and horses—in short supply.

The employment of cavalry to strike far in the enemy's rear is the more interesting since in Europe at that time cavalry were seldom used for such an operation. Napoleon had said that the secret of war lay in the communications, as Genghis Khan and other great masters of war had discovered before him, but it was a theory to which only lip service had been paid so far as European cavalry were concerned. It has a peculiar significance today, now that the airplane has become the vehicle for wide-range raids into the rear areas. The parachutist and the helicopter-borne trooper are the modern equivalent of Mosby's Rangers, infinitely more expensive and complex than a tough and independent horseman armed only with the repeating rifle, but if correctly employed a battle-winning factor of incalculable importance.

A realization that cavalry could best be used to disrupt communications, man the outposts, and impose delay on an advancing enemy did not come overnight. During the first year of the war both Federal and Confederate cavalry leaders hankered after shock action, the thunder of the charge, and the cut and thrust of saber against saber. Two factors militated against such cavalry engagements, one being the ground, which did not favor the employment of cavalry in mass, and the other, the lack of training and discipline. It was not just a question of training the raw recruits how to ride and maneuver with precision, but of equal importance was the training of the horses. Unseasoned horses straight from the farms and the prairies required months of careful training before they could be handled as Frederick the Great's troopers handled theirs, and time was always at a premium. Nor is discipline easy to instill when each man considers himself the equal of his neighbor and when the need for every soldier to take his place in the firing line overrides the requirement to train him first

in the elementary military virtues. As a Confederate general
has said:

> The difficulty of converting raw men into soldiers is en-
> hanced manifold when they are mounted. Both men and
> horses require training. . . . There was but little time,
> and it may be said less disposition, to establish camps of in-
> struction. Living on horseback, fearless and dashing, the
> men of the South afforded the best possible material for
> cavalry. They had every quality but discipline. . . ." [7]

Only at Brandy Station in Virginia on June 9, 1863, did a
cavalry battle approaching the European scale take place, and
even there the scope for massed maneuver was considerably
hampered by the terrain.

Brandy Station was a hamlet in Virginia on the main railway
between Alexandria and Charlottesville and four miles south of
the Rappahannock River. The Rappahannock formed the
boundary between the Federal Army of the Potomac and the
Confederate Army of Northern Virginia, which, under Lee,
was covering the approaches to Richmond from the north. The
country around Brandy Station was gently rolling, thickly
wooded, and intersected by the numerous streams which flow
into the main river. The farms dotting the countryside consisted of fields cleared from the forests, and fenced to protect
the crops so that even the few cultivated areas presented an
obstacle to the free movement of cavalry. Seven miles farther
down the line from Brandy Station was the township of
Culpeper Court House. Lee's army was mainly concentrated
around Fredericksburg, watching the Army of the Potomac
under Hooker, which lay at Falmouth on the opposite bank
of the Rappahannock. Major General Jeb Stuart commanded
Lee's cavalry, and his patrols were watching the fords across
the river, the rest of the Cavalry Corps being bivouacked in
the woods and farms around Brandy Station. On the far bank
of the Rappahannock, the Federal cavalry under General Alfred
Pleasanton were keeping a keen watch on the Confederates'

[7] Henderson, *op. cit.*, p. 269.

every move. Pleasanton was still smarting from the memory
of his encounter with Stuart during the previous October when
he had tried to intercept the latter on his return from a raid
into Pennsylvania. The Federal cavalry had reached one of
the Potomac fords first but had been brushed aside and severely
handled by Stuart's troopers. This failure did not, however,
interfere with the rapid promotion of the ex-captain of dragoons, who had risen fast in the two years since he brought
his detachment back from Utah for the Union.

Lee had given the Federals a beating at Chancellorsville
during the first week in May, 1863, and hopes ran high on the
Confederate side. Early in June an impressive parade took place
at Brandy Station when everyone who mattered in Confederate
society attended a review of Stuart's cavalry. Twelve thousand
magnificently mounted horsemen with twenty-four galloping
guns were drawn up in glittering array while their handsome
young general cantered slowly down their ranks, accompanied
by a glittering staff, and then led them past the visiting digni-
taries at a walk, a trot, and finally in an awe-inspiring and
exhilarating gallop. The parade was followed by a barbecue
and ball graced by the loveliest in a land famed for the beauty
of its women, and victory seemed to be just around the corner.
It was an occasion which has often been compared with the
ball given by the Duchess of Richmond on the eve of Waterloo,
and like that night of revelry it too had a bloody sequel.

For across the Rappahannock there was uneasiness lest Lee
might slip away from Hooker's guard and strike against Washington. Hooker was unhappy about the concentration of
Confederate cavalry at Brandy Station and was worried by
memories of Stuart's previous raids right round the flank of
the Army of the Potomac. It was important to find out what
was happening across the Rappahannock, and accordingly
Pleasanton was ordered to carry out a reconnaissance in force as
far as Brandy Station and Culpeper Court House. To do this
he had about fifteen thousand cavalry, divided into three divisions, and a small contingent of infantry, all of which were
set in motion sometime on June 8. This movement was reported to Stuart by spies, and he accordingly issued orders for

his cavalry to close up to the Rappahannock at dawn on June 9, and oppose the Federal crossing.

Pleasanton beat him to it and as the sun rose the scattered Confederate patrols saw the long lines of Federal cavalry splashing through the Rappahannock at Kelly's Ford and at Beverly. These two fords were some six miles apart, and Pleasanton had split his force into two columns; the northern column, crossing at Beverly, was directed on Brandy Station from the north, while the southern column was to split after fording the river at Kelly's, one division moving direct on Culpeper Court House, and two divisions wheeling right-handed and heading for Brandy Station.

The column crossing at Beverly was checked at first by Stuart's advanced posts, but eventually the superior weight of the Federals pushed the Confederates of Jones's brigade back through the thick woods as far as St. James's Church, two miles from the Rappahannock and halfway between the river and Brandy Station. Much of this was dismounted fighting, rifle against rifle, although Pleasanton brought up some artillery to shift the Confederates from their breastworks. The Confederate resistance stiffened as they fell back to St. James's Church where Stuart had come up with fresh troops and occupied a strong position. Three dismounted brigades were covering the church, entrenched behind stone walls and with their flanks protected by mounted regiments. The Federals were disorganized after their hard fighting through the woods and were in considerable confusion. Stuart's artillery positioned around the church was now doing considerable execution, and a Confederate charge against the Federal flank forced them to give ground, whereupon Stuart's men followed up with great *élan*. The situation was critical and it looked as if the northern column of Pleasanton's force would be driven back pell-mell into the river. Only the silencing of the guns could save the situation, but between the Confederate artillery and the forward positions of the Federals was about eight hundred yards of open and bullet-swept ground. The guns themselves were concealed by walls and breastworks and the thick swirling smoke made it difficult to pinpoint their exact positions, while the Confederate shelling and rifle fire interfered with any attempt on the Federal side to form up the cavalry in preparation for a charge.

The 6th Cavalry were regulars, but formed only in 1861. They were better-disciplined than their Confederate opponents, certainly no less brave, but equally certainly worse-mounted. "Cavalry! Attention! Draw sabers!" was the order, and then the regiment trotted slowly forward in column of squadrons, the nature of the terrain preventing them from wheeling into line. This mass of closely packed blue-clad troopers and horses was received with a murderous fire as it emerged from the cover of the trees, and almost at the same moment the high notes of the trumpet shrilled out the "Charge." With a wild cheer the leading squadron burst into the open, its officers out in front and turning in their saddles to encourage the ranks behind them. There was no room to maneuver; this was an old-style knee-to-knee affair, snorting, roaring, plunging horses fighting for their heads as their riders struggled to control them.

As the Confederate guns spewed canister, horse after horse crashed to the ground. Those following behind either jumped over the fallen bodies or crashed into them and were brought down themselves. Riderless horses milled about in the ranks while others, crazed with fright, went galloping off to the flanks and rear. Confederate musketry took heavy toll of dismounted men trying to regain the Federal lines, and the whole charge lasted only a few minutes; but for those who took part, and who survived, it seemed longer than a lifetime. It was a charge made in the highest tradition of the regular army of the United States, and an eyewitness said of it:

> It was made over a plateau fully 800 yards wide, and its objective point was the artillery at the Church. Never rode troopers more gallantly than did those steady regulars, as, under a fire of shell and shrapnel and finally of canister, they dashed up to the very muzzles, then through and beyond our guns. Here they were simultaneously attacked from both flanks and the survivors driven back.[8]

[8] *Ibid.*, p. 270.

All their gallantry and all their training were of little avail. The 6th Cavalry had no room to maneuver, those following behind merely telescoped into their comrades who had reached the guns and who were engaging the Confederate gunners with their sabers, and a swirling mass of horsemen disintegrated in the face of the Confederate fire. Like a wave piling up against a concrete breakwater, their force was spent, and those who still survived were merely scattered individuals cutting and slashing amid the dust and confusion. Finally they wheeled their terrified horses and went back the way they had come. The Confederates still held St. James's Church, their guns still fired, and a good regiment had been thrown away with little to show for all their gallantry.

Meanwhile, away to the south, Pleasanton's other column was faring more successfully. They had experienced little difficulty in crossing the Rappahannock at Kelly's Ford, Stuart's outposts merely exchanging a few shots and then retiring towards Brandy Station, and soon one division was moving off rapidly in the direction of Culpeper while the other two divisions rode for Brandy Station. They made good time, hastened by the heavy firing they could hear from St. James's, and they had worked their way round the southern flank of the enemy before they were spotted by Stuart's adjutant general. That officer had stationed himself on Fleetwood Hill, about half a mile to the north of Brandy Station, which Stuart had chosen as the position for his headquarters, and at the time when the Federal cavalry came into view there were only a few staff officers, orderlies, and a solitary howitzer protecting the Confederate rear. Stuart himself had gone forward to command the battle raging round the church, and his flank was wide open. The Federals had the game in their hands if only they had attacked at once.

An orderly was sent galloping posthaste to Stuart to warn him of the danger, and the few Confederates on Fleetwood Hill disposed themselves as best they could for the hill's defense. The howitzer was brought into action and its opening rounds had an effect that was as surprising as it was unexpected. The advancing Federal cavalry halted and waited for their horse artillery to deploy and come into action. Precious minutes ticked away as the gunners came forward, unlimbered, and then opened fire, and while all this was happening Stuart had received his adjutant general's message and the 12th Virginia were galloping back *ventre-à-terre* to his assistance. Hot on their heels came a second Confederate regiment, and soon after them Jeb Stuart in person.

The 12th Virginia were only just in time. As their leading files crashed up the gentle slopes of the hill, they passed the Confederate howitzer withdrawing; it had done its work magnificently. Immediately below Fleetwood Hill a complete regiment of Federal cavalry was advancing in well-drilled column of squadrons, the guidons whipping in the breeze and every saber drawn and flashing in the bright sunlight. The mad dash back from the church had strung out the 12th Virginia over half a mile of country and the colonel found he had only a few troopers up with him; without hesitation he led them straight at the enemy, but they were brushed contemptuously aside and the Federals stormed the crest. A wild melee followed, and the Confederates were driven off Fleetwood Hill. The other Confederate regiment which had been following up the 12th Virginia was also thrown into the fight, but their horses were winded by the hard gallop and the ranks were disorganized. The Confederates were compelled to withdraw out of range, reorganize, and then charge again, but with the same result. The Federal cavalry drove them back and retained their hold on the hill. Then two squadrons of the Confederates galloped round the west side of the hill in an attempt to capture the Federal horse artillery which was deployed in that area, but the gunners stood their ground and Confederate carbine and pistol met their match in the staunch artillerymen.

By this time Stuart was withdrawing his troops from the area of St. James's Church. As the Confederate cavalry debouched from the woods, one regiment came upon several hundred Federal horsemen who were in the act of retiring; the Confederates immediately charged, although they were less than two hundred strong, broke through the Federals, and rode down some guns. They were driven back again, once the

Federals had had time to reorganize, but the temporary respite had been invaluable for the Confederates. Stuart now appeared, galloping hard for Fleetwood Hill, followed by four regiments in column of squadrons. Two of these regiments were launched straight at the hill, and they took it with their sabers alone. The Federals seem to have been unnerved by the vigor of this charge and they withdrew off the hill in considerable disorder, but their retreat served them ill. As they were trying to reorganize on the level ground between Fleetwood Hill and Brandy Station they were ridden into the ground by two other Confederate regiments which had swung left round the hill and crashed right into them:

> This charge was as gallantly made and as gallantly met as any the writer witnessed during nearly four years of active service. Taking into estimation the numbers of men who crossed sabres in this single charge (being nearly a brigade on both sides), it was by far the most important hand-to-hand contest between the cavalry of the two armies. As the blue and grey riders mixed in the smoke and dust, minutes seemed to elapse before its effect was determined. At last the intermixed and disorganised mass began to recede, and we [i.e. the Federals] saw that the field was won by the Confederates.[9]

It was now about noon and neither side could really claim the victory. Stuart had been forced to pull back from St. James's Church, and he had only just been in time to push the Federals off Fleetwood Hill. He had, however, driven the enemy out of the railway station, and Pleasanton had withdrawn the majority of his southern column to link up with the rest of his force which was still positioned near the church. Why the northern column failed to follow Stuart when he withdrew from St. James's is difficult to explain, but it was probably due to a fear lest the line of withdrawal to Beverly Ford should be cut. A Confederate brigade was positioned near Cunningham farm and was threatening the open right flank of the Federals. Whatever the reason may be for the

[9] *Ibid.*, p. 272.

Federal inaction, it gave Stuart time to reorganize his defenses to cover Brandy Station, and he was even able to withdraw the brigade from Cunningham farm and extend his left flank to the high ground overlooking Thompson's house.

Both sides were now very tired and there was a dangerous gap between Stuart's left flank and the river. Pleasanton bent all his energies to work round this flank, and a great deal of skirmishing between individual companies and regiments followed. Two Federal regiments made a very gallant charge near Thompson's house but they were met and broken by the 9th Virginia, dismounted and fighting from behind the protection of stone walls. The 9th Virginia were forced back by superior numbers, but the 10th and 13th Virginia came up in their support, gave their "rebel yell," and then dashed forward in an irresistible charge. Soon the whole Federal line was withdrawing on the Rappahannock, covered by some infantry which Pleasanton had brought up to cover his retreat. Stuart made little effort to follow up, and his men were probably too exhausted to do so.

The force detached to reconnoiter as far as Culpeper Court House was intercepted by two Confederate regiments near Stevensburg, and some stiff dismounted fighting then took place. One of the Federal regiments was caught while changing formation, and a comparatively weak Confederate charge, made in column of sections, was completely successful. The result of this action caused the Federal commander to withdraw back across the Rappahannock with his mission unaccomplished.

Pleasanton's reconnaissance in force had achieved very little and at considerable cost to himself. His total casualties amounted to 936, almost twice those of the Confederates, and he also left behind three guns. Brandy Station has been described as "a swirling hugger-mugger of an affair," [10] which is possibly as good a description as any for an old-style cavalry-versus-cavalry action fought over a wide frontage and lasting for over eight hours. It was the largest purely cavalry battle fought during the Civil War, and the nature of the country,

[10] Herr and Wallace, *op. cit.*, p. 95.

when coupled with the difficulty of co-ordinating the action of the northern and southern Federal columns, caused it to be mainly a series of skirmishes and charges launched on the initiative of individual regimental and company commanders. But if it did nothing else, the Battle of Brandy Station showed that at long last the Federal cavalry were getting into their stride, and it certainly has earned Pleasanton a niche in history which might not otherwise have been his—at one moment it seemed quite possible that he had the redoubtable Jeb Stuart whipped.

CHAPTER SEVEN

Mars-la-Tour

AUGUST 16, 1870

"Tod oder Ruhm"

METZ is one of the most famous fortress towns in Europe. Standing on the banks of the Moselle, it guards the gateway into France from southern Germany, and this way have passed Romans and Goths, Burgundians and Spaniards, Austrians and Russians and Germans, and from beyond the seas, the armies of America. And this way, too, through the town's narrow, cobbled streets, have poured the impulsive, intelligent, swaggering soldiers of France, their kettledrums rattling out the step as they marched to subdue vast provinces for Bourbons, *La Révolution*, and Bonaparte.

Not always, however, has Metz been the jumping-off spot for a victorious campaign—it has seen defeat as well. On August 14, 1870, the Army of the Rhine was withdrawing through the town with the armies of Prussia and her allies

close on its heels. Two days previously the Emperor, Louis
Napoleon III, had quitted the command of the Army of the
Rhine, for which he had never possessed the slightest quali-
fication, and was waiting at Longueville, just outside the town,
for the escort which was to ride back with him to Paris. The
command had then devolved on Marshal Bazaine, the soldier
who had risen in thirty-five years from private in the 37th
Infantry of the line to marshal of France, and who was to
surrender his command eighty days later to the King of Prussia,
together with three marshals of France, 173,000 officers and
men, and nearly 1,400 guns.

France had declared war on Prussia on July 19. The pretext
had been the offer of the crown of Spain to a Prussian prince,
but the real reason had been the fear that Prussia, under the
driving genius of Bismarck, was growing too powerful. The
sick and vacillating Napoleon III desperately needed some success to offset the decline in his own authority and the increasing influence and faction of his politicians. The French army,
which had distinguished itself on the battlefields of Magenta
and Solferino during the 1859 campaign against Austria,
thought itself the best army in Europe. The war against Prussia
would be a walkover.

It had not worked out that way. The Army of the Rhine,
which was to advance on Frankfurt, separate Prussia from her
south German allies, and then defeat her at leisure, had never
even reached the Rhine. Nor had any success attended the
other French army, under Marshal MacMahon, which had
invaded Germany from Strassburg. Both the armies had been
defeated, and MacMahon's was in precipitate retreat towards
Châlons-sur-Marne, miles in the rear. Bazaine, if he were not
to lose complete touch with MacMahon, would have to retreat
likewise, and the orders for this withdrawal went out on August
13. It was only two days before the annual celebration in Paris
of the *Fête Napoléon* which was planned to be an even greater
ceremony than usual, for Napoleon III had expected his armies
to be well on the road to Berlin by August 15.

Bazaine had approximately 200,000 men under his command,
and they comprised the flower of the French army. The soldiers

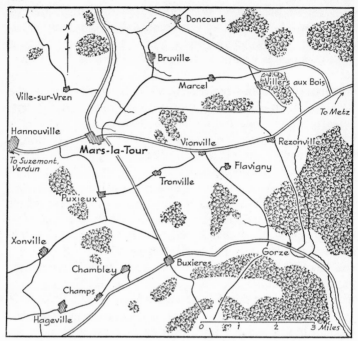

were brave enough, as were the regimental officers, but the High Command was incompetent, riddled with politics, and lacking in resolution. Staff work was bad and administration was overcentralized. Favoritism influenced promotion far more than professional efficiency, and it was far too easy for the well-to-do to escape the rigors of conscription by finding, and then paying for, substitutes; in the call-up of 1869 there were 42,000 substitutes out of a contingent of 75,000.

The French soldier was dressed in the most colorful of uniforms, formed into regiments with such romantic titles as zouaves, voltigeurs, and chasseurs, and armed with the *chassepot* rifle which was reputed to be the finest in the world. He had fought in the Crimea, in Italy, in Mexico, and in a hundred campaigns against Algerians and Indochinese, but even this battle experience could not offset the incompetence of the staffs. This is best exemplified by the story of the commandant at Marseilles who telegraphed the War Ministry: "9,000 reserves here; I do not know what to do with them. In order to give me room I shall ship them all on board the transports in harbour for Algeria." Small wonder that French mobilization was a chapter of accidents from beginning to end.

Bazaine intended to disengage his army from contact with the Prussians during the night of August 13, and then fall back through Metz to Verdun, sixty-five kilometers to the west. This westward movement did actually start as planned, and the first troops to clatter through the streets were the 3rd Cavalry Division of General De Forton; at their head rode General Prince Murat, commander of the dragoon brigade, and the bearer of one of the greatest names in the history of cavalry. The rest of the Army of the Rhine was to follow them during the 14th of August, but Bazaine was compelled to fight an inconclusive action with the enemy at Colombey before he could disengage, and this delayed his plan by over twenty-four hours. Time is money in war, and Bazaine could not afford the delay, since it enabled the Prussians to work round his flank and block the escape routes to the west.

These ran across the plateau which rises steeply from the west bank of the Moselle. Metz lies in the valley, but the high road to Verdun climbs up to the plateau at Longueville, five kilometers from Metz, and then divides at Gravelotte. The southern road passes through the villages of Rezonville, Vionville, and Mars-la-Tour; the northern route through Doncourt and Jarny. Bazaine, with three army corps, was to take the southern route, while two army corps were to march by way of Doncourt.

The plateau of Mars-la-Tour is ideal terrain for the employment of cavalry. It is a countryside of rolling downland, of thick woods lying along the spurs, and of quiet villages nestling in the hollows. Prosperous farms dot the landscape, but for the most part the farms are concentrated around the villages—Gravelotte, Rezonville, Vionville, Flavigny, and Mars-la-Tour. The names ring out like a roll of drums. They are blazoned on the colors of many a French and German regiment, and for their possession men fought and died throughout the hot and thirsty daylight hours of August 16, 1870.

The eastern edge of the plateau, where the ground falls steeply to the Moselle valley, is thickly wooded and in places almost an escarpment. This is infantry country, but once the heights have been gained, the road to Verdun is almost within rifle shot. It was vital to the success of Bazaine's plan that the Prussians should not be allowed to form up in those woods, and then debouch onto the plateau across his path. He knew that the Prussian advance guards were already approaching the east bank of the Moselle around Pont-à-Mousson on August 13, and he surely must have realized that he would have to drive his infantry to the limit of their marching powers if they were to avoid encirclement. Yet the orders he issued for the withdrawal made no mention of any need for urgency, and the whole operation was carried out in the most dilatory fashion.

The reverse was true of the Prussians. The armies of Prussia, Saxony, Bavaria, and Württemberg, were under the supreme command of King William of Prussia, but the driving force behind them was the chief of staff, Von Moltke. He had realized some time earlier that the French did not intend to fight it out to the bitter end round Metz, but meant to fall back into France. He decided therefore to bring Bazaine to battle before he reached Verdun, and accordingly the First Army was ordered to pin Bazaine at Metz, while the Second Army crossed the Moselle at Pont-à-Mousson, thirty kilometers south of Metz, scaled the escarpment, and rolled up the Army of the Rhine from the west. These orders went out almost simultaneously with Bazaine's for withdrawal, but in contrast with the French, were carried out with ruthless efficiency. Prussian infantry marched day and night for the Moselle, their cavalry patrols had crossed it and were ranging far to the west of Mars-la-Tour before the French advance guards had even begun to scale the escarpment from Metz, and the Prussian First Army attacked on August 14 east of Metz and delayed Bazaine's plan for disengagement.

De Forton's cavalry division had left Metz on the evening of the 13th, but by the 15th had covered only the thirty kilometers

to Vionville. Such slow progress could be excused only if the
dragoons and cuirassiers had been reconnoitering every inch
of the way, but in fact virtually no reconnaissance was performed, although De Forton was well aware that the Prussians
had reached the Moselle and that some of their cavalry patrols
had been reported west of Mars-la-Tour on the Verdun road.
He seems, however, to have been blandly oblivious of any need
for information about the enemy, and the same is true of Du
Barrail's cavalry division which was moving on the northern
route, and at much the same pace. Du Barrail had reached
Doncourt by the 15th, and had halted there for the night.

As the sun came up on August 16 the French troopers
scrambled out of their bivouacs, rolled their blankets, and
stood-to their horses. While they were waiting for the order
to move off they could hear the bugles of Frossard's Second
Corps rousing the infantry from their slumbers around Rezonville, two kilometers away to the east and hidden from the
cavalrymen by the rising ground. Marshal Canrobert's Sixth
Corps was on the northern road and about parallel to the
Second, and the Third Corps under Marshal Leboeuf was
echeloned to the right rear and slightly north of the Sixth.
The Imperial Guard, consisting of one cavalry and two infantry
divisions under General Bourbaki, were still at Gravelotte, as
was Bazaine's headquarters. At 4:30 that morning Napoleon
had left with an escort of cavalry by the northern route for
Verdun.

The order to advance was a long time in coming, and De
Forton's men loosened their horses' girths and began to talk
about breakfast; the horses were feeding, so why not the riders?
Then down the road came the sound of a galloping horse, and
one of Bazaine's orderly officers drew up in a flurry of dust.
He brought fresh orders from the marshal to De Forton.
There had been difficulty during the night; the marching
columns had become inextricably mixed up in the narrow
streets of Metz; artillery had missed the right road and the
transport drivers were all over the place; some of the infantry
had been marching in circles all night and were badly in need
of rest; the arrangements for getting away the wounded had

broken down. It would take time to sort out the muddle. Any
further withdrawal would be postponed until that afternoon,
and in the meantime the troops might repitch their *tentes
d'abris* and get some rest. Of course, the order said, commanders of divisions would take the usual precautions as
regards reconnaissance; it failed, however, to give any information about the enemy, although Bazaine must have known
by this time that the Prussians had crossed the Moselle in force.

De Forton seems to have been infected with the same inexplicable optimism as his commander in chief. He at once
gave orders for horses to be unsaddled and watered, for bivouacs
to be set up, and for the camp kitchens to prepare *petit
déjeuner*. His aide-de-camp saw that the General's table was
placed in the shade—it was already very warm—and that
preparations for breakfast were in hand; then he went off to
invite Prince Murat and other senior officers to join the divisional commander at breakfast—it was such a lovely morning!

The only discordant note was a plea from an overkeen officer
that he might be permitted to take out a patrol and investigate
some small bodies of troops which could be seen on the high
ground to the southwest. De Forton had a look at them through
his field glasses and then shook his head. *Non!* He had been
told that Mars-la-Tour was clear of the enemy, and that village
was seven kilometers away to the west. The troops moving
about on the skyline must be vedettes from Du Barrail's division up in the north. They were probably scouting a bit
farther south than was necessary. He returned to his omelet
and the aristocratic company of Prince Murat.

Vionville lies in a hollow, and to the north there is a broad
and shallow valley. In this valley were Murat's two regiments
of dragoons, some horse artillery, and De Forton's headquarters
staff; in all about 3,000 horses. The cuirassier brigade of the
3rd Cavalry Division was bivouacked farther to the rear, between Vionville and Rezonville. The whole area was a scene
of bustling activity as officers' servants unpacked shaving kits,
set up tents, and hurried off to the village to find rooms where
their masters might wash and brush up. The dragoons removed
their heavy brass helmets, unbuttoned their tight jackets, and

unslung their sabers. Then they laid the horse blankets on the ground, placed the saddles at one end, and lay down with their backs cradled against the saddles. Some of them led their horses down to the village to water at a pool, while others waited for the coffee to boil. It was more like maneuvers than war.

But war was creeping up on De Forton a good deal faster than he realized. Owing to his failure to reconnoiter during the previous day, he did not know that infantry of the Prussian 6th Infantry Division had crossed the Moselle and had occupied the village of Gorze on the evening of August 15. Gorze, which is no more than six kilometers from Vionville, lies below the escarpment and is surrounded by thick woods. It was an admirable assembly area for infantry, but they could not have arrived there unobserved if De Forton had taken the most elementary precautions.

Nor did De Forton know that at six o'clock that morning a strong force of Prussian cavalry had started to move towards Vionville and Mars-la-Tour. This was General Rheinbaben's 5th Cavalry Division. It had been ordered forward by the commander of the Prussian Third Corps, Count Alvensleben, who had passed a much uneasier night than De Forton.

His orders from Prince Frederick Charles, the "Red Prince" and commanding general of the Prussian Second Army, were to pursue the retreating French, get across their line of retreat, and to delay them until the rest of the Second Army could arrive. In accordance with these orders he had crossed the Moselle during the night of August 15 with his 5th and 6th Infantry Divisions, and had sent out cavalry patrols as far as Mars-la-Tour during the same afternoon. The patrols returned without making contact with the French, nor had they found any evidence that the French had passed through Mars-la-Tour. They had, however, seen what looked like a considerable body of troops encamped near Rezonville.

Alvensleben was puzzled. He knew that the French had begun their withdrawal two days previously, and it was unbelievable that they had been unable to march the distance between Metz and Mars-la-Tour. It was not much more than thirty kilometers, and a Prussian infantryman would cover

that distance easily in twenty-four hours. He therefore assumed
that the French must be retiring on Verdun by the northern
road through Doncourt, and not by the Mars-la-Tour route.
The force reported at Rezonville must be the rear guard to the
main force, and unless he acted quickly Bazaine would slip
through his hands. He immediately sent for Rheinbaben and
instructed him to take the 5th Cavalry Division on a reconnaissance in force as soon as it was light, on August 16, and,
in case the reconnaissance developed into a running fight with
the rear guard, he sent forward two additional horse artillery
batteries to join the 5th Cavalry Division.

Rheinbaben's cavalry started soon after 6:00 A.M. on the
16th, and reached the edge of the plateau about an hour later.
Led by Redern's hussar brigade,[1] the Prussian cavalry moved
cautiously across country in the direction of Vionville, and by
8:00 A.M. their leading scouts rode slowly forward onto the
ridge just west of the village. To their utter astonishment they
found themselves looking down on De Forton's division less
than half a mile to their front, and, so far as they could see,
completely oblivious of their presence. They were probably
too far away to be able to smell the coffee boiling, but they
could clearly see the jacketless dragoons sauntering about in
the sunshine, or leading their horses to and from the water.

It was the opportunity of a lifetime, and the more surprising
since the dust they must have raised during their advance
across country had apparently gone unnoticed. Redern ordered
forward his horse artillery, and they unlimbered rapidly. Within
a few minutes of eight o'clock shell after shell burst among
the French bivouac. Some squadrons were watering their
horses at a pond, others were slowly leading them back to
the horse lines, and a considerable number of them were without saddles. Officers were breakfasting, the narrow streets and
yards of Vionville were jammed with wagons, carts, and pack
animals, and soldiers were buying eggs and vegetables from
the civilian inhabitants.

The result was disaster. Men jumped barebacked onto their
horses and galloped off in panic; officers ran wildly backwards

[1] 10th, 11th, and 17th Hussars.

and forwards, trying to rally their men, searching for their grooms and horses, buckling on their sabers, shouting out orders but unable to find anyone willing to listen to them. The civilian transport drivers fled in a body across the fields, accompanied by the inhabitants of the village, and followed by many a dragoon whose heavy knee boots had not been designed for such an exercise on foot. Murat's dragoon brigade disappeared over the horizon in a regular *sauve-qui-peut*, galloping over their own infantry which had stood-to at Rezonville the moment they had heard the firing, and De Forton did not succeed in rallying them until they were almost at Gravelotte.

The German cavalry did not attempt to complete the rout by charging after the fleeing dragoons. This was partly due to the fact that Redern believed that there were concealed infantry positions beyond Vionville, and partly to the fact that the cuirassier brigade of De Forton's division had managed to withdraw in fairly good order. But as the last dragoon disappeared in a cloud of dust, the Prussian hussars cantered down into Vionville and across the bivouac area, to find the ground littered with dragoon helmets, saddles, officers' kits, tables laid for breakfast, and coffee pots simmering on the camp kitchens. They had drawn first blood in the battle of Mars-la-Tour.

The infantry of Frossard's Second Corps, which was bivouacked around Rezonville, deployed hurriedly to receive the expected cavalry charge, but as they did so fresh firing broke out on their left. This came from the horse artillery of the Prussian 6th Cavalry Division which had been following up Rheinbaben's 5th. Soon a vast semicircle of horsemen ringed the French from Mars-la-Tour in the west to the Bois de St. Arnould above Gorze, and by ten o'clock the cavalry had been joined by two infantry divisions of Alvensleben's Third Corps. As the infantry appeared through the woods they began to run forward towards the Mars-la-Tour road, and to the astonished French they seemed to be coming from every direction at once. The speed with which the Prussian artillery came into action added to the French confusion: "everywhere Prussians emerging from woods on the skyline and surrounding us with

fire." Yet these same Prussians had been within a few miles of
the French for the past twelve hours without being located.

There is always confusion in war. No one ever knows exactly what is happening "on the other side of the hill." The
rolling nature of the terrain made it hard for either French
or Prussians to estimate accurately the forces engaged, field
glasses were still in their infancy, and the clouds of dust thrown
up by bursting shells or the movement of horses made observation difficult. So did the black smoke from guns and
rifles which drifted slowly in the still air.

Alvensleben was still convinced that he was dealing with
the French rear guard, and it was not until after eleven o'clock
that it suddenly dawned on him that his two infantry divisions,
supported only by two cavalry divisions, had run up against
the 200,000 horse, foot, and guns of the Army of the Rhine.
Instead of making contact with the French rear guard, he was
now faced with the French advance guard, and behind it were
marching sixteen infantry divisions and six of cavalry. Meanwhile the nearest Prussian reinforcements were the Tenth
Corps, and they were still crossing the Moselle and unlikely
to reach the battlefield until late that afternoon.

It was an unpleasant situation, but Alvensleben did not
hesitate. His task was to delay the withdrawal of Bazaine's
army, and he was prepared to see his own corps destroyed if
necessary. He ordered the 6th Infantry Division, at that moment advancing north towards Vionville, to wheel to the right
and advance eastward towards Metz astride the main road.
By 11:30 A.M. he had secured Vionville itself, and by midday
his two infantry divisions had linked up in the little hamlet
of Flavigny, a mile south of Vionville. The road to the west
was blocked—for the time being, at least.

The French were equally confused about the Prussian intentions. Bazaine had galloped forward from Gravelotte as
soon as he heard the firing, and had joined General Frossard
on the high ground just east of Rezonville. As he arrived he
could see the infantry of Frossard's corps streaming back towards Rezonville, and over behind him, in the low ground
northeast of Rezonville, he saw thirteen cavalry regiments

drawn up in column of squadrons and awaiting orders. They were from De Forton's division, now re-formed and burning to avenge their disgrace of earlier in the day, and from the *chasseurs à cheval* and dragoons of Valabrègue's cavalry division. Marching up from the rear were the divisions of the Imperial Guard which Bazaine had set in motion before he had left Gravelotte, while Canrobert's Sixth Corps were hastening down from the north to join in the battle. Bazaine had plenty of soldiers.

For some inexplicable reason however he misunderstood the Prussian mission. Instead of assuming the obvious, that they intended to cut off his retreat to Verdun, he conceived that they were trying to work round his left flank and cut him off from Metz. This *idée fixe* played right into Alvensleben's hands, since it led to Bazaine strengthening his left flank where it rested on the wooded edge of the escarpment, and it was not until much later in the day that he tried to use his superior numbers to roll up the very exposed flank of the Prussians where it rested on Mars-la-Tour and Vionville. By the time he got around to doing this, it was too late, and the Army of the Rhine was trapped.

While Bazaine and his staff were thus reasoning things out, General Frossard was growing increasingly agitated. His infantry were streaming back towards Rezonville and at any moment they might break into panic flight. If the Prussians followed them up and took Rezonville, everything might be lost; and in the meantime there were upwards of five thousand French sabers standing about and doing nothing. He tried to convince Bazaine of the urgency of the situation, but the commander in chief remained blandly indifferent; all he seemed to be concerned about was his left flank. Frossard could stand it no longer and galloped off to the two nearest cavalry regiments—the 3rd Lancers and the cuirassiers of the Guard. He at once gave orders to the cuirassiers to charge, but there then followed a ridiculous argument between Frossard, the colonel of the cuirassiers, and Bazaine, during which the colonel argued that he could not charge without first obtaining permission from his brigade commander.

Finally, Bazaine was heard to mutter, "Yes, we must sacrifice a regiment; we must stop them," and an orderly officer was sent at the gallop to order the 3rd Lancers to charge. Presumably this regiment was selected because there were fewer strings attached to its use than there were to a regiment of the Guard, but whatever the reason there was no attempt to assign the lancers an objective, no attempt on their part to reconnoiter their route, and no attempt to support them with artillery fire.

The 3rd Lancers were a good regiment, and a popular one. As they cantered forward the infantry cheered them with shouts of *"Vivent les lanciers!"* and they came over the rise in a formation worthy of a review. Directly in their path lay the impedimenta left by Murat's dragoons in their panic flight earlier in the day, and as they swerved to avoid the obstacles a terrific fire greeted them from the Prussian infantry. Almost at the same time an order was given to wheel to the right—by whom, it has never been established—and the lancers wheeled across the front of the Prussians and back to their start line without accomplishing anything.

Frossard then ordered the cuirassiers of the Guard to charge. Their brigade commander objected that they would only succeed in riding down their own retreating infantry, that the Prussian infantry was over a mile away, and that failure was certain unless they were supported by heavy artillery fire. "Attack at once, or we are all lost!" retorted Frossard, and the cuirassiers obeyed. The two leading squadrons were thrown into confusion by the same obstacles that had impeded the lancers, the two squadrons following collided into them, and into this jumbled mass of plunging, rearing horses, the Prussians poured volley after volley of aimed fire at fifty paces distance. The French colonel and his adjutant managed to break into one of the Prussian squares, but the rest of the regiment was decimated. The cuirassiers of the Imperial Guard left 22 officers, 208 cuirassiers, and 243 horses on the field of battle after this ill-fated charge, which was delivered against only two companies of the 52nd Brandenburg Infantry Regiment.

Bazaine watched the charge through his field glasses, and as soon as he saw it begin to go wrong he ordered up a battery of guns to cover the cuirassiers' retirement. Watching also from behind the burning village of Flavigny was Colonel Von Caprivi, chief of staff of the Prussian Tenth Corps, and as the French cavalry fell back in disorder, Caprivi urged the colonels of the 11th and 17th Hussars to pursue them; it was the moment for which the hussars had been eagerly waiting.

The 17th "Black" Hussars of Brunswick were one of Prussia's oldest and most famous regiments. They had been raised in 1809, and, as the "Black Troop," had marched from Bohemia to Oldenburg in the campaign against Bonaparte. They had been forced by overwhelming French forces to embark for England, and there had taken service under George III in the King's German Legion, fought under Wellington in Spain, and again at Waterloo, where they lost their commanding officer, the Duke of Brunswick, on the field of Quatre Bras. The hussars returned to Brunswick in 1816, and were absorbed into the Prussian army in 1867, the year when Hanover became part of Prussia. They were allowed to retain their emblem of the "Death's Head" as well as the battle honors won under British command—including "Peninsula," "Sicily," and "Waterloo." They were to add to them at Mars-la-Tour.

Together with a squadron of the 2nd Dragoons of the Guard, the 17th Hussars moved out of Flavigny, wheeled to the right, and charged after the French cuirassiers. Behind them, and to the right, the 11th Hussars swept over the French infantry, which was falling back in disorderly fashion towards Rezonville. Most of the French cuirassiers who had succeeded in remaining in the saddle broke safely away, but as the 17th Hussars swept across the ridge they suddenly saw the battery brought up by Marshal Bazaine preparing to come into action. They immediately charged the guns, the artillerymen gallantly remaining with their pieces and firing canister shot at point-blank range at the charging horsemen.

A furious melee ensued, involving Prussian hussars, French artillerymen, and Marshal Bazaine and his staff. The French commander in chief drew his sword to defend himself, displaying throughout the personal bravery which had always been one of his most marked characteristics, but it seemed certain that he would be either killed or captured. His nephew, who was acting as his aide-de-camp, galloped off to summon Bazaine's personal escort of chasseurs, but on the way fell in with a squadron of the 5th Hussars. This was the regiment which had distinguished itself during the French expedition to Mexico in support of the ill-fated Archduke Maximilian, and it came galloping forward with great *élan* to the rescue of Bazaine. Behind galloped the 3rd Lancers, and the two French regiments succeeded in driving back the Prussian hussars and rescuing Marshal Bazaine. The 17th Hussars withdrew to Flavigny, leaving seventy-four dead horses behind them.

An interesting sidelight on this action is that sixteen years before, at Balaklava, and at almost exactly the same time of day, two of the British cavalry regiments which thundered up the "valley of death" were the 11th Hussars and the 17th Lancers. The 17th Lancers also wore the badge of the "Death's Head" in their lance caps, and their motto, "Or Glory." At Mars-la-Tour the 11th and 17th Prussian Hussars charged together, and the motto of the latter regiment was *"Tod oder Ruhm."*

More than five hours had passed since the first shells had fallen among Murat's breakfasting dragoons. The Prussian infantry were exhausted and Alvensleben had no reserves left in his Third Corps. The French, on the other hand, were getting a better grip of the situation; their first panic reaction was over, and Bazaine was moving troops down from the northern road to strengthen his right flank. He had two army corps within easy reach, whereas Alvensleben could not call up even a fresh platoon. The situation was growing hourly more critical for the Prussians.

Both sides had been fighting under conditions of extreme heat. The sun had been blazing down all morning, the parched ground was very dusty, and there was very little water. What water there was had been fouled by dead animals, and water bottles were empty. Most of the Prussian infantry had been forced-marching for the preceding forty-eight hours in tight and uncomfortable uniforms and carrying large quantities of ammunition and heavy packs. The horses, especially, were in a pitiable condition. They had been on the move since dawn, carrying fully equipped cavalrymen weighing, with all their saddlery and weapons, over 280 pounds, and many of them had been wounded by bayonet or bullet. Every farmhouse was full of wounded, lying side by side in the blood-stained straw, while outside on the middens were the amputated limbs thrown there by the surgeons. Ammunition was very short, and little was coming forward from the rear.

It seemed as though Alvensleben's Third Corps had shot its bolt. It had barred Bazaine's retreat throughout the long morning, but it had been fought to a standstill while doing so. At any moment now the French must surely launch an attack on the exposed Prussian left flank between Vionville and the Tronville copses, and there was nothing left with which to meet it. No wonder Alvensleben told one of his staff officers that he felt like Wellington waiting at Waterloo for Blücher to come up from Ligny to relieve the appalling pressure on his overstretched line: "Would to God that either night or the Tenth Corps would come."

But night was still six hours away, and the Tenth Corps could not arrive on the battlefield for at least another hour. Somehow the Prussian corps commander must gain time and forestall the threatened attack against his left flank.

This left flank extended from the village of Vionville for about a thousand yards northwest to the Tronville copses. These copses were thick woods, with even thicker undergrowth, overlooking the main road from Mars-la-Tour to Rezonville, which was still held by the French. A ridge of high ground ran in an easterly direction from the copses, and along this ridge there had once been a Roman road. Numerous French batteries were now deploying on the crest of the ridge, from where they could shell the Prussian-held villages of Vionville and Flavigny, while the French infantry were beginning to infiltrate through the wood north of the Roman road and down into the Tronville copses. Once the copses were in their hands they would be able to attack Vionville from the rear, clear the ground between that village and Mars-la-Tour, and the road to Verdun would then be open. From the high ground just west of Vionville the commander of the Prussian 6th Infantry Division anxiously scanned the battlefield to his front. He saw immediately to the east of the village what remained of his 24th Infantry Regiment, extended in a single line from the main road to the Tronville copses. They were without any reserves and unable to dig themselves any cover in the hard ground, and it was almost impossible to evacuate their wounded. Beyond them, and about two thousand yards away, General Von Buddenbrock could see the French infantry deployed in two lines with the field guns coming into action to their left. It was an apparently hopeless situation and only a matter of time before the 24th Infantry were overrun.

Von Buddenbrock himself was almost at the end of his tether. He had hardly slept for three days, and most of his waking hours had been spent on horseback. Turning to his aide-de-camp he said, "I am so tired I am going to sleep; call me if you notice anything." Without dismounting he fell asleep on his horse's back.

He was wakened some minutes later by the aide-de-camp, who had seen some French cavalry gallop up to the ridge north of Rezonville and had assumed that they were about to charge the weakened Prussian infantry. He suggested that he should gallop off to find some Prussian cavalry to charge first, but Von Buddenbrock objected, pointing out that cavalry could not be expected to charge unshaken infantry. Eventually, however, he gave in to the pleadings of the younger officer, realizing that the 24th Infantry were doomed unless something was done to save them.

Lieutenant Pohl, the aide-de-camp, accordingly rode off to find some cavalry, and on the way fell in with the chief of staff of the Third Corps, to whom he explained the situation. Like Von Buddenbrock at first, the chief of staff demurred at the idea of sending cavalry out on such a deadly mission, but when the situation had been fully explained to him he ordered Pohl to find General Von Bredow and order him to charge with his cavalry brigade.

Pohl found the heavy cavalry brigade drawn up in the low

ground west of Vionville, and to the south of the road which
runs from Vionville to Mars-la-Tour. Von Bredow had with
him the 7th (Count Bismarck's) Magdeburg Cuirassiers and
the 16th Uhlans of Altmark, neither of which had yet been
involved in the battle. In order to ease their horses the cavalrymen had dismounted and were standing beside them, while
Von Bredow and his staff were watching the battle through
their field glasses. Pohl immediately explained the order, and
Von Bredow shook his head. It was a crazy order, he said;
cavalry cannot charge unbroken infantry, and that at the end
of nearly three thousand yards' gallop. And against guns as
well—the flashes were clearly visible along the line of the
Roman road—it just could not be done.

Pohl was a subaltern of eight years' service, and Von Bredow
was one of the most distinguished cavalry officers in the Prussian army. Pohl was about to ride back to his general with his
mission unaccomplished when the chief of staff of the Third
Corps joined them. He brought orders from General Alvensleben that the heavy cavalry brigade was to be sacrificed
in order to save the infantry, and Von Bredow argued no
longer. Raising his sword in salute, he ordered his trumpeter
to sound the call to "Mount"; then he rode forward a few
hundred yards to have a closer look at the ground.

He looked down on what must have seemed to him to be
"suicide alley." At the far end of the alley were the French
infantry, occupying well-chosen fire positions and armed with
the best rifle in Europe, and with artillery behind them. On
the left flank were the Tronville copses which were supposed
to be occupied by more enemy infantry, and it seemed, therefore, that the Prussian cavalry would be exposed to enfilade
fire, as well as to fire from their direct front. Even the Light
Brigade at Balaklava had not been called upon to execute a
more desperate charge, and in their case the order had been
given in error. But there was no error here. The order had been
given in explicit terms by Alvensleben's chief of staff, and
Lieutenant Pohl had been there to witness it.

The main worry was lest the cavalry should be caught by
enfilade fire while forming line to charge—always a tricky

maneuver to perform at the gallop—and Von Bredow decided
that he must mask the Tronville copses on his left flank. It
was a task that would inevitably mean heavy losses, since the
troops detailed for the duty would be under heavy shell and
rifle fire for most of the time. The flanking squadrons were
therefore selected by drawing lots, and one squadron from each
regiment was chosen, with the task of covering the heavy
brigade's flank, and if need be they were to fight their way
on foot through the thick woods to prevent any interference
with the charge.

This left six squadrons, amounting to less than 800 sabers, to
charge the French infantrymen and guns. They trotted forward
across the high road, and then dipped down into the shallow
valley running almost due north of Vionville. This valley provided cover from artillery observation, and so far there had
been no fire from the Tronville copses, towards which the
flanking squadrons were galloping. Arrived in the valley, Von
Bredow gave the following orders, which were intended to
wheel the brigade until it faced east (until then they had been
trotting north), and then deploy the regiments from squadron columns into line for the charge:

> Front eastward—left wheel [in order to make use of the
> low ground]—right wheel by divisions—take intervals
> while riding forward—form line to the front—*Charge!*

The drill movement took very little time to execute. Indeed,
Lieutenant Pohl had not yet had time to rejoin Von Buddenbrock, when the heavy cavalrymen swept past him at a thundering gallop. Riding knee to knee, and stretched out over the
horses' necks, the cuirassiers and uhlans burst over the crest
and into the astonished French infantrymen. The charge seems
to have come as a complete surprise, since several of the
French batteries were in the act of withdrawing from the
firing line to make room for fresh batteries coming up from
the rear. Dense clouds of dust mingled with the smoke of
shells, and the plunging of wounded and screaming horses
added to the confusion.

No attempt seems to have been made to open fire at point-blank range at the cuirassiers and uhlans, who were therefore able to cut down the French artillerymen. The reason for this failure on the part of the French artillery to open fire was due to the very strict French artillery regulations which forbade any change to a fresh target without first getting permission from superior authority. When one artillery colonel saw the cavalry approaching he sent for permission to open fire on them, but before it arrived the Prussian cavalry were into them. The French had not fired a single shell.

Having burst right through the line of batteries, Von Bredow's cavalrymen galloped after the fleeing infantry and artillery, spearing and sabering as they went. Before the galloping horses, the battlefield disintegrated into a confused mass of men, crouching and running, falling and stumbling, scattered hither and thither like leaves blown by a sudden wind. And the lancers leaned even farther from their saddles to reach out at those who hugged the earth as tightly as any leveret sheltering from a hawk.

Some distance to the flank was De Forton's re-formed cavalry division which had been watching the progress of the Prussian charge with something more than just professional interest. There was the shameful episode of the morning to be avenged. De Forton turned to Prince Murat, waved in the direction of the Prussian cavalry with his sword, and left the rest to the dragoons. They required no urging.

As the Magdeburg cuirassiers and the Altmark uhlans came down into the dip beyond Rezonville, at the end of their long gallop, they were met head-on by the French dragoons, and almost simultaneously two French cuirassier regiments charged them from the rear. There now followed the first of a long series of cavalry-against-cavalry combats which have gained for Mars-la-Tour the description as "the greatest cavalry battle of modern times." French dragoon and Prussian lancer, Prussian cuirassier and French cuirassier, were locked together in the fury of hand-to-hand combat. Jousting against each other were the 7th Cuirassiers of Prussia and the 7th Cuirassiers of France, and at one stage the rival regiments were represented in almost single combat; a huge Prussian cuirassier was locked in a saber duel with an officer of the French cuirassiers—in all the splendor of casque and breastplate and waving horsehair plumes. Then the maelstrom surged back round the two combatants and drove them apart.

Von Bredow's brigade was now in deadly peril. Outnumbered five to one by the French cavalry, their horses were exhausted, and so were the riders. Many horses were wounded, and nearly all of them were half-demented by the noise of battle and the excitement of the charge. The troopers—blackened with smoke and dust, maddened with thirst, and reeling in their saddles from fatigue—were now faced with ever-increasing numbers of French horsemen, for Valabrègue's cavalry division was hastening up to help De Forton's. Either the Prussians withdrew at once or remained to be ridden right into the ground.

The recall was sounded, and what remained of the Magdeburg cuirassiers and the Altmark uhlans heaved their horses round by main force, and galloped back the way they had come—back past the overturned guns, the scattered wagon lines, the empty shell cases, the debris, the dead, and the dying. Behind them they left over half their strength: 16 officers, 363 men, and 400 of the finest horses that have ever come out of Germany.

They rallied at last behind Flavigny, not far from the place they had left not long before to make their charge. It has become the most famous charge in German history—the "*Todtenritt*," or "Death Ride." The way they had gone was plain for all to see; both the advance and withdrawal was marked out in white across the fields of stubble—the white tunics of the Magdeburg cuirassiers who lay there silent beside their still horses.

They had not died in vain. The French threat to the Prussian left flank was eased for the time being, and the guns which had been pouring out such a murderous fire from beyond the Roman road were silenced. Von Buddenbrock's infantry had been saved, but at the price of two regiments of Prussia's finest cavalry.

The French had suffered severely as well.

Every one of the gunners of the first battery were cut down or pierced [wrote Count Von Schmitten, who led his 7th Cuirassiers in the "Death Ride"]. In approaching the second battery my helmet was pierced by two bullets, and my orderly officer thrown from his horse wounded in two places. Lieutenant Campbell, the Scottish officer, when the French cuirassiers fell upon ours, seized the eagle of the regiment with his left hand, which was at once shattered by a bullet, and he was surrounded by the French horsemen, but some of our own cuirassiers cut their way desperately towards him and saved him.[2]

The charge of the Prussian cavalry up the narrow valley from Vionville was watched by a man who sixteen years before had been an eyewitness of a similar charge up the "valley of death." He was Marshal Canrobert, whose Sixth Corps was hastening down from the north to the rescue of Frossard's Second, and as he saw Von Bredow's thunder across the crest he must have thought back to that day when he stood beside Bosquet at the edge of the Chersonese, and heard Bosquet utter his immortal epigram: *"C'est magnifique, mais ce n'est pas la guerre."*

For a time a lull settled over the battlefield, but as the dust thrown up by the milling cavalrymen began to settle, a fresh threat began to develop against the Prussian left. Two French army corps had been marching as fast as they could to the sound of the guns, and about 3:00 P.M. they began to deploy on the battlefield. Almost at the same moment the advance guards of the Prussian Tenth Corps appeared from

[2] H. B. Franklyn, *The Great Battles of 1870* (Trübner, London, 1887), p. 73. Campbell of Craigneish, later Baron Campbell, was serving with the Prussian cavalry. He was severely wounded in the charge and owed his rescue to Pemberton, *Times* correspondent with the Prussian army, who rode in the charge as a *spectator*. He galloped alongside one of the troop leaders, escaped unhurt, and picked up and carried back across his saddle the badly wounded Campbell. Pemberton's coolness and self-possession made a great impression on all who saw him, and his conduct at Mars-la-Tour was in the great tradition of war correspondents which we have seen since on innumerable battlefields, and most recently in Korea. Pemberton was subsequently killed outside Sedan, by a stray bullet, some time after the French surrender.

the southeast, and a fierce struggle now ensued for the possession of Mars-la-Tour village. This culminated at 5:00 P.M.
with the advance of the Prussian 38th Infantry Brigade, drums
beating and colors waving, across the high road to assault the
French infantry which were concentrating north of the Tronville copses.

Five battalions of Prussian infantry ran forward in dashes of
100 to 150 yards, only to find themselves halted by a steep
ravine. As they scaled the far side, they came under a withering fire from the French infantry, and the Prussians, weighed
down by heavy packs and extra ammunition, were thrown
back. After a terrible mauling they struggled back out of the
ravine, but were too exhausted to fall back any farther. They
had marched for twenty-seven hours to reach the battlefield,
and had hardly slept for days; they were hungry, thirsty, and
bewildered, and their rifles were outranged by the French.
They had called up their last reserves of stamina, physically
and mentally, and had reached that crucial stage in a soldier's
existence when morale hangs by a thread. Once again on
August 16, the cavalryman was to come to the rescue of the
infantry.

Among the barns and farmyards on the southern outskirts
of Mars-la-Tour were five squadrons of Prussia's elite cavalry—
the dragoons of the Guard. General Count Brandenburg, who
commanded them, was ordered to protect the left flank of the
infantry attack, and as soon as it was clear that the attack had
failed, Brandenburg led his squadrons forward to cover the
withdrawal.

It was 6:00 P.M. when the squadrons trotted across the Mars-
la-Tour road, wheeled to the northeast, and deployed for the
charge. The ground in front of them was far less suitable for
cavalry than it had been earlier in the day for Von Bredow's
brigade. There was a maze of hedges and ditches surrounding Mars-la-Tour, and the dragoons of the Guard were pre-
eminently heavy cavalry, who required a good deal of space in
which to work up speed. Yet despite the unsuitable terrain the
Prussian cavalry deployed in good order, and they smashed their

way through the hedges, jumped the ditches, and halted the French advance.

They paid a heavy penalty for doing so. There were 204 horses killed outright, others were wounded and made the battlefield hideous with their screams, and 132 officers and men were killed or wounded. The commanding officer of the 1st Dragoons of the Guard, Count Von Auerswald, was mortally wounded and pinned to the ground beneath his horse. Before he died he handed over command of his regiment to the junior captain, Prince Hohenzollern, and called on the dying around him to give three cheers for their king.

Once again the danger to the Prussian left flank was temporarily halted, but the French redoubled their efforts to capture Mars-la-Tour. They brought up the bulk of their cavalry in an attempt to release the stranglehold on their escape route, and there followed a medley of cavalry actions which swept backwards and forwards across the open downland that lies due north of the village. Bazaine had collected over five thousand sabers on his right flank, whereas the Prussians could only scratch together three thousand to oppose them. The French were fresher too, and had their attacks only been properly coordinated they must have driven the Prussian cavalry from the field. But as it was, the battle degenerated into a welter of furious charges, regiment against regiment, squadron against squadron, and troop against troop. And on occasions even individual horseman against horseman.

In a battle of this sort the superior training and discipline of the Prussian cavalry was bound to tell. Their horsemanship was better than the French, and their horses were bigger and stronger. They also made better use of the ground. Montaigu's hussar brigade found this out when they charged the Prussian 13th Dragoons, drawn up on a ridge outside Mars-la-Tour.

Montaigu had first suggested that his hussars should open fire on the Prussians with their carbines before they charged home with the sword, but the divisional general, Legrand, was anxious to strike home. "*Non,*" he shouted, "*au sabre!*" So the hussars on their wiry little horses plunged down the slope at a

gallop, and up the other side towards the skyline, where the
Prussians were drawn up to receive them, *comme des colosses*.
The dragoons waited until the hussars were almost upon them,
opened fire with their carbines, and then, drawing their swords,
crashed down onto the shaken and winded French. The Prussian cavalry had everything in their favor, and the hussars were
cut to pieces. As they reeled back the way they had come, they
were set upon from the flank by yet another Prussian cavalry
regiment which had been waiting its opportunity, and in a
matter of minutes the hussar brigade had ceased to exist as a
fighting entity. Legrand, whose impulsiveness had sent the
brigade to almost certain defeat, died from a saber thrust as
he led up another regiment to try to rescue the broken regiments.

During the last hours of daylight the cavalry battle increased
in intensity. There were over five thousand horsemen milling
over the open downs, enveloped in a dense cloud of dust, and
uncertain who was friend and who was foe. A French regiment
of lancers was cut to pieces by another French regiment which
had mistaken its light-blue uniform for Prussian; another French
regiment opened fire at close range with its carbines against
some of its own side withdrawing across its front.

One of the last charges of the day was made by the Chasseurs
d'Afrique, the pride of the French cavalry, against the 13th
Uhlans, a regiment which had first seen service under the British flag in Spain. As the 1st Light Dragoons of the King's German Legion, the 13th Uhlans had charged at Garcia Hernandez
under General Bock, and they still bore the battle honor on the
front of their lance caps. As the two regiments crashed into each
other, Bazaine threw into the struggle the lancers, dragoons,
guides, and carabiniers of the Guard, but the Prussians held
firm. The Westphalian cuirassier regiment galloped up, and the
French began to retire slowly to the northeast. The battle was
over.

Mars-la-Tour was still in Prussian hands when darkness fell.
The road to Verdun remained blocked, although Bazaine
could have switched his withdrawal to the northern route, which
was under his control. The possibility never seems to have

occurred to him, for he was still obsessed with the belief that the Prussian aim was to cut him off from Metz.

So ended the greatest cavalry battle of modern times. There would be campaigns in the future when even larger forces of cavalry were involved, but it was the last battle in which great bodies of horsemen were locked together in the cut and thrust of close combat. It was also a battle in which cavalry played a predominant part. Between dawn and dusk they charged home on eighteen separate occasions, in troops, squadrons, regiments, and even brigades. Cavalry first discovered the French, pinned them to the ground until the infantry could come up, and then saved that infantry from almost certain destruction on two separate occasions. And at the close of day it was the cavalry on the French side which sought to wrest victory from defeat, as it was the cavalry on the Prussian side which prevented them from doing so.

The moon came up to light a battlefield on which there lay thirty-two thousand dead, dying, and wounded. It is an astonishing figure when one considers that man had yet to perfect the diabolical killing powers of his weapons. In the whole of their long retreat in Burma in 1942, the British casualties did not amount to half this figure.

Out there, too, in the hedges, ditches, and stubble, lay hundreds and hundreds of dead horses. Horses, still and silent as the dew fell upon them, that had been killed by bullet or bayonet, saber cut or lance thrust, or that had been blown to eternity at the muzzle of the guns, or had just collapsed from sheer exhaustion.

They also had earned their Mention in Dispatches.

CHAPTER EIGHT

Little Big Horn

JUNE 25, 1876

"There were a great deal too many Indians who were powerful good shots on the other side . . . and they were fighting for all the good God gives anyone to fight for."

CAPTAIN F. W. BENTEEN

IT WAS barely a year after Lee's surrender when Congress paused in its gigantic task of disbanding the volunteer army of the Union and authorized the formation of four new cavalry regiments for service on the Indian frontier. The senior of these new regiments was the 7th Cavalry, and to it was assigned Lieutenant Colonel (and Brevet Major General) George Armstrong Custer.

They were a remarkable collection of men who joined the 7th Cavalry at Fort Riley during the summer and autumn of 1866. Almost every officer was a veteran of the Civil War and many of them had held high rank in the Union army; among them were a Prussian, a half-breed Indian, a former papal Zouave, an ex-judge, a Frenchman, and a grandson of Alexander

Hamilton.[1] The soldiers were no less mixed in their nationalities and backgrounds, and they were a tough, colorful, and independent-minded body of men, requiring as their commanding officer someone who was at least as tough and as colorful as they were. They found the man in Custer.

Custer's military career had been astonishingly successful, and "Custer's luck" was something of a legend. He had only just left the Military Academy at West Point when the Civil War began, and by the time he was twenty-five he had five times been brevetted for gallantry and had reached the acting rank of major general. The 3rd Cavalry Division, which he commanded, had played the leading part in harassing the retreating Confederates in 1865. And it was Custer who so delayed the movements of Lee's army that the infantry of the Army of the Potomac were able to overhaul the battered gray columns and finally bar their retreat at Appomattox Court House. By the end of the Civil War, Custer was certainly one of the best-known military figures in North America, and his sudden rise to fame was in the best tradition of the American "success story."

This was the man who arrived at Fort Riley in September, 1866, to mold the heterogeneous collection of soldiers of the 7th Cavalry into a disciplined and well-trained regiment.[2] He brought with him a brilliant reputation as a soldier but a doubtful one as a man. He was brave, ruthless, flamboyant, and conceited, and determined to get his own way in everything. Still only twenty-eight, he would have been more than human had his rapid promotion not gone to his head. There were, however, other officers in the 7th Cavalry who had achieved almost as quick promotion during the Civil War; one of them was Major Robert Reno, who had risen from lieutenant to colonel "for gallant and meritorious service," and another was

[1] Captain Louis McLane Hamilton was killed riding beside Custer at the battle of Washita in 1868.

[2] Congress had appointed Brevet Major General A. J. Smith to command the 7th Cavalry, but he was subsequently assigned to command the local military district. Custer, although nominally second-in-command, commanded the regiment.

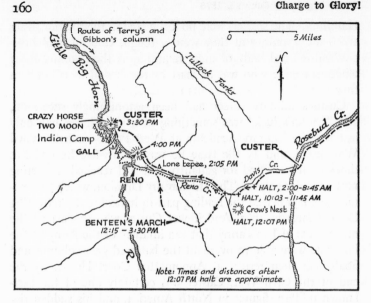

Captain Frederick Benteen, who had also reached the rank of colonel by the end of the war. Both these officers had dropped several grades in rank and they resented Custer's superior airs.

The years between 1866 and 1886 were the years of the Indian Wars. The great expansion westward across the prairies was gathering momentum, and the Indians were making desperate attempts to keep the white men out of their territory. There had, of course, been wars against the Indians ever since the first white men settled in Virginia, and the few regular regiments in the United States army had spent most of the first half of the nineteenth century campaigning against the Indians. But it was not until after the Civil War that the Indians fully realized the dangers which were threatening their traditional way of life, and from then onwards for the next twenty years they fought with all the fury of despair.

It was hard, brutal, and relentless war, stained by massacre, torture, and rape, and with little quarter given or asked on either side; a war of companies, troops, and patrols, of ambushes and sieges of isolated posts, and of long marches carried out over vast distances in extremes of heat and cold. There were

those among the white men who saw in these frontier skirmishes the opportunity to get rich quick, and huge fortunes
were made by trading modern rifles and revolvers to the Indians.
The standard price of a rifle was one hundred dollars' worth
of robes, hides, or furs, and a single cartridge might be priced
as high as twenty cents. The profits were vast, the risk of detec-
tion in that wilderness negligible, and the knowledge that the
weapons would be used against fellow Americans of little or
no consequence. Naked savages were thereby enabled to take
the field with better weapons than were provided for the soldiers by a parsimonious and antimilitarist Congress.

There, along the Indian frontier, was forged the military tradition of the United States, and for the most part it was forged
by junior captains and lieutenants, commanding their small
detachments with no hope of advice or support from their
seniors, who were usually several days' ride away. Older-established armies are sometimes inclined to think that the regiments
of the United States army lack military tradition, but they are
wrong. A fine tradition was built up during the Indian Wars
which will stand comparison with that of any other army in
the world.

Custer played his full part in forging that tradition, but first
of all he had to build his regiment. Like all true cavalrymen
he was a great believer in *panache,* and he set himself to drill
and train the 7th Cavalry until it was one of the most efficient
and smartest regiments in the army. In order to achieve this he
drove his men hard, and his methods were not calculated to
add to his popularity. Many of the enlisted men had joined the
7th because the regiment was stationed at the gateway to the
Far West, and therefore provided the opportunity of free transportation to the gold fields. They would desert at the first opportunity and trek westward across the mountains, and it was
said of the 7th Cavalry that by the end of five years in Kansas
enough men had deserted to fill the ranks of a division.

Custer had been with the 7th only a few months when he
led out four troops against the Indians, and by the time they
returned to Fort Riley the hard-bitten troopers were muttering
among themselves that service under Custer was far more

rugged than fighting Indians. He had driven them so hard that forty men deserted in one night, and a few days later several others succeeded in slipping away. They were seen by Custer, who sent out some of his officers to bring them back "dead or alive," and in the course of their doing so two or three of the soldiers were shot. Later, when Custer was court-martialed for indiscipline, among the charges leveled against him was unnecessary harshness towards his deserters.

Yet there could be no doubt about his powers of leadership. His stamina and vitality were abnormal, as is so often the case with born leaders of men. He thought nothing of marching from dawn until dark, his soldiers reeling in their saddles with fatigue while Custer rode up and down the column, laughing and joking. Then, when the column had bivouacked for the night, he would sit up half the night writing letters or reports, until he felt it was time to snatch two or three hours' rest. But at dawn he would be the first into the saddle, as fresh as a daisy, and he could keep this up for weeks on end as the 7th Cavalry scoured the Great Plains after the hostiles.

The principal enemy was the Sioux confederation of tribes, who with the Cheyennes were probably the most formidable of all the Indian tribes in North America. The Sioux have been described as the "finest light cavalry in the world," which is possibly rather extravagant praise from an officer who won his spurs fighting against them, but they certainly possessed in full measure the good cavalryman's eye for terrain, as well as tactical ability and horsemanship. They were mobile, well armed, and more often than not better shots than the regulars. When on the warpath they thought nothing of covering fifty miles a day, and they had in their war chief—Ta Shunka Witko, or Crazy Horse—an inspired military leader who deserves his niche in the pantheon of North American military heroes. Crazy Horse was undoubtedly the ablest of all the Indian war chiefs, and was grudgingly respected by the soldiers who took the field against him.

In 1868, General Sheridan was appointed to command operations along the Indian frontier, and one of his first acts was to recall Custer from suspension. He had been suspended by a court-martial eight months previously, after being charged with leaving his regiment without permission in order to visit his wife, and with undue harshness towards his deserters. Sheridan had been Custer's superior during the Civil War and he knew Custer's worth as a soldier; he was equally aware of Custer's shortcomings, but needed him to command an expedition against the Cheyennes in Oklahoma.

The original suspension was for twelve months, but Sheridan managed to have this reduced to eight, and on October 30, 1868, Custer rejoined the 7th Cavalry at Fort Dodge on the Arkansas River. Sheridan was one of the few senior officers whom Custer respected, and he accordingly did what Sheridan told him. In return, Sheridan stood up for Custer when his outrageous behavior had Washington thirsting for his blood.

One month later Custer led the 7th Cavalry through a blizzard to surprise and attack an Indian camp on the Washita River. The Indians, like other nomads, tended to disperse into family groups when conditions were good, and to congregate into tribes or subtribes when conditions were difficult. The climate that November was so severe that the thermometer had fallen to 7 degrees below zero and the Indians must have believed it most unlikely that the soldiers would venture far from their posts.

Despite the atrocious weather, Custer was in uproarious spirits as he led the 7th Cavalry out from Fort Supply. Their guidons were whipping in the breeze, and the unfortunate musicians in the regimental band raised their instruments to their cracked and bleeding lips and blared out the regiment's marching song, "Garry Owen." This tune, adopted by Custer as the 7th's own, has since become one of the best-known military tunes in America. To this day the 7th Cavalry are known as the "Garry Owens" throughout the United States army, and there is a town with the same name in the valley where Custer made his last stand. Custer was not the first, however, to march his soldiers to war to the lilting refrain of "Garry Owen." It was a popular marching tune long before Custer got hold of it, and Wellington's lighthearted Irish regiments trudged halfway across Spain to the same strain.[3]

For five days the 7th Cavalry plunged through snow drifts and across frozen streams until scouts reported a camp ahead on the banks of the Washita. So far as was known the Indians did not know of Custer's approach. Halting about a mile from the village, Custer divided his regiment into four parties and surrounded the sleeping village under cover of darkness. Then they waited, wrapped only in a blanket, through hours of freezing cold, until at daybreak the numbed and shivering bandsmen crashed once more into "Garry Owen" and Custer led his troopers forward in the charge. The Indians were completely surprised and lost many killed, but they rallied in time to cut off a detachment of the 7th under Major Elliott, which had galloped off down the valley. Elliott's detachment was killed to a man, and soon other Indians from encampments farther along the Washita hurried to the assistance of the attacked village. Custer's force was outnumbered and in grave danger of being overwhelmed.

Even if common military prudence, not one of Custer's most marked characteristics, did not advise withdrawal, the shortage of ammunition did. He had left his supply train forty miles behind, and it was guarded by only eighty men. His base was five days' march away and he had several wounded men, as well as eighty-seven prisoners, to carry back safely. Nevertheless he did endeavor to discover what had happened to Elliott's detachment. Ordering the band to strike up "Ain't I glad to get out of the Wilderness," Custer marched the 7th Cavalry boldly down the Washita in the direction in which Elliott had disappeared, and where the Indians were massing to destroy his meager force.

As soon as darkness fell, however, Custer ordered the column

[3] "Garry Owen" is the regimental march of the Royal Irish Fusiliers in the British army. Most of the immigrants who first enlisted in the 7th Cavalry were Irish and it appears that many of them were former members of the 5th Royal Irish Lancers, whose favorite song was "Garry Owen." Custer heard them singing the song and liked it so much that he established it as the regimental march. One squadron of the 7th Cavalry has now formed a pipe band on the same lines as those in the Irish regiments of the British army to perpetuate this Irish connection.

to turn about, and by forced march through the freezing night he regained his supply train. A few days later the 7th were back at Fort Supply and rode proudly in review in front of General Sheridan, with the bandsmen still blowing away indefatigably; they must have been the hardest-worked of all the hard-worked members of the 7th Cavalry!

Although the engagement on the Washita could scarcely be called a battle, it made Custer's reputation as an "Indian fighter." From then onwards he became as famous a figure along the frontier as he had been among the ranks of the Union cavalry during the Civil War. At the same time there were those who condemned him for withdrawing before he had been able to establish the fate of Elliott's detachment, and some of his most bitter critics were to be found among his own officers —there was a distinctly "anti-Custer" faction among the 7th's officers, just as there were those who hero-worshiped the flamboyant colonel in his buckskins and with flowing yellow hair.

Custer never let the fact worry him. He merely drove his regiment the harder in the campaign against the Indians. For the next three years he hunted and harried the Indians across the rolling plains, in fair weather and foul, and between times he waged war with his senior officers. He wielded a bitter pen and must have been an impossible subordinate, but his courage was unquestioned. By the time the 7th Cavalry were withdrawn from the frontier and sent to Kentucky and South Carolina in 1871, they were probably the best-known regiment in the army. This does not necessarily mean that they were the happiest, for men of Custer's temperament make as many enemies as they attract admirers, but they never lacked for recruits. Custer's reputation as a soldier brought eager young Americans from all over the country to enlist in the 7th Cavalry.

The 7th Cavalry returned to the frontier in 1873 to find that the Northern Pacific Railway had reached as far as Bismarck in North Dakota. Soon it must be continued even farther west and open up Montana, and every Indian knew what that would mean: the building of white settlements and the end of the Indian way of life. The tribes were growing daily more suspicious and hostile, particularly the powerful Sioux, whose finest buffalo hunting grounds lay directly in the projected path of the railway. So dangerous was the situation that in 1868 the United States government had decided to conclude a treaty with the Sioux which set aside their favorite hunting grounds, the Black Hills, and certain other territory in Montana and North Dakota as Indian reserved territory. This allayed Sioux suspicions for a time, but only for a time. Into this caldron of fear, suspicion, and hate, Custer dropped the last essential ingredient to trigger off the greatest Indian rising of all—he found gold.

Up in the Black Hills of Dakota, pledged by treaty to the Sioux, there was reputed to be gold. Soon after the 7th Cavalry returned to the frontier, Custer was ordered to march through the Black Hills and prospect for gold. From July to September, 1874, the 7th Cavalry marched through the area and found gold in several places. Custer's telegram to headquarters reporting the find became public property within a few hours. A gold rush began a few days later, and despite all attempts to cordon off the Black Hills, the prohibited territory was soon swarming with prospectors. Not long afterwards congressmen were being petitioned to lift the prohibition on entry into Indian territory, and a public demand for the reduction in size of the Indian reservations gathered strength.

Every effort to keep the Black Hills for the Sioux failed before the insatiable lust for gold. Miners in the thousands poured into the area, and there was a growing crop of incidents in which isolated mining camps were attacked by Indians defending their own. Custer was one of the many officers who warned the government that it was playing with fire:

> The Indians are quiet now and offering no armed resistance, because they have been told by the military officers that the government will keep its word. But the moment they think that it is not acting in good faith, there will be a rising of every tribe between the Missouri River and the Rocky Mountains.[4]

[4] Frazier Hunt, *Custer* (Cosmopolitan, New York, 1928).

By December the situation had become critical for both the Indians and the white men. Sullen and angry, the Sioux had rallied behind their medicine man, Sitting Bull. Collected in the Bad Lands around the Yellowstone River were the tribes which made up the great Sioux nation: Hunkpapa and Oglala, Blackfoot and Brûlé, Sans Arcs and Miniconjou, Yanktonai and Santee. And hastening to join them came the Cheyenne and the Arapaho, determined to stem this white invasion for once and for all—or to go down fighting. The time was past for counsels of caution or for counting the cost, and in any case, men sometimes fight the best when the odds are at their worst.

A badly scared Department of the Interior warned the Indians that they would be regarded as hostile if they failed to come in by January 31, 1876. The Indians hardly deigned to consider the matter. Sitting Bull took up the challenge and the Indian rising began according to the usual pattern. Isolated farmsteads and prospectors' camps were attacked, massacred, and sacked by Indian bands. Stage coaches were ambushed, white women raped, and government posts besieged. Throughout the vast territory inhabited by the Sioux and the Cheyenne the tribes were up, and at a time which was vastly inconvenient for the commanding officer of the 7th Cavalry. Not for the first time was he under suspension for indiscipline.

He had been talking too freely of his suspicions that Secretary of War Belknap was involved in graft affecting army supplies. Ordered to Washington to testify before a congressional committee, he became the star witness against the secretary. President Grant was furiously angry with his former cavalry general, and he took steps to make his displeasure felt where it would hurt the most. He forbade Custer to accompany the 7th Cavalry on their forthcoming operations against the Sioux.

For once the ebullient, devil-may-care, independent Custer was rocked back on his heels. He tried every means to persuade the President to rescind his order, but without success. Finally he sent the President a telegram through the adjutant general of the Division of the Missouri:

I have seen your order transmitted through the general of the army, directing that I be not permitted to accompany the expedition against the hostile Indians. As my entire regiment forms a part of the proposed expedition, and as I am the senior officer of the regiment on duty in this department, I respectfully, but most earnestly request that, while not allowed to go in command of the expedition, I may be permitted to serve with my regiment in the field. I appeal to you as a soldier to spare me the humiliation of seeing my regiment march to meet the enemy and I not to share its dangers.[5]

Long before he became president, Grant had been a soldier. Custer's appeal was too much for a soldier to resist. The ban was lifted and Custer was allowed to march with his 7th Cavalry—on the last march of his life.

That march was to lead him from Fort Abraham Lincoln, near Bismarck, North Dakota, and through the Bad Lands of the Little Missouri into the buffalo plains of Montana. The turbulent and treacherous Yellowstone River crosses those plains on its way to join the Missouri on the eastern border of Montana, and during its course is joined by a number of tributaries flowing south from the Big Horn Mountains in Wyoming; among these tributaries are the Powder, the Tongue, the Rosebud, and the Big Horn. Thirty miles upstream of its junction with the Yellowstone, the Big Horn River branches into two, and the eastern branch is called the Little Big Horn.

The entire region is a tangle of creeks, rivers, knife-edged ridges, sudden precipices, and deep valleys. Somewhere among these valleys the hostile Indians were grazing their huge herds of ponies, and moving slowly from camp to camp. No one knew exactly where the Sioux were concentrating, and during April and May, 1876, a series of military columns had been combing through this difficult country. There had been skirmishes with roving bands of Indians, but nothing definite had been found. On May 17, the 7th Cavalry left Fort Abraham Lincoln to join in the game of hide-and-seek.

[5] *Ibid.*

It was not until June 19 that any worthwhile information was obtained. Major Reno, Custer's senior major, had been scouting through the valleys which lie along and between the Tongue and the Rosebud when he came across an abandoned Indian camp on the Rosebud, and a little farther on there was a clearly defined Indian trail leading out of the Rosebud valley and across the hills towards the Big Horn.

As soon as General Terry, who was commanding the operations against the Indians, received Reno's report, he called a conference on board the river steamer *Far West*, anchored in the Yellowstone just below the junction with the Rosebud. His plan was comparatively simple. A force made up mainly of infantry under Gibbon was to march west along the north bank of the Yellowstone, cross over at the junction with the Big Horn, and then carry out a sweep to the south up the valley of the Big Horn. Meanwhile Custer was to take his 7th Cavalry south, up the valley of the Rosebud, until he reached the Indian trail reported by Reno. He was to satisfy himself that this trail did in fact lead into the valley of the Little Big Horn, but he was not to follow it directly. Instead, he was to proceed farther south until he reached the headwaters of the Tongue, and then swing to the west, timing his marches so that the 7th Cavalry would enter the Little Big Horn valley from the south at the same time Gibbon's force approached it from the north. Terry's object was clear—to trap the Indians between his two converging columns and so force them to battle or surrender.

General Terry's written instructions to Custer were as follows:

Camp at the Mouth of
Rosebud River,
June 22, 1876.

Lt. Col. Custer, 7th Cavalry:
Colonel:

The Brigadier General commanding directs that as soon as your regiment can be made ready to march, you proceed up the Rosebud in pursuit of the Indians whose trail was discovered by Major Reno a few days ago. It is, of course, impossible to give you any definite instructions in regard to this movement, and were it not impossible to do so, the Department commander places too much confidence in your zeal, energy and ability to wish to impose upon you precise orders which might hamper your action when nearly in contact with the enemy.

He will, however, indicate to you his own views of what your action should be, and he desires that you should conform to them unless you shall see sufficient reason for departing from them. He thinks that you should proceed up the Rosebud until you ascertain definitely the direction in which the trail above spoken of leads. Should it be found, as it appears to be almost certain that it will be found, to turn toward the Little Big Horn he thinks that you should still proceed southward, perhaps as far as the headwaters of the Tongue, and then turn toward the Little Big Horn, feeling constantly however to your left so as to preclude the possibility of the escape of the Indians to the south or southeast by passing around your left flank.

The column of Col. Gibbon is now in motion for the mouth of the Big Horn. As soon as it reaches that point it will cross the Yellowstone and move up at least as far as the forks of the Big and Little Big Horn. Of course its future movements must be controlled by circumstances as they may arise; but it is hoped that the Indians, if upon the Little Big Horn, may be so nearly enclosed by the two columns that their escape will be impossible.

The Department Commander desires that on your way up the Rosebud you should thoroughly examine the upper part of Tullocks Creek, and that you should endeavour to send a scout through to Col. Gibbon's column with information of the result of your examination. The lower part of this creek will be examined by a detachment from Col. Gibbon's command.

The supply steamer will be pushed up the Big Horn as far as the forks of the river are found to be navigable for that space, and the Department Commander, who will accompany the column of Col. Gibbon, desires you to re-

port to him there not later than the expiration of the
time for which your troops are rationed, unless in the
meantime you receive further orders.

Respectfully,

E. W. SMITH,

Capt. 18th Infantry,

Acting Ass. Adjt. Genl.[6]

These orders have since been subjected to almost microscopic
examination in order to determine whether they were clear or
ambiguous, whether Custer was justified in departing from them,
and whether they contained sufficient information on which
Custer could act. The answer must surely be that they were a
general directive, based on Terry's guess of the Indians' reac-
tions once they learned of his approach, and that they left a
good deal to Custer's own judgment. This is hardly surprising
in view of Custer's distinguished reputation as an "Indian
fighter," and it must also be remembered that when they were
drafted, Terry still lacked definite information concerning the
Indians' exact location and their strength.

Terry did, however, express some concern about Custer's own
strength, and he offered to accompany the 7th Cavalry, bringing with him the detachment of the 2nd Cavalry which had
been operating with Gibbon. Custer declined the offer, believing that the 7th Cavalry were fully capable of dealing with any
Indians that they might encounter, and he also refused the
offer of a battery of Gatling guns. He told Terry that the battery would slow down the speed of his march up the Rosebud.

Custer left the mouth of the Rosebud at noon on June 22,
1876, with twelve companies of the 7th Cavalry—nearly six
hundred strong—and some forty Arikara and Crow Indians
acting as scouts. The column was carrying fifteen days' rations,
and twenty-four thousand rounds of reserve ammunition loaded
on pack mules. Each trooper carried one hundred rounds of
rifle ammunition and twenty-four rounds of pistol, and every
horse carried extra oats. As an afterthought Custer ordered that

[6] W. A. Graham, *The Story of the Little Big Horn* (Century, New
York, 1926).

the regiment should take along an extra supply of salt; it might be necessary to live on horse meat before the operations were successfully over.

Experience had shown that the Indians rarely stood and fought it out. The only way to bring them to battle was to take them by surprise, and for this reason the advance up the Rosebud was to be carried out as swiftly and as quietly as possible. Every trooper in the 7th Cavalry was fully confident of the regiment's ability to defeat the Indians, always providing they could be caught before they melted away into the mountains, and various guesses put the Indians' strength at between fifteen hundred and two thousand. There were, it is true, an unusually high proportion of raw recruits riding into battle with the 7th for the first time, but Custer did not let this affect his plans. All that mattered was to surprise the Indians, and the 7th Cavalry would do the rest.

Ninety miles were covered by 9:00 P.M. on the 24th, and in the gathering darkness Custer assembled his officers and told them that the Indian scouts had found the trail leading westward towards the Little Big Horn. He also told them that he proposed following up the Indians that same night, and the 7th Cavalry were to march at once in order to reach the foot of the divide separating the two valleys before dawn on the 25th. The regiment was to halt east of the divide, conceal itself during the daylight hours of the 25th while the scouts located the Indian camp, and the surprise attack on the Indians was to be launched at dawn on the 26th. All this was a clear departure from the orders Custer had received from General Terry, but the trail was so clear and well marked that it seemed evident that Indians had passed along it only a few hours previously. Custer would not have been Custer, nor a major general before he was twenty-five, if he had failed to engage his enemy at the first available opportunity.

Slowly the regiment picked its way through pitch darkness until at 2:00 A.M. it was only twelve miles from the divide. Then they halted until the sun rose and the scouts could search the valley ahead of them.

As soon as it was light enough to see, the scouts sent back their message—an Indian encampment had been seen fifteen miles away to the south, on the banks of the Little Big Horn. Custer at once rode forward to the highest point on the divide, called the Crow's Nest, and searched the valley through his glasses. They told him nothing, although the sharp eyes of the Indians had picked out the great herds of ponies which were grazing round the encampment, and he returned to the regiment entirely unconvinced by their report. There might be Indians ahead, but it was at best a fifty-fifty chance. The regiment was ordered to continue the advance to the divide.

The column halted again at noon, still on the Rosebud side of the divide, and Custer once again searched the valley. He was still uncertain whether the Indians were in the valley, although the half-breed chief of the scouts, "Mitch" Bouyer, assured him that they were; but in any case he knew that the advance of his column had been reported. A box of rations had been dropped during the night march and the sergeant who rode back to retrieve it had surprised a party of Sioux examining it. They had made off on his approach, as had another party of Indians who were seen watching the column during the early morning. Further concealment was therefore useless; the only way to surprise the Indians, if indeed they existed at all, was by pushing on at full speed.

Custer accordingly split his regiment into three parts, or, as he termed them, battalions. Three companies were formed into a battalion under Major Reno; three more were placed under the command of Captain Benteen; five were retained by Custer under his own command; and one company was assigned as escort to the pack train. Once this reorganization had been carried out, the 7th Cavalry crossed the divide and proceeded on a reconnaissance in force. It was then 12:15 P.M.

Benteen was given a detached mission. He was to take his battalion off to the left and search the creeks and bluffs on that flank. He was ordered to "pitch into anything he might find," and soon after moving off he was lost to sight among the brushwood and the rocks. Custer later sent two gallopers to order

Benteen to scout even farther to the left, and this he proceeded
to do. Meanwhile, Custer and Reno moved off down the valley
towards the Little Big Horn.

In those days of no radio, and when communication was
dependent largely upon gallopers, a commander who moved far
beyond "the other side of the hill" was soon out of touch.
Custer had no idea how strong the Indians were, nor was he
certain of their location. He did not know that only a week
before, a column under General Crook had been checked on
the Rosebud by these self-same Sioux; but even had he known,
it is doubtful whether he would have altered his plan. He had
always experienced success in battle and he was supremely confident that "the Seventh can handle anything it meets." Benteen was covering his left flank, and with Reno's battalion and
his own he believed that he was strong enough to deal with
anything the Indians might have in the valley.

A stream flows down from the divide to join the Little Big
Horn, and for about two hours Custer's force followed along
it, Reno's battalion riding parallel with Custer's along the opposite bank. The pack train came plodding along in the rear,
the heavily laden mules finding it impossible to keep up with
the horses.

Some time later Reno recrossed the creek to join Custer, and
the two battalions went on together until they were about three
miles from the Little Big Horn. It was then that they came
across what looked like the remnant of a recently abandoned
Indian village; only one tepee was still standing, and it was
burning fiercely. Inside the tepee was the body of an Indian,
and while Custer was examining the body his interpreter, Fred
Girard, rode to the top of a small knoll. Directly to his front
he saw a party of Sioux who appeared to be riding away, down
the valley, and he immediately turned in his saddle and shouted
to Custer: "Here are your Indians—running like devils."

Custer's immediate reaction was to order his Indian scouts
to go in pursuit, but they refused. Unlike Custer, they were certain that the hilly country ahead of them concealed far more
Indians than was healthy. So Reno was ordered to follow up
the Indians as quickly as possible, and he was told that he

would be supported by "the whole outfit." He was also informed that the Indian village was on the far bank of the Little Big Horn, three or four miles farther downstream, although it was still hidden from view.

Reno left Custer and moved off rapidly, alternating between trot and gallop, while Custer followed on behind at a more leisurely pace. Girard accompanied Reno, but as he reached the ford across the river he saw that the Sioux were streaming up the valley from the village to attack. Knowing that Custer was under the misapprehension that the Sioux were running away, Girard galloped back up the trail and reported that the Sioux were coming up the valley in force. There can be no doubt, therefore, that Custer knew by 2:30 P.M. that the enemy were present in large numbers and that they had no intention of running away.

Meanwhile Reno and his battalion of about one hundred men crossed the Little Big Horn and pressed on towards the village. As they drew nearer, more and more Indians came swarming out at them, and Reno soon found himself seriously outnumbered. There was no sign of Custer following him up, and Benteen was even farther away; Reno therefore dismounted his men and took up a defensive position less than half a mile from the village. The ground was not particularly favorable for defense, being heavily timbered and intersected by numerous dry watercourses, and the thick undergrowth aided the infiltration tactics of the Indians. They lost no time in attacking Reno, who seems to have lost his head and ordered a panic withdrawal back to the ford. A *sauve-qui-peut* followed and it was checked only after Reno had lost nearly half his force. He then took up a defensive position on some high ground on the opposite side of the Little Big Horn, and about three miles upstream of the village. There he was rapidly followed up by the Indians and pinned down by their fire. He was completely in the dark concerning Custer's whereabouts, and he had no idea of Custer's plans.

Reno had moved off from Custer about 2:15 P.M. He had reached the vicinity of the Indian village about forty-five minutes later, and he was back behind the Little Big Horn by 4:15.

All he had to show for the past two hours was the loss of three officers and twenty-nine enlisted men, together with the expenditure of more ammunition than he was able to replace. He had also lost all touch with his commanding officer, who seemed to have vanished into thin air.

There is no doubt that Reno's command was in a tight spot. Men and horses were exhausted after their gallop down to the village, and the panic scramble back from it. It was extremely hot, water bottles were empty, and the route from Reno's position down to the river was under heavy fire. Things would have gone hard with them had not Benteen suddenly appeared from the north, bringing with him his three companies and the news that the pack train was an hour behind him up the trail.

Benteen's comment on Reno's command when he came up with it is a masterpiece of understatement: "Reno's men appeared to be in good order, but pretty well blown, and so were the horses. They were not in line of battle, but were scattered around, I suppose to the best advantage. They all thought there was a happier place than that, I guess." [7] In fact, one of Benteen's troop commanders was greeted by Lieutenant Hare, who had been involved in the fight down the valley, with the words, "We've had a big fight in the bottom, got licked, and I am damned glad to see you."

There was still no sign of Custer, and Reno and Benteen immediately discussed what they should do next. There were large numbers of Indians skulking in the brushwood and ravines, and more could be seen on the high ground ahead. Reno's men were very short of ammunition and there was the problem of the pack train, which might be ambushed unless Reno and Benteen waited for it to catch up with them.

While they were talking, heavy firing broke out from downstream. The Indians around them heard it too, and soon they could be seen hurrying off to the south. The pressure on Reno's position relaxed, and some of his officers grew impatient at the delay. They believed that Custer was now engaged with the Sioux, and they knew their place was with their commanding officer. The firing grew heavier and heavier, and without wait-

[7] E. A. Brinstool, *The Custer Fight* (privately printed, 1940).

ing for orders Lieutenant Weir moved off with his troop to a ridge about a mile downstream from Reno's position.

By the time Weir reached the ridge the firing ahead of him had ceased, and when Benteen joined him some minutes later all he saw to the south was a village of about eighteen hundred tepees and the swirling dust kicked up by the Indians' ponies. There was no sign of troops or fighting. Reno then began to move forward with his command to join Benteen and Weir, but the advance was slow. The wounded had to be carried, and this meant slinging them in blankets which were carried between six mounted troopers. There was also the pack train to slow down the advance; it had come up just before Reno moved off, and there was no longer any problem over ammunition.

The Indians were now streaming back up the valley to attack Reno and Benteen, and it was decided to withdraw to Reno's original position, which in Reno's view was more easily defensible than the ridge selected by Weir. They regained the position only just in time, for within a few minutes they were being attacked from every side. They could see nothing to shoot at, but any man who exposed himself was immediately shot, and the Indians crept so close to the position that they were able to throw clods of earth at the defenders.

The fighting died down during the night, and Benteen took advantage of the respite to erect some cover from the Indians' fire. Boxes of biscuit and ammunition were used to make a breastwork. The only tools were three spades and two axes, and the troopers were compelled to dig their holes with clasp knives and spoons. The ground was brick hard and they were all suffering from thirst, while around them in the darkness lay wounded and moaning soldiers. Many of the horses had been wounded, and the problem of disposing of the carcasses seemed insuperable.

The main topic of conversation that night was the fate of Custer. Strangely enough, it does not seem to have occurred to any of Reno's and Benteen's men that Custer had been defeated—they were convinced believers in "Custer's luck." Rather, they seem to have thought that their colonel had withdrawn down the Little Big Horn to join forces with Gibbon's column, and there were those who grumbled that Custer had abandoned half his regiment to its fate.

Only Benteen seems to have suspected the truth, and he was far too busy organizing the defense to worry about anything else. Had he not been there to inject some fire into the badly shaken Reno, and to impose his personality on the exhausted troopers, it is virtually certain that no 7th cavalryman would have left the valley of the Little Big Horn alive. All through the night he was organizing the defenses.

As the sun came up, the Indians attacked. Hour by reeling hour the weary troopers fought off the Indian attacks. Blackened by powder, tortured with thirst, and with the screams of wounded horses ringing in their ears, they stubbornly defended Reno Hill. Benteen was the leader who put heart into the defenders, led the exhausted troopers in a dismounted charge, and by sheer leadership staved off what must have seemed inevitable defeat.

Suddenly—at midday on June 26—the attacks ceased. To the amazement of the defenders the firing died down, and soon parties of Indians were seen slipping away down the valley. By late afternoon all the Indians had withdrawn to the village, and as evening fell, the astonished Reno and Benteen saw the great mass of Indians, with their families, tents, ponies, and impedimenta, disappear towards the Big Horn Mountains. Only then did they realize the odds. The ponies they estimated between fifteen and twenty-five thousand, and the fighting strength of the village from three to five thousand. It was the largest gathering of Indians ever seen on the plains.

As night fell Reno and Benteen counted the cost. Eighteen men had been killed on Reno Hill, and fifty-two had been wounded; many of the wounds had been caused by arrows and were rapidly festering. The animals, exposed to heavy fire throughout the siege, had suffered terribly, and the stench from the dead bodies was appalling. For most of the day both men and animals had been raging with thirst, and the first action was to move nearer the river. The next was to bury the dead— and the next was to speculate on Custer's whereabouts. What had become of him? Could he have deserted them in their hour of trial? Or was he at that very moment riding to their rescue with Terry and Gibbon?

They never knew the full story, and neither shall we, but certain of the facts seem clear. After detaching Reno to cross the Little Big Horn and attack the Indian camp, Custer swung to the right. He had with him 225 officers and men—C, E, F, I, and L Companies—and some forty Arikara and Crow scouts. He led them off at the gallop, and so killing was the pace that two of the overdriven horses foundered and had to be left behind with their riders.

But Custer's object seems clear enough. He wanted to arrive somewhere in the vicinity of the village as nearly as possible at the same time as Reno's battalion reached it along the opposite bank of the river. Then both Reno and Custer could repeat the tactics of the Washita battle, and take the village from the flanks.

As soon as he was within sight of the village, Custer halted his sweating horses and perspiring troopers and rode up onto the nearest high ground to plan the next move. It was while carrying out this reconnaissance that he was seen from across the Little Big Horn by Lieutenant DeRudio of Reno's battalion, who at the time was watching the river flank of Reno's skirmishing line. At that precise moment Reno had dismounted his command to repel the Indians' attacks, and it must have been clear to Custer that Reno would get no farther. It must have been equally clear that he had seriously miscalculated the Indians' strength. The Indian village was nearly two miles long, and the bottom below Custer was blanketed with the dust kicked up by the ponies as they galloped towards Reno. This was no handful of runaway Sioux.

Shortly before this reconnaissance, Custer had sent a sergeant galloping back up the trail with orders for the pack train to come on "straight across country." The sergeant met Benteen's battalion on its way down the valley, and Benteen had sent him on to the pack train. At this time Custer had no reason to suppose that Benteen was anywhere near him, since Benteen's instructions had been to scout to the west, but Ben-

teen had decided to rejoin Custer. He thought he was wasting
his time looking for Indians among the gullies and ravines west
of the Little Big Horn. It was like looking for a needle in a
haystack, and in any case he was certain that "the Indians had
too much sense to go to any place over such rugged country."
It was fortunate for Reno that he did decide to return, but the
decision to do so was Benteen's alone.

Once Custer saw the village, he was under no delusions. He
needed Benteen badly, and he needed him quickly. Trumpeter
Martin, an eighteen-year-old Italian who had served under Gari-
baldi as a drummer boy, was sent back with a message for
Benteen: "Benteen—Come on—Big Village—Be quick—bring
packs." The message was signed by Cooke, adjutant of the 7th
Cavalry, and after his signature he added a "P.S. Bring Pacs." [8]
Martin immediately galloped back along the trail and was the
last man to see Custer alive. Sometime later he came up with
Benteen, delivered the message, and survived the battle under
Benteen's command.

The country where Custer had halted his men was seamed
and broken with ravines and gullies running down from the
mountains into the Little Big Horn. The cavalrymen were compelled to keep to the low ground where the going was easier
for their horses, and they were thus at a disadvantage when
compared with the lightly equipped Indians who were swarming above them in the rocks and brushwood. It was evident
that if Custer were to hold them off until Benteen reinforced
him, he would have to find a position where he could meet the
Indians on less unequal terms. No sooner had he dispatched
Martin with his message than he galloped off to look for such
a position.

The time was now about 3:30 P.M. Reno was involved in his
withdrawal on the opposite bank of the river, Benteen was
nearly an hour's march away up the trail, and the pack train
was even farther off. Had he set out to do so deliberately, Custer could not have succeeded in dispersing his available force
more effectively; not one of the three battalions into which he
had divided his regiment was capable of supporting another.

[8] *Ibid.*

This fatal dispersion must have been noticed by Crazy Horse and the other war chiefs. The majority of the Indians galloped off down the far bank of the river, keeping parallel with Custer's movements, while another party, under Gall, crossed the river and crept up the ravines leading from it. Only a few were left to follow up the retreating Reno, which probably explains how that harassed officer succeeded in extricating his battalion. There were certainly enough Indians around to have wiped out Reno, but Crazy Horse was after bigger game—Custer himself.

Custer's last fight, which probably ended shortly after 4:30 P.M., is lost in the realm of conjecture and surmise. No one survived to tell the tale. In Benteen's opinion, Custer was overwhelmed before he had even been able to deploy for battle:

> The position of the bodies on the Custer battle field indicated that the officers did not die with their companies, for only three officers were found with their companies. That shows that they did not fight by companies. All the officers, except Keogh, Calhoun, and Crittenden were on a line with Custer. That would not be the fact if the command was overwhelmed making a stand. If there had been a charge the officers would have led it; there is no royal road to death in a charge.
>
> The officers' bodies, including General Custer's, were in a position which indicated that they had not died in a charge; there was an arc of a circle of dead horses around them.
>
> Lines could have been formed, but lines were not formed; they probably had not time to form lines. General Custer might have fled the field and saved a part of his command; and I think discretion would have been the better part of valour had he done that.[9]

Unfortunately Benteen's known dislike for Custer, coupled with the anxious search for a scapegoat once the disaster became known, has made his opinions suspect. Yet for any soldier studying the battle, Benteen's comments seem to be pure common sense. What seems clear is that Custer, once he saw

[9] *Ibid.*

Reno's battalion withdrawing in disorder, had only two courses open to him. He could withdraw, either upstream towards Benteen and the pack train or downstream towards Terry and Gibbon, or he could attack the Indians in the hope of driving them from the field. A withdrawal upstream might have meant the annihilation of what was left of Reno's battalion, while a withdrawal downstream would have left Reno, Benteen, and the pack train at the mercy of the Indians; and in any case he had no clear idea of the whereabouts of Gibbon and his infantry column.

In the event, it seems that he decided to fight it out with the Indians on ground of his own choosing. His record of success against the Indians probably led him to underrate their advantage in numbers, and he probably underestimated those numbers since many of the Indians were hidden from his view by the broken ground.

The likelihood is that Custer was forced by the Indians to dismount his command in a hurry. Once dismounted his force was reduced by a third, as one man in three was out of battle as a horse-holder. The Indians were able to stampede the horses by firing into them, and once the horses had panicked, Custer lost all mobility. The Indians were no worse marksmen than the soldiers, and it must be remembered that horsed cavalry was always limited by the amount of ammunition a trooper could carry. Once that ammunition was expended, there was no alternative but to fight it out hand to hand, and when it came to cold steel, only numbers could prevail. It was the payoff.

General Terry, advancing up the Little Big Horn, received news of the disaster during the early afternoon of the following day. At first he did not believe it, but he urged his weary infantry forward by forced marches so that by the same evening they bivouacked only five miles below the battlefield. It is now known that it was the approach of Terry's column which caused the Indians to abandon their attacks on Reno and Benteen and move off with their families to the mountains. Terry was too late to save Custer, but he did save what was left of the 7th Cavalry; twelve hours more and he would have been too late to save anyone.

At dawn on June 27 the leading scouts of Terry's force rode on to the battlefield and found the naked bodies of the 225 soldiers who died with Custer. Some had been mutilated, but Custer's body was untouched. Only one living thing moved among the dead bodies of men and the carcasses of horses, and that was a buckskin sorrel named Comanche, which had carried Lieutenant Keogh in his last battle.[10]

From their observation post farther up the valley, Reno and Benteen watched the approach of Gibbon's marching infantry. As soon as they were certain that the dust clouds did not mean the approach of yet more Indians, a party was sent off to make contact with the advancing column. Their first question was about Custer. Why was he not with the column? It was then, for the first time, that half the 7th Cavalry learned that the other half of the regiment had been massacred to a man, and less than five miles away.

The news of Custer's defeat stunned American public opinion. It seemed barely credible that naked savages could have defeated the best-known "Indian fighter" in the United States army, and a wave of anger swept through the country, akin to that which swept through England when the news of Gordon's death at Khartoum became known. No one has ever had cause to offer excuses for a victory, but a defeat will produce nearly as many excuses as there are corpses. In the search for a scapegoat both Reno and Benteen came in for much criticism, although the opinion was not shared by those of the 7th Cavalry who survived the battle and who petitioned the President that Reno should be promoted in Custer's vacancy, and Benteen in Reno's.

The reasons for Custer's defeat are perfectly clear. He underestimated his enemy, dispersed his own force, and then lost mobility by dismounting and fighting it out on foot. His reconnaissance was bad, he failed to carry out the instructions given him by General Terry, and he seems to have had no clear plan for dealing with the situation; or if he had, he certainly never explained it to his subordinates, Reno and Benteen. As the

---

[10] Comanche was never saddled again. For the rest of its life Comanche was more than a regimental mascot—for the 7th Cavalry the horse was a living symbol of the regiment's battle against overwhelming odds.

British were to do later against the Zulus, he made the mistake
of believing that savages will always run away, and he paid the
inevitable price for his miscalculation.

Possibly Benteen put the whole thing into a nutshell when
he said: "There were a great deal too many Indians who were
powerful good shots on the other side. We were at their
hearths and homes; they had gotten the bulge on Reno; their
medicine was working well, and they were fighting for all the
good God gives anyone to fight for." [11]

Custer's one defeat has damaged his reputation to such an
extent that his many successes have been overlooked. He has
been described as one of the most overrated generals of all time,
a mountebank on horseback, and a complete incompetent. No
man rises to the rank of major general by the age of twenty-five
and merits such a rating, nor could such a man have built up
the 7th Cavalry until its reputation was second to none in the
United States army. He was vain, aggressive, and conceited; he
had got on a good deal too fast and was arrogant and high-
handed. Yet he had outstanding qualities of leadership, and he
possessed that indefinable quality which inspires men. The
United States army has never lacked colorful characters, as
witness Generals MacArthur and Patton, but there have been
few as colorful as Custer.

Ever since he commanded them, the 7th Cavalry have been
known as the "Garry Owens" or "Custer's Own." It seems
strange, and a little sad, that their tradition, which was forged
on horses, is no longer perpetuated in the mobile role. They
fought as infantry in World War II, and again as infantry in
Korea, but still as "Custer's Own."

Custer would surely have felt that this was his finest memorial.

[11] *Ibid.*

CHAPTER NINE

Beersheba

O CTOBER 31, 1917

"General Grant's action forms a notable landmark in the history of cavalry, in that it initiated that spirit of dash which thereafter dominated the whole campaign."
THE DESERT MOUNTED CORPS
BY R. M. P. PRESTON

THE death knell of horsed cavalry was struck at some unrecorded moment on September 13, 1914. By that date the German advance on Paris had been held up and then thrown back, and the Battle of the Marne had been won. A French cavalry corps under General Conneau was poised to strike at the wide-open lines of communication of the Second and Third German Armies, and the fate of millions of ordinary men hung in the balance. But Conneau never moved. The Germans were given time in which they could dig their trenches, set up their machine guns, and then wire them in with the deadly barbed wire that was to hog-tie the battlefield, as in later years it was to cramp the English hunting field. Soon every front-line soldier in Europe was burrowing like a mole, throwing up parapets and paradoses, revetting and wiring, erecting strong

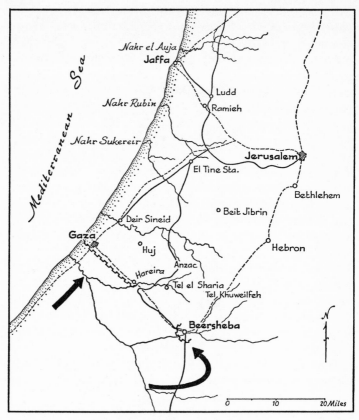

points and excavating dugouts, and abandoning the battlefield
to the domination of the machine gun until man's inventive
genius thought up the tank.

Horsed cavalry experienced their moments on the Western
front, but those moments were few and far between—for most
of the time they were kept waiting for opportunities which
never came. German and Austrian cavalry on the wider and
more open spaces of the Eastern front were still able to test
their worth against the cossacks of Russia, but even in Galicia
and Poland the machine gun and barbed wire restricted their
mobility. It is therefore something of a paradox that the war
which saw cavalry reduced to virtual impotence should also

have produced one of the greatest cavalry campaigns of all history. Between October 27 in 1917 and October 28 in the following year the cavalry divisions of General Allenby advanced from the frontiers of Egypt to the borders of Anatolia and won a campaign as classic in its conception as it was superb in its execution. The Great War of 1914-1918 may indeed have reduced the art of war to a bloody slogging-match from trench to trench, and yet no other general in history has made a greater virtue out of mobility than Allenby did in Palestine; Wavell, who was no mean handler of mobile troops himself, has written of Allenby's generalship: "There is no parallel in military history to so deep an adventure by such a mass of cavalry against a yet unbroken enemy." [1]

An interesting sidelight on the brilliantly successful cavalry campaign in Palestine is the fact that none of the regular regiments in the British cavalry took part in it. The regiments which had tumbled the Imperial Guard to ruin at Waterloo, ridden up the "valley of death" at Balaklava, and charged and charged against the Sikh squares at Aliwal were either kept hanging about in France waiting for the chance of shock action that never came or were employed in India or Mesopotamia. The only regular cavalry regiments with Allenby were provided by the Indian army. The remainder of his cavalry were yeomanry regiments from Britain, and the light horse and mounted rifles regiments of Australia and New Zealand— "hostilities only" [2] soldiers of a quality and character that the mounted arm has never seen surpassed.

The yeomanry had a tradition which was almost feudal in origin. Most of the regiments could trace their ancestry back to the times of the French Revolution, when invasion seemed imminent and when the landowners and country gentlemen raised their own troops of horsemen to take service under the leading noblemen of the county. They undertook to mount, dress, and equip their troops at their own expense, and they

---

[1] Field Marshal Earl Wavell, *Life of Lord Allenby* (George G. Harrap, London, 1940), pp. 224-225.

[2] An expression used during the 1914-1918 war to differentiate the wartime enlistment from the regular.

were welded together with their men by the bonds which have always united master and man in rural England. When the Middlesex Yeomanry was first raised in 1797, the Earl of Berkeley hunted a country stretching from London in the east to Bristol in the west, and the fox-hunting farmers flocked to join the yeomanry. Many of the officers and men in the yeomanry regiments in Palestine could trace a direct connection with their regiments for over a hundred years, and acceptance into their ranks was by strict selection, many yeomanry regiments being a good deal more exclusive than the regular cavalry regiments. A high proportion of the ordinary troopers mounted themselves on their own horses and considered that as yeomen they were not like ordinary soldiers. The Earl of Dudley, who took the Worcestershire Yeomanry to Gallipoli in 1915, actually *armed* his regiment at his own expense. He provided them with the modern type of sword in place of the old-fashioned cavalry saber with which the War Office equipped the yeomanry. If a Worcestershire yeoman was wounded and sent back to the rear, it was the regimental medical officer's responsibility to make certain that his "Dudley sword" did not go down the line with him. The British army's order of battle in 1914 included fifty-five yeomanry regiments, and of these, thirty-six took part in the Palestine campaign. Half of them served as infantry in the 74th (Broken Spur) Division, and the remainder with their horses served in the Yeomanry Division. In the spring of 1918 many of these yeomanry regiments were sent to France and were replaced in Palestine by the Indian cavalry.

There was nothing feudal about the Australian and New Zealand mounted regiments. They were probably the most democratic soldiers who have ever taken the field in defense of democracy, and the stories of their escapades when in Cairo on leave have now been hallowed by legend.[3] Discipline sat lightly on them and they were quick to detect the pretentious

[3] During the Anglo-Egyptian dispute over the Suez Canal zone in 1952 an Arab asked me in all seriousness why the British did not send a few Australian troops to Port Said. "The Cairo shopkeepers would at once persuade their government to allow the British to remain, providing the Australians went home," he said.

and the condescending. Yet in some strange way they shared an
affinity with the stolid and law-abiding English yeomen and
the straight-backed Indian sowars. Most of them were country
men with their roots deep in the soil, and the soil formed a
bond between them. The Australians and New Zealanders
were farmers, sheep men and cattle ranchers, and accustomed
to the wide horizons of the "Outback." They had been brought
up with horses since their earliest childhood, and they judged
a man by his character and not by his position and rank. The
normal conventions which erect a barrier between leaders and
led meant little to them, but they could appreciate a joke
against themselves. There is a story of a monocled British
officer who was sent to take temporary command of a regiment
of Australian light horse. The morning after his arrival he rode
on parade to find that every light horseman had a monocle
gleaming in his eye—whereupon the Englishman removed his,
tossed it nonchalantly in the air, and caught it neatly in his
eye. "Bet you can't do that," he said, and from then on he
could do anything with them. But he was a good soldier as
well as a good monocle-juggler.

There were two Australian and New Zealand divisions in
Palestine by 1917—the Australian and New Zealand Mounted
Division, usually called the Anzac Division, and the Australian
Mounted Division. When Allenby arrived to assume command
of the Egyptian Expeditionary Force one of his first acts was
to group these two divisions with the Yeomanry Division to
form the Desert Mounted Corps under Lieutenant General
Sir Harry Chauvel, himself an Australian.

British operations in the Palestine theater had begun in
January, 1915, when a Turkish force advanced across the Sinai
Desert. The Turks intended cutting the Suez Canal and in-
vading Egypt, but their attack was badly planned and ill-co-
ordinated. The British drove them back without much difficulty, and by February 5 the Turks were in full retreat across
the desert. It was during this action along the banks of the
Suez Canal that a young captain in an Indian regiment, the
62nd Punjabis, underwent his baptism of fire. Twenty-seven
years later he returned to Egypt as a full general and com-

mander in chief, but the likelihood is that Field Marshal Sir
Claude Auchinleck remembers the first battle more clearly than
any other of the many battles he was to fight. One's first experience under enemy fire is not altogether unlike one's first
experience of love. Both seem to stick in one's memory.

The British allowed the Turks to withdraw to their bases
along the Palestine-Egyptian frontier without pursuit, and a
lull then settled over the Palestine front. The campaigns in
Gallipoli and Mesopotamia were in full swing and the British
had no desire to become further involved in Palestine, but by
the following year they were forced to think again. The attempt
to force the Dardanelles had ended in failure, there had been
disasters in Mesopotamia, and British prestige in the Middle
East had sunk extremely low. Over a quarter of a million
British troops were living in tented camps along the banks of
the Suez Canal, or in the desert around Cairo, and morale
was not as good as it should have been. Cairo was living up
to its reputation as a "stew pot," [4] and the camps were full of
angry and disillusioned men who thought that the authorities
should have shot *at least one* general for the hideous bungling
at Gallipoli. The angriest were the Australians, who resented
British army discipline and distrusted British staff officers.
Their views on base areas have been echoed in a book by an
American who fought in Burma during World War II:

> The Marauders had had the experience, common in all
> armies but characteristic above all of the United States
> Army, of finding that the farther back you went from the
> thinly tenanted front lines the more soldiers you met until,
> a thousand miles to the rear, you could hardly shoulder
> your way through the press of them.[5]

It would be difficult to find a better description for the
Australians' attitude towards the British staffs in Egypt during

[4] Winston Churchill described Cairo as a "stew pot" of intrigue during the doubt-filled weeks which followed the news that Rommel had
captured Tobruk—the period which has gone down in British history as
"The Flap."
[5] Charlton Ogburn, Jr., *The Marauders* (Harper, New York, 1959), pp.
273-274.

the bitter and disillusioning months of 1916. Rumors that the Turkish troops released by victory at Gallipoli would be employed in a fresh attempt to invade Egypt decided the British to reoccupy the desert area between the Suez Canal and the Palestine frontier. This would forestall any Turkish moves and might serve to distract attention from the Arab revolt which had just broken out in the Hejaz under the inspiration of T. E. Lawrence. A slow and cautious advance then began into Sinai, the pace being governed by the time it took the engineers to lay a water pipeline and railway behind the forward troops, but by Christmas Day, 1916, the British had occupied El Arish on the Mediterranean coast and had established themselves once more along the Egyptian frontier. Unkindly critics, blessed with the advantages of hindsight, have compared the speed of this advance with that of a glacier.

General Murray's advance to the frontier may have been slow but it was at least successful, and it inspired the British government to order the advance to be continued into Palestine. Lloyd George and his advisers were frantically seeking a way to win the war which would not involve murderous frontal assaults across "no man's land" in France and Belgium, and these supporters of "the other way round" school of strategy clutched at the chances of victory over the Turks. Murray was ordered to push on but was warned that he was to take no risks and that the cost in troops was to be kept as low as possible. The result was disaster at Gaza where in two abortive battles, in March and April, 1917, the British were thrown back with heavy casualties. The Palestine front then settled down to positional warfare on much the same lines as in France, only that it was very much hotter and dustier in Palestine, and there were far more flies.

The position of Gaza is a very strong one, and its natural defenses had been further strengthened by pick, shovel, sandbag, and wire.

> Gaza itself had been made into a strong, modern fortress, heavily entrenched and wired, and offering every facility for protracted defence. The remainder of the enemy's

line consisted of a series of strong localities, viz: the Sihan group of works, the Atawineh group, the Abu el Hareira-Abu el Teaha trench system (near Sharia), and, finally, the works covering Beersheba. These groups of works were generally from 1500 to 2000 yards apart, except that the distance from the Hareira group to Beersheba was about four and a half miles. . . . By the end of October these strong localities had been joined up so as to form a practically continuous line from the sea to a point south of Sharia. The defensive works round Beersheba remained a detached system, but had been improved and extended.[6]

Two Turkish armies were deployed along the Gaza-Beersheba defense line: the Seventh Army under a German, General Kress Von Kressenstein, and the Eighth Army under Fevzi Pasha. The Turks had available about 49,000 men and 360 guns, and most of their senior staff officers were German, as were the officers of the engineer and supply services. The air force and the heavy artillery were German-manned, and there were a few German and Austrian infantry battalions to stiffen the already formidable qualities of the Anatolian Turk as a defensive fighter. The Turkish right flank rested on the sea at Gaza, and their left on the open desert and barren hills east and southeast of Beersheba. A metaled road between Gaza and Beersheba enabled the Turks to switch their reserves rapidly, and two branches of the Palestine-Syria railway had been constructed from Junction Station on the Jaffa-Jerusalem line to carry troops and stores down to Gaza and Beersheba. The Turkish plan was to defeat the anticipated British attack on their defenses, and then use the Gaza-Beersheba position as a base for their advance into Egypt.

War in the desert has often been likened to war at sea, but as both the British and Germans learned in World War II, there are dangers in carrying this analogy too far. It is true that flanks often have to rest on no other obstacle than the open desert and that positions can frequently be turned by mobile forces. But operations in the desert are almost

---

[6] General Allenby's dispatch, dated December 16, 1917.

invariably governed by the availability of water, and this was particularly the case when armies were mainly dependent on animals for their means of transportation. An outflanking force, however mobile it may be, must either be self-contained for water for the duration of the operation or be certain of capturing a water supply before thirst brings its operations to a grinding halt. The Turks had destroyed the few and inadequate wells during their withdrawal across Sinai in 1915, and the British had had to bring their water with them by means of the pipeline built across the desert from Ismailia on the Suez Canal. Subsequently their engineers had supplemented this water supply by repairing wells in Sinai, but water was always in short supply. The real significance of Beersheba was that it contained seven good wells, and the success of any operation aimed at turning the Turks' desert flank would be dependent on capturing those wells.

The Turkish High Command, fully aware of the importance of Beersheba's water supply to any enemy force moving round their flank, had turned the town into a fortress. The town lies on a plain about four miles long and three miles wide, and is completely surrounded by a jumbled mass of rocky hills, steep, seamed with deep and precipitous wadis, in many areas impenetrable except to a man on foot, and utterly waterless. Not a tree breaks the skyline and from May to October the sun beats down at a mean temperature of 110 degrees in the shade, frequently soaring to 120 or more. When the Psalmist wrote of "the wilderness" he was referring to the wild and tangled country lying to the south and east of Judaea; it is some of the worst campaigning country in the world.

The Turks had added to the obstacles provided by nature. Two lines of defenses had been constructed, and the inner line was a continuous trench system that completely encircled the town. The trenches were protected by barbed wire, but there was an unconfirmed report that those facing east had not yet been wired. The outer defenses were strongest to the southwest, west, and northwest, where they rested on the high ground running in a rough semicircle about seven thousand yards from the town. Northeast, east, and southeast, where the terrain was even more rugged than to the west, there was not a continuous series of defenses; instead the Turks had constructed strong points on the hills which jut out above the ravines and ridges like slag heaps in a coal-mining countryside. These hills, or "tels" as they are called in Arabic, provided excellent observation for calling down artillery and machine-gun fire.

Beersheba was a drab little desert settlement which owed its small importance to the perennial water supply from its wells. With the railway, however, had come German technicians and an increase in the garrison, and a few stone houses and some barracks had been built alongside the railway station. There was even a hotel, and talk of transforming Beersheba into "the Gateway to Sinai."

In June, 1917, the British replaced General Murray by General Allenby as commander of the Egyptian Expeditionary Force. Allenby was a cavalryman with a reputation for ruthlessness. He was a big, heavy, and rather forbidding man, known to his soldiers as the "Bull." As an army commander on the Western front his reputation had not been particularly high, but he was to show in Palestine a readiness to take risks and an ability to handle large numbers of troops, which placed him in the front rank of the commanders of World War I; his understanding of mobile warfare and the skill with which he employed his mounted troops also entitles him to a place among the great cavalry leaders of all time. His directive from the British War Cabinet was to break the deadlock in Palestine and to capture Jerusalem.

The troops available for this task amounted to about 76,000 men, of whom 20,000 were mounted, and 550 guns. The British therefore considerably outnumbered the Turks, particularly in cavalry, but they were dependent on a desert line of communications with Egypt and were short of water-points. Their vast preponderance of cavalry was also of doubtful value unless the Turkish infantry could be driven out of their fortifications and back into the coastal plain of Philistia beyond, and before this could happen the Turkish defenses would have to be stormed frontally or their desert flank would have to be turned. Twice already a frontal attack on Gaza had failed, and the terrain on the desert flank was hardly conducive to the employment of cavalry.

Yet this was where Allenby decided to employ his horsemen. Cavalry and infantry were to seize Beersheba and the high ground to the west and northwest. Once this phase of the operation was successfully accomplished, the enemy's left flank would be exposed, and the main infantry attack would go in at Hareira to roll up the enemy defenses from east to west. The Turks would then be forced to withdraw across the open country towards Jerusalem and the Judaean hills, and the whole of Allenby's mounted corps would be perfectly positioned to sweep out from Beersheba and take them in the flank. The success of the operation hinged on two things; first, the ability of the British to conceal from the enemy the real point of the main attack, and second, the capture of Beersheba within twenty-four hours. Without Beersheba and its wells, Allenby would be unable to water his cavalry and would have to call off the whole operation.[7]

The British took immense pains to obtain surprise. Part of their cover plan involved an attack on Gaza, preceded by a week's bombardment by all available artillery, to persuade the Turks that they intended to make yet another frontal assault on the town. Various ruses were also employed to deceive the enemy, and perhaps the best known of them is the story of an officer who rode out towards the Turkish lines, was fired on, and who galloped off swaying in his saddle and dropping his

[7] Allenby's plan has some remarkable similarities with that adopted by Rommel to defeat the British Eighth Army in Libya in May and June, 1942. On that occasion the British occupied a line of defenses stretching from the Mediterranean to Bir Hacheim, forty miles inland. Rommel began his operations by sending his Afrika Corps (15th and 21st Panzer and 90th Light Divisions) round the desert flank of the British, and later swung them north to threaten the Eighth Army's communications with Tobruk and Egypt. He then launched a frontal attack against the Sidi Muftah position in the center of the British defenses and breached the British mine fields, broke into the main defenses, and in a series of armored actions destroyed most of the British armor, eventually forcing them to retreat. Rommel had one great advantage over Allenby however; he had no animals to worry him and he could carry all the water he needed.

haversack as he disappeared in a cloud of dust.[8] The haversack contained £20 in notes with a letter to his wife, a copy of a letter from General Headquarters to the Desert Mounted Corps informing them that a staff officer was going out on patrol, and a letter from a staff officer criticizing the commander in chief for making Gaza and not Beersheba the main objective of the attack. The Turks retrieved the haversack and seem to have been taken in by a ruse of almost childish simplicity. They seem to have been convinced that the main attack would be made on Gaza, and they may well have been influenced by their knowledge that the bulk of the British cavalry was thirty-five miles away to the southwest. They did not consider it possible for cavalry to make an approach march of that distance over such rugged terrain, and be in a position to attack Beersheba without the Turks receiving prior information of their advance.

The land bombardment of Gaza began on October 27, 1917, and as soon as night fell on October 30 the Desert Mounted Corps began its wide sweep round the Turkish desert flank. The Anzac Mounted Division was in the lead, closely followed by the Australian Mounted Division, and the horses tripped and stumbled as they picked their way along the stony wadis and across the rock-strewn ridges. Fortunately there was a bright moon, and the thirty-five-mile approach march was accomplished successfully by dawn. The Anzac Mounted Division had seized its first objectives by eight o'clock on October 31 and was working its way round to the east and northeast of the main Beersheba defenses. Simultaneously the Twentieth Corps, which included the 74th dismounted Yeomanry Division, was launching an infantry attack on the Beersheba defenses from the west.

There is no doubt that the Turks were completely surprised by the sudden appearance of the Desert Mounted Corps. Ismet Bey, commander of the Beersheba garrison, was sitting in his

[8] The staff officer's name was Meinertzhagen. He was later to acquire fame as an ornithologist and as the world's leading authority on birds of the Middle East.

battle headquarters on a hill west of the town watching the British infantry attack. He was not in the least concerned, since he still had several regiments of infantry and the 3rd Cavalry Division in reserve, and he was quite confident of his ability to defeat the British attack. This was about eleven o'clock in the morning. Five or ten minutes later, happening to look round, he saw the plain behind Beersheba covered with cavalry. He sent his personal aide-de-camp off at a gallop to find out the reason for this unexpected activity, but that unfortunate officer was soon rounded up by an Australian cavalry patrol. Ismet had not long to wait before he had the answer to his question, for by 11:30 the Anzac Mounted Division was advancing in dismounted action against the Turkish defenses northeast of Beersheba.

By one o'clock the British infantry of the Twentieth Corps had secured their objectives to the west and were consolidating their positions. So far so good, but the battle was slowing down to the east and northeast. The plain was swept by machine-gun fire and by artillery concealed in the town of Beersheba, and the Turkish defenses on Tel Saba enfiladed any advance from the east. The Australians and New Zealanders were trained more as mounted infantry than for shock action, but they lacked the heavy weapons to support them forward once they dismounted and took to their feet. For the next two sweltering and thirsty hours they inched their way forward from wadi to wadi, and from one boulder-covered ridge to the next, as they worked their way close to the Turkish strong points. Tel Saba was captured at the point of the bayonet shortly after three o'clock, and the last of the outer defenses were taken. Three miles away across the wide open plain was Beersheba and its precious water, but the inner line of defenses was still intact and in less than two hours it would be dark. It seemed possible to General Chauvel, watching the progress of his troops from an observation post on Khassim Zanna ridge, that the onset of darkness might cheat him of the prized possession of Beersheba.

At 4:00 P.M. on October 31, the 4th Australian Light Horse

Brigade[9] was resting and feeding its horses behind the protection of the Khassim Zanna ridge, which runs roughly from north to south about six miles east of Beersheba. One regiment of the brigade—11th Australian Light Horse—had been detached to the southwest to watch the left flank of the Australian Mounted Division. The brigade was comparatively fresh and had not been involved in the battle, but the heat, thirst, and flies had driven both horses and men nearly crazy. The more senior of the officers had been able to watch the progress of the battle from the crest of the ridge, but most of the troops had spent the day dreaming of long cold drinks and searching for patches of shade.

Brigadier General Grant, who commanded the brigade, had spent the afternoon on the top of a nearby hill, watching the dismounted troopers of the Anzac Division working their way forward across the broken terrain to the north. He was there when his divisional commander came clambering up the hill to join him shortly after four o'clock. "It's your turn now to go in, Grant," said Major General Hodgson. "Come and see the corps commander." The two men then made their way to the headquarters of the Desert Mounted Corps where General Chauvel was waiting for them.

General Chauvel had decided that the time was ripe for an all-out assault but was undecided whether to use his reserve yeomanry brigade or the 4th A.L.H. Brigade for the final *coup de grâce*. He knew that the yeomen were armed with swords whereas the Australians carried rifles and bayonets, and a sword would be a more useful weapon than a bayonet in a mounted attack. His mind was made up for him by the fact that the Australian brigade was nearer at hand and closer to the objective. "Go right in and take the town before dark," he told Grant, and although Chauvel did not specifically mention a mounted attack, Grant was certain that his brigade was expected to take Beersheba by shock action.

Not much more than an hour's daylight remained and speed was vital. Grant sent orders for the 4th and 12th Regiments to

[9] The brigade consisted of the 4th, 11th and 12th Regiments, Australian Light Horse.

saddle up immediately and to be brought forward by their seconds-in-command to an assembly area south of the track running east from Beersheba. He then galloped forward with his two commanding officers, brigade major, and four orderlies to look for an assembly area which would not be overlooked and shelled by the enemy. If the charge was to be successful it was vital that the horses, already tired after the long hours of waiting, should not be panicked by enemy shell fire.

There was no time for a detailed reconnaissance, nor time to bring up artillery and machine guns to support the attack. Messages were, however, sent to the two nearest batteries of horse artillery instructing them to do what they could to assist, and the artillerymen at once limbered up and galloped forward, coming into action in the open about twenty-five hundred yards from the Turkish trenches. Simultaneously the 4th and 12th Regiments moved from their positions of assembly, about three thousand yards from the objective, and at 4:30 P.M. the brigade trotted forward in column of squadrons with brigade headquarters following behind them. Each trooper carried his bayonet in his hand, with his rifle strapped to the saddle. Grant had decided that the bayonets were to be used as swords, but not fixed to rifles; there was a danger of the mounted man losing both bayonet and rifle if bayonets were fixed.

As the two regiments swept out of their assembly area into the open, they were bombed and machine gunned by two enemy airplanes, but they were moving so rapidly by then that little damage was done. The enemy artillery opened fire at the same time, but they misjudged the range and most of the shells exploded harmlessly behind the charging horsemen. Machine-gun fire from the Turkish trenches was silenced by the accurate fire of the horse artillery battery which found their target with the second ranging round, and in one dust-drenched, cheering, thundering mass the Australians surged towards the Turkish trenches and the town beyond.

By then the short eastern twilight had almost ended and the gathering darkness was lit by the flashes of the defenders' rifle and artillery fire, and shells exploding in the air. A dense

cloud of dust billowed up above the charging horsemen, re-
ducing visibility and hiding the ground ahead, and at the back
of every man's mind there hammered the unanswered question:
what if the Turkish trenches were protected by barbed wire?
And between the Australians and the town ran the Wadi
Saba which was unreconnoitered. What if its banks were as
steep and the wadi as deep as those they had crossed on their
long approach march of the night before? The leading wave
would tumble into ruin, and those following behind would
crash down on top of them, in a wildly kicking jumble of
broken legs, screaming horses, and shattered bodies. Perhaps it
was as well that dust and darkness hid all but the comrade on
left and right.

Fortunately the trenches in that particular sector had not
been wired, either because the Turks had never expected them
to be attacked or because there had not been sufficient time to
complete the defenses. As the light horsemen came suddenly
upon them they put spurs to their horses and leapt the obstacle
like steeplechasers. Then they threw themselves from their
horses and plunged into the trenches to finish off the action
with the bayonet. Over half their sixty-four casualties were
killed during this hand-to-hand fighting in the half darkness,
and most of the remainder had fallen wounded before ever
the trenches were reached. Within ten minutes the trenches
were in their hands, and Grant was able to reorganize his two
regiments.

He ordered the two regiments to gallop on into the town and
capture as many prisoners as possible. It was now quite dark
and the horsemen swept on through the streets, riding down
the scattered bunches of enemy and keeping them on the run.
Great gouts of flame swept skywards as the Turks blew up
their wells and dumps, and the darkness was lit by the burning
railway station. By six o'clock, two hours after Grant had
ridden up to Chauvel to receive the orders for the attack,
Beersheba was in British hands, and with its capture the first
part of Allenby's plan had been successfully accomplished.
The 4th Australian Light Horse Brigade had captured nearly
twelve hundred prisoners, ten guns, and great quantities of

stores and animals. Ismet Bey, the Turkish commander, managed to escape in his car only a few minutes before the victorious Australians came thundering down the streets on their way to surround his headquarters.

Much of the success of this charge was due to the speed with which it was carried out. It took the Turks by surprise, since it was the first time in Palestine that shock action had been used against them. The other cavalry attacks that day had been dismounted ones, the Anzacs using their horses to carry them forward to forming-up positions, and thereafter dismounting and fighting their way forward on foot. Just before the charge came in, the Turks had been engaged with the dismounted New Zealanders on Tel Saba, and they were not only looking in the wrong direction when the Australians galloped into them but their rifles were sighted to fire at long ranges. When they were examined afterwards all of them were found to be sighted to fire at eight hundred meters, and as a result most of the rifle fire passed over the Australians' heads.

Quite apart from the vital part they had played in the capture of Beersheba, the charge of the 4th Australian Light Horse Brigade set the standard for the rest of the campaign. It had shown that under certain circumstances cavalry might still be used for shock action, and it inspired a spirit of dash and daring which the rest of Allenby's cavalry was quick to emulate. When Allenby finally smashed his way into Gaza on November 8 and the pursuit across Philistia began, the Desert Mounted Corps went after the retreating Turks like foxhounds after a fox. At Huj, ten troops of the Worcestershire and Warwickshire Yeomanry charged and captured twelve guns and broke the resistance of the Turkish rear guard, and on November 13 at El Mughar the 6th Mounted Brigade[10] charged a Turkish position across fifteen hundred yards of open country, capturing over one thousand prisoners, two guns, and fourteen machine guns. It was in this celebrated charge that Lieutenant Colonel Freddy Cripps, commanding officer of the 1st Royal Buckinghamshire Hussars, after galloping over a mile in the

[10] The 6th Mounted Brigade was a yeomanry formation consisting of the Dorset Yeomanry, Buckinghamshire Hussars, and Berkshire Yeomanry.

face of aimed machine-gun fire, jumped a wadi at the foot of
the enemy position from bank to bank while traveling at top
speed. The aftermath of these charges was described rather
graphically by a British noncommissioned officer who said he
looked back after it was all over and saw: "Dead 'uns, dead
'orses, shell 'oles, and the 'undred other 'orrors what goes to
make up the pageant of war!"

Ten months later, after Jerusalem had been captured, and
Allenby launched his final attack which rolled up the Turkish
right flank and began a pursuit which did not end until Aleppo,
five hundred miles to the north, there were over ten occasions
when cavalry charged riflemen and machine guns in position
and were successful. A British cavalry brigade commander said
later that he was absolutely convinced that, tactically, success
was entirely due to a bold use of the sword, where possible
with the covering fire of artillery and machine guns! That
this was not a view confined to a British cavalryman is shown
by the opinion expressed by Brigadier General Wilson of the
3rd A.L.H. Brigade, who has said:

> The Cavalry sword was issued to all ranks of the Aus-
> tralian Mounted Division prior to the general offensive [in
> September 1918]. The Division had received a fair amount
> of training in the use of the bayonet as a sword for shock
> action. The bayonet was not, however, satisfactory. The
> issue of the sword was, I consider, more than justified. I
> consider that the sword has a great moral effect both on
> the man carrying it and on the enemy. One of the chief
> values of the sword is the spirit of progress it inspires in
> the carrier. He does not allow himself to be bluffed by
> slight opposition. He rides on feeling that he has a weapon
> in his hand and nineteen times out of 20 finds the op-
> position only a bluff.[11]

These views were expressed in 1922, six years after the first
tank had appeared on the battlefield, and they were upheld

[11] Col. G. A. Weir, "Reflections on the Cavalry Campaign in Palestine,"
Journal of the Royal United Service Institution (London), May, 1922,
p. 226.

by many distinguished soldiers. "I am convinced," said General Lord Horne that same year, "that clear thinking will lead us to decide that the day is not yet when mechanical and other contrivances can take the place in war of either the man with the rifle, or the man on the horse," and he was supported by General Godley, whose view was that "whatever modern inventions and mechanical appliances there may be, you may always, in the end, have to fall back on the combination of the man and the horse." [12]

The fact that Allenby's successful employment of cavalry in Palestine set back the clock of mechanization in most armies for nearly twenty years should not, however, obscure the brilliance of his victory. If horsed cavalry had first appeared on the battlefield with a bang in 333 B.C. at the Battle of Issus, they certainly made their exit in a resounding crescendo under Allenby's direction in Palestine. His 5th Cavalry Division ended their five-hundred-mile pursuit of the Turkish armies at Aleppo, not far from the place "where Alexander the Great first showed how battles could be won by bold and well-handled horsemen," [13] and in Allenby, Alexander would have found a cavalry commander after his own heart.

The pattern of it all was set by the 4th Australian Light Horse Brigade at Beersheba on October 31, 1917, when they raised the curtain on what was to prove to be the last magnificent appearance of horsed cavalry on the modern battlefield. Every true admirer of *l'arme blanche* will remember them with gratitude for having done so.

[12] *Ibid.*
[13] Wavell, *op. cit.*, pp. 245-246.

CHAPTER TEN

Moreuil Wood

MARCH 30, 1918

"Je n'oublie pas l'héroisme de la vaillante Brigade de Cavalerie Canadienne."

MARSHAL FOCH

NORTHERN FRANCE saw little of the sun on March 21, 1918. The wide fields, rolling hills, and drab industrial towns of Picardy were blanketed in fog, swirling in the valleys and shrouding the hilltops, and the fog was to continue with scarcely a break for the next four days. That would be sufficient time for the German army to smash a fifty-mile-wide hole through the British and French defenses on the Western front and come very close to winning the war at the eleventh hour.

The German assault had been preceded by a lull in operations, which had lasted since January. The British were licking their wounds after the appalling casualties they had suffered at Passchendaele the previous autumn, while the French were still recovering from the mutinies of April and May, 1917;

both armies were waiting for the time when the full strength
of the American army had been assembled in France and was
ready to play its part in a general offensive. The Allied line
ran without a break from Switzerland to the North Sea, and
the British sector lay between the coast and the River Oise.
From the Oise eastwards the French held the line, and the
junction point between the two armies was at La Fère, a town
on the Oise and some eighty miles northeast of Paris.

Three years of war on two fronts had told heavily on the
Germans, but by the end of 1917 they no longer had any need
to worry about Russia. Lenin had overthrown Kerensky and
the Russians were systematically tearing themselves to pieces.
Germany could now switch her full weight to the Western
front and open the way to Paris before the American army
was in a condition to take the field. For the first time, as
Helferich told the Reichstadt, the whole German manhood
was united in a single theater of war, ready to strike with the
strongest army that the world has ever known.

In the total wars of this twentieth century it has proved
virtually impossible to conceal the preparations for a great
offensive; there are too many men and machines to be moved,
too many roads, airfields, and railways to be constructed, and
too many dumps to be established. From the air, from agents
in enemy territory, from radio intercepts, and from other
sources of information, it soon becomes possible for the Intelligence Services to build up a picture of the preparations being
made "on the other side of the hill." Fog, darkness, smoke,
and other natural and artificial aids may help a commander to
achieve tactical surprise, but modern means of surveillance
are such that strategic surprise is extremely difficult to obtain.
The Germans had concentrated 192 divisions on the Western
front by March, 1918, and sixty-four of these were assembled
opposite the sector they intended to attack. The movement of
such numbers of men, animals, and guns was perfectly well
known to the British and French, but what they did not know
was the time and date chosen for zero hour.

The German plan was to strike at the junction between the
British and French armies, somewhere between St. Quentin

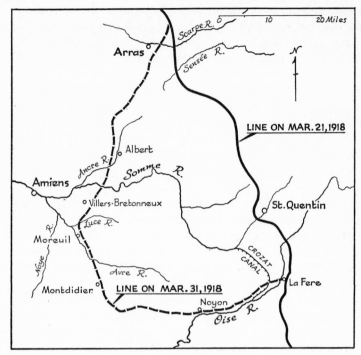

and La Fère, and force the British northward towards the
sea. The exposed left flank of the French army could then
be rolled up and the way to Paris would be clear. The brunt
of the blow would fall on the British, whose Third and Fifth
Armies held the line from just north of Arras to the junction
with the French Sixth Army at Barisis, four miles south of
La Fère. The total length of line held by these two British
armies amounted to about seventy-five miles, and forty-one of
these lay within the sector of the Fifth Army. The commanders
of both the Third and Fifth Armies were cavalrymen—Generals Sir Julian Byng and Sir Hubert Gough. During World
War I, which was essentially an infantryman's war, a remarkable number of cavalry officers rose to high rank in the British
army, whereas in World War II, which saw mobility restored
to its proper place on the battlefield, nearly all the leading

British generals were infantrymen. There must be a moral in this somewhere!

The main German effort was to be directed against the Fifth Army, and by dawn on March 21 they had succeeded in assembling thirty-seven divisions within three thousand yards of the British outpost line. Against this overwhelming strength the commander of the Fifth Army could muster only fourteen infantry and two cavalry divisions, and in an attempt to offset this disparity in numbers he had disposed his troops in three zones of defense. The forward zone was a line of resistance, intended to check the German advance and throw them off balance, and it consisted of a trench system, heavily wired and protected by outposts, and strengthened at two-thousand-yard intervals by redoubts armed with machine guns. The gaps between the machine-gun posts were covered by artillery. Farther back, at distances varying from one-half mile to three miles, was the battle zone, which had been prepared on the same principle as the line of resistance. The final defensive zone lay farther back still, but it was only partially completed; the Fifth Army had taken over the sector in January and there had been only seven weeks in which to complete the elaborate defenses.

The work had not been helped by the paucity of troops available to dig the trenches, erect the barbed wire, and build the strong points. The severe casualties incurred the year before at Passchendaele had cost the British commander in chief the confidence of his prime minister. Lloyd George believed that Haig was destitute of tactical skill and that his only recipe for victory was head-on assaults against the German trenches; fearful lest the massacres of Passchendaele should be repeated, he deliberately withheld the reinforcements which his commander in chief repeatedly requested. Both Haig and Gough were therefore having to make bricks without straw, and it is hardly surprising that the house collapsed as soon as the wind blew with sufficient force.

The Fifth Army sector was particularly important, not only because it linked up with the French on the right, but also because it covered Amiens. This communications center on the River Somme was a nodal point on the lines of communication of the British armies in France, as well as being an obvious key town on the approach route to Paris. If the Germans could punch a hole between Amiens and the Oise there would be virtually nothing to stop them and the British would be forced to withdraw northwards to safeguard their communications with England. In view of this there is no doubt that the Fifth Army should have been considerably reinforced, but Haig was unwilling to weaken the other sectors of his front to provide the men needed. He had no reason to suppose that the Germans would not attack elsewhere as well as opposite the Fifth Army, and he gambled on the hope that the Fifth Army would be able to hold out. It was a calculated risk and he lost.

The fog came down during the afternoon of March 20, and at 2:00 A.M. the next morning Gough was warned that the attack would probably come that day. He had sent out orders to man the battle zone, and the Fifth Army were already in their positions when they learned without any possible doubt that "today is the day." At 4:30 A.M. a storm broke loose. Four thousand German guns plastered the British defenses with a hail of steel. Barbed wire was flattened, sandbagged redoubts demolished, and entire trench systems filled in as if by some gigantic bulldozer. Under cover of the fog the German infantry infiltrated forward in small groups, unseen and unsuspected until they loomed out of the murk to close with the shell-blasted and pulverized British infantry. The British artillery, unable to see more than fifty yards ahead of them, fired aimlessly into the swirling gray mist, and the British machine gunners were equally without targets until the Germans were so close that only the bayonet mattered. German artillery firing on targets previously registered from the map were not hampered by the fog, and their shells came down with deadly precision on communication trenches, assembly positions, and the villages behind the lines where harassed staff officers were hastily scraping together reinforcements.

By nightfall on March 21 the Germans had overwhelmed the Fifth Army's carefully prepared forward zone. They brought up fresh troops during the night, attacked again at dawn on March 22, and by that night had breached the Fifth Army's rearmost line of defense south of St. Quentin. There was no lack of leadership and gallantry on the part of the British, but the fog which lapped them on every side forced them to fight a series of unco-ordinated and isolated actions. The complex system of communications, largely dependent on the field telephone, which had been built up during three years of siege warfare, had been wrecked by the German bombardment and no one knew what was happening on his right and left. The rear areas were congested with hordes of noncombatants employed on the lines of communication. There were Chinese, Burmese, Annamese, Senegalese, and a dozen other nationalities all milling around in hopeless confusion, spreading rumors, blocking the roads, and seeking safety in flight. Through this flotsam and jetsam the few available reserves were struggling desperately to march to the sound of the guns, along roads jammed with transport of every description and in many cases already under fire from the enemy artillery.

During the night of March 22 information reached Gough that the Germans had got behind his right flank south of St. Quentin. The report was incorrect but it caused Gough to order a withdrawal to the River Somme, and this shortening of the line meant that the Fifth Army had lost contact for the time being with the French Sixth Army. If the Germans had taken advantage of this loss of contact and thrown the whole weight of their attack between St. Quentin and La Fère, the entire course of World War I might have been changed. In the event, however, they made their main effort to the north where the British Third Army was struggling desperately to maintain contact with the Fifth, and so cover Amiens. The Germans spent six precious days hammering at the junction between the Third and Fifth Armies and this gave the French time to switch their reserves to the left flank where the danger was growing from hour to hour. By March 27 the German Eighteenth Army under General Hutier had reached Montdidier, twenty miles southeast of Amiens as the crow flies, and had penetrated the Fifth Army's right flank to a depth of forty miles. Here was the opportunity for which the Germans had been waiting—they had only to reinforce Hutier's army and direct him to swing north. He would then be able to roll up Gough's flank and threaten Amiens from the southeast. Instead, they ordered an attack on Amiens by the Second Army under Von der Marwitz, which had been fighting its way forward in a westerly direction.

A great opportunity was lost thereby, for by March 28 the German attack was losing its impetus. The fog had lifted and the British artillery was able to slow down the German advance. The air force was attacking German communications and the Fifth Army front had been shortened sufficiently for Gough to pull out troops to form a reserve. The chaos of the battlefield across which they had to advance was hampering the Germans, as was the loot which they found in every shell-torn village and vacated British billet. Whole companies drank themselves insensible as they ransacked the *estaminets* behind what had been until a few days previously the British front line, and looting was becoming a serious problem. The Germans were still advancing across the rolling downland of the Somme, but their cohesion was departing. It is often said that in battle it is the last quarter of an hour which counts, and it will always be to the eternal glory of the young Canadian army that it was during that last quarter of an hour that they outfought and outlasted the most formidable and experienced soldiers in the world.

When dawn broke on March 21 the Canadian Cavalry Brigade were bivouacked around the village of Devise, ten miles behind the front line. The brigade consisted of two regular regiments, the Royal Canadian Dragoons and Lord Strathcona's Horse (Royal Canadians), and a militia regiment, the Fort Garry Horse; its two batteries of Royal Canadian Horse Artillery were also part of Canada's small regular army, or Permanent Force as it was then called.[1] On the night when the shelling

[1] The Fort Garry Horse are now a regular regiment. The senior regiment of the Canadian army is the Royal Canadian Dragoons, who were raised in December, 1883, as the Cavalry School Corps. In May, 1892, their title was changed to Canadian Dragoons, and the prefix Royal was granted in 1893. The Royal Canadian Dragoons took part in the South African War, where at Lilliefontein they were nearly ambushed by a Boer commando. It was while approaching the ambush that the dragoons

began the brigade commander was in London dining with Prime Minister Lloyd George, a form of entertainment not usually indulged in by humble brigadier generals, but then, Jack Seely was no ordinary personality. He was a member of the British House of Commons, had held high office in the British government as secretary of state for war, had fought in South Africa with his yeomanry regiment, had practiced at the Bar, and had been for many years a member of a famous lifeboat crew. He threw up everything in 1914 to become a soldier, and was selected by Lord Kitchener in 1915 to command the Canadian Cavalry Brigade which was then being formed in England. Few men in British public life could boast of such versatility, and of those few one was his great personal friend Winston Churchill.

From the moment when it arrived in England, the Canadian Cavalry Brigade had shown that it was a formation of exceptional quality. The Permanent Force of the Dominion of Canada was young in years and only a few thousands strong, but it had based its tradition on the regiments of the British army, from which it had sprung. It was an entirely volunteer force, and behind it was the militia, a volunteer and part-time force, which had also adopted the regimental system of the British army. Shortly after Seely took command of the brigade he was sent for by Kitchener, the secretary for war, and asked if he would find volunteers to go out to France as infantry to fill the breach made in the British line by the first German gas attack. Every man in the brigade volunteered without a moment's hesitation, and the Canadian cavalry's first experience of fighting in France was as infantry in the water-logged trenches of the Ypres salient.[2]

During the first few days of fighting on the Fifth Army's front in March, 1918, the Canadian Cavalry Brigade spent

---

noticed a springbok leaving the area, and its behavior aroused their suspicions. The Canadians deployed for action and during the ensuing battle the dragoons gained no less than three Victoria Crosses for supreme gallantry. Subsequently the regiment adopted the springbok as its badge; and ever since, the anniversary of Lilliefontein has been celebrated as the "regimental day."

[2] The Fort Garry Horse replaced King Edward's Horse in 1916. Their second-in-command was a crack shot who used to shoot fish with his pistol.

much of their time plugging gaps. They provided a dismounted battalion which fought with great gallantry to stem the German advance, while the remainder of the brigade, with their horses, were hurried from place to place, hastily occupying positions and holding them until infantry could be scraped together and rushed up to relieve them. During this critical time the Canadians found themselves commanded at various times by both British and French commanders, but finally on March 27 the Fifth Army front was beginning to stabilize, and some order was coming out of the preceding six days of confusion. The brigade was ordered to concentrate at the village of Arsy, a few miles from Compiègne and thirty-five miles in a direct line from where they had been in bivouac when the German attack first began. In the ensuing six days they had marched four times that distance and been in almost constant contact with the enemy, but their morale was as high as ever. Their versatile brigade commander had rejoined them on March 24, having crossed the Channel on March 22, commandeered some staff officer's car at Calais, driven across France, and finally arrived with his brigade when confusion was at its height. How he managed to discover its location in the fog and make his way to it through the flood of refugees in the disorganized rear areas is one of the more remarkable feats of a remarkable career.

The Canadians left Arsy at 6:30 A.M. on March 28. They had spent only a few hours in the place but some weeks later they received a claim from the French for 20,000 francs. This bill covered the loss of a horse and cart, bedding, crockery, and a fantastic quantity of ladies' underclothes! They were able to point out that soldiers marching to meet the enemy were unlikely to burden themselves with cups and saucers, feather pillows, petticoats and panties, even though they might have had the forethought to appropriate a horse and cart for conveyance of their loot, and the bill was returned to the sender. It was the last ever heard of the claim.

The German threat to Amiens grew in intensity during March 28 and 29. The French had succeeded in blocking the threat from Hutier's army at Montdidier, but the Germans were working their way forward across the rolling country lying between the rivers Somme and Avre. Once across the Avre, which flows northwest to meet the Somme at Amiens, they would be able to cut the main railway line from Amiens to Paris, and Amiens would be in danger of encirclement. By the evening of March 29 the German advance had reached the ridge looking down onto the village of Moreuil in the Avre valley, and the front line had been forced back to the River Luce, only ten miles from Amiens. The Luce joins the Avre just below Moreuil, and the woods along the Moreuil Ridge were swarming with German infantry. British and French reinforcements were being rushed forward to hold the line of the Luce, but it took time to do this when mechanical transport was still in its infancy, and when speed was something which depended on the length of a man's marching pace and his ability to keep it up and still arrive in battle with sufficient stamina left to fight.

On the evening of March 29 the Canadian Cavalry Brigade were bivouacked in some woods ten miles west of Moreuil. At two o'clock the next morning they were ordered to be ready to move at dawn, and at 6:30 they saddled up and stood-to. General Pitman, commander of the British 2nd Cavalry Division, arrived to see Seely at 8:30 and told him the situation was critical. "The Germans," said Pitman, "have captured Mezières and are rapidly advancing on Amiens. I want you to cross the Avre as quickly as possible and engage and delay the enemy." His final words were, "Go to the support of the infantry just beyond Castel, this side of the Moreuil Ridge. Don't get too heavily involved—you will be needed later." Seely in reporting this conversation later said that he knew the situation must be pretty desperate if it had alarmed a general as cool and as poised as Pitman.

The brigade advanced at a trot across country, Seely galloping on ahead with his brigade major, Connolly of Lord Strathcona's Horse, and his aide-de-camp, Prince Antoine of Orléans. Prince Antoine was as romantic a figure as the general he served—a sort of Aramis to Seely's D'Artagnan. As a member of the French royal house he was forbidden by law to serve in the

French army and had therefore received his military training in the Austrian army. The Emperor Franz Josef of Austria had promised that if ever France and Austria were at war, he would give Prince Antoine a safe conduct to return to his country, which he did in 1914. President Poincaré refused to allow him to join the French army, but King George V accepted him in the British army, although he was given no rank. Seely knew him and managed to get him a commission in the Royal Canadian Dragoons, where he served with great distinction as aide-de-camp and intelligence officer in the cavalry brigade. He was a born soldier, completely fearless, and the finest type of aristocrat. The British gave him the Military Cross for gallantry, and he was invested by General Foch with the order of a Chevalier of the Legion of Honor for his bravery at Moreuil Wood. He was killed shortly afterwards.

Crossing the Avre by the bridge at Castel, Seely and his two companions rode through the village streets and down the valley towards Amiens and the Allied front line along the River Luce. Castel was under enemy fire as they cantered through it, for above them and to their right the Germans held the spur of the Moreuil Ridge, the crest heavily wooded and affording observation over the Luce and right up the Avre valley as far as Amiens. If the Germans were allowed to establish themselves firmly on the Moreuil Ridge the thinly held line on the Luce would be untenable, and the railway to Paris would be within easy striking distance. An insignificant wooded hill in a remote corner of rural France had acquired an importance that in this utilitarian age is normally conceded only to a desirable piece of real estate in the heart of New York or London; but in war, good observation is more precious than rubies, and the possession of the ground which provides that observation may mean all the difference between victory and defeat.

Seely had immediately appreciated the importance of the Moreuil Ridge. On the outskirts of Castel he came unexpectedly across a French general whose division was holding the right flank of the Allied defenses. From him Seely learned that the Germans were still advancing in great strength, that they had already started to work their way into Moreuil village two miles farther up the valley, and that at any moment they were expected to cross the Avre and begin to envelop the open flank of the French division. The French general had already given orders for his troops to pull back out of Moreuil village and to withdraw on Amiens to avoid being outflanked.

> I saw at once that the position was desperate, if not fatal [wrote Seely]. If the enemy captured the ridge which I had just left, the main line from Amiens to Paris would be definitely broken, and I knew already that when that happened the two armies—the French and the British—would be compelled to retire; the French on Paris, and our Army on the Channel Ports. All our sea power, even the great host of determined soldiers now crossing from the United States would not avail to save the Allied cause. All that we had fought for, and bled for, for nearly four years would be lost.[3]

He told the French general that the ridge must be retaken. The Frenchman agreed but said that he had no troops available for the task. Seely then told him that he had ample troops to capture the ridge, but the Frenchman was not deceived—"but your poor little force cannot do it. The Germans have a whole division in the wood this side of the ridge." Seely persisted, and at last the skeptical Frenchman gave in. He sent orders to his troops in Moreuil village to hang on for the time being, and Seely, his heart high, galloped off to deploy his brigade for the battle. In the life of every man of action there comes a supreme moment—Seely's had come on March 30, 1918, and he was to share that supreme moment with Canada.

Moreuil Ridge is about one hundred meters high, sloping gently in the north to the valley of the Luce, and rather more steeply on the west to the valley of the Avre. The slopes and crest above Moreuil village are thickly wooded and the Bois de Moreuil extends down the slope as far as Moreuil village. At the northernmost point of the ridge a smaller wood adjoins the main Moreuil Wood, and Seely established his headquarters on the edge of this smaller wood. From there he could look down

---

[3] J. E. B. Seely, *Adventure* (Heinemann, London, 1930), p. 300.

on the rest of his brigade as they crossed over the Luce, passed through the British front line, and then galloped up the slopes of Moreuil Ridge. It was typical of Seely that he should have led the way with only a few signalers, and as he galloped past the infantry, hugging the earth in their hastily scraped trenches, he called out to a young captain: "We are going to retake the ridge. Fire on both sides of us, as close as you can, while the rest of us go up." His nickname, "Galloper Jack," sums up the man.

The Royal Canadian Dragoons were the leading regiment in the brigade. They were ordered to gallop a squadron to the right of Moreuil Wood and clear the southwest corner. Thereafter they were to try to make contact with the French still holding out in Moreuil village. The other two squadrons were to gallop round the other side of the wood, one to clear the northwest face of the wood, while the other moved right round to the southeastern corner.

Lord Strathcona's Horse, comprising the second wave, were to detach one squadron to gallop round the wood and prevent German reinforcements from approaching from the east, while the two remaining squadrons were to dismount, leaving their horses near Seely's headquarters, and fight their way through the wood from the northwestern edge. The Fort Garry Horse were to remain in reserve. It was a simple enough plan in its essentials, involving the encirclement of the Bois de Moreuil by mounted men, followed by a sweep into the wood by men on foot. The danger lay in the fact that the wood was full of German infantry, better armed for close hand-to-hand fighting than dismounted cavalry, and with the terrain in their favor. The Germans, moreover, had their reinforcements close at hand, while the Canadians, once they dismounted, would immediately have reduced their fighting strength by at least a third: one man in every three would be required to hold horses.

Captain Nordheimer's squadron of the Royal Canadian Dragoons thundered up the open slopes of the ridge, and swung to the left as it reached the crest. It crashed into the wood at the northwest corner, engaged the enemy in close combat, and killed a large number of Germans who refused to surrender. Behind the leading squadron came Captain Newcomen's squad-

ron, heading for the southwest corner, but they were received
with heavy machine-gun fire from the Germans in Moreuil village. Horses and men pitched to the ground like rabbits in a
farm shoot, and Newcomen was forced to dismount his squadron and occupy a position inside the wood and about halfway
along its southwestern face. The third squadron of the dragoons, under Major Timmis, galloping round the wood to the
southeastern corner, met such heavy fire that it was compelled
to wheel away to the north where it found some cover below
the crest. The dragoons had managed to get a footing on either
side of the wood, but they had suffered heavy casualties while
doing so, and were unable to get round to the southern face
which the Germans were still able to reinforce.

Lord Strathcona's Horse were now arriving on the ridge, and
as soon as their leading squadron, under Lieutenant Flowerdew, arrived, Seely rode up to him and told him his task. It
was the most difficult and adventurous of all the tasks given
to the Canadians that day, for he was to lead his squadron
right round the wood at the gallop, reach the southern face,
and cut off the Germans. Seely emphasized the importance of
Flowerdew's task, and Flowerdew replied with a smile, "I know,
sir, I know, it is a splendid moment. I will try not to fail you."
He led his squadron at the gallop round the corner of the wood,
and the other two squadrons of Lord Strathcona's threw themselves off their horses and began to fight their way into the
wood.

As Flowerdew's squadron burst round the wood they suddenly came across a very steep bank. This was held by the Germans who had been forced out of the wood by the Royal
Canadian Dragoons, while another column of Germans was
marching across the open towards the wood. Flowerdew
wheeled three of his four troops into line and charged the
reinforcements, scattered them, and then charged the enemy
holding the bank. In the course of this most gallant action
Flowerdew was fatally wounded—he had two bullet wounds
through his chest and was shot through both thighs—but he
still called to his men, "Carry on boys. We have won." For his
gallantry on this, his last battlefield, Lieutenant Flowerdew received the posthumous award of the Victoria Cross:

For most conspicuous bravery and dash when in command of a squadron detailed for special services of a very important nature. On reaching his first objective Lieutenant Flowerdew saw two lines of enemy, each about sixty strong, with machine guns in the centre and flanks; one line being about two hundred yards behind the other. Realising the critical nature of the operation and how much depended on it, Lieutenant Flowerdew ordered a troop under Lieutenant Harvey V.C.,[4] to dismount and carry out a special movement, while he led the remaining three troops to the charge. The squadron (less one troop) passed over both lines, killing many of the enemy with the sword; and wheeling about galloped on them again. Although the squadron had then lost about seventy per cent of its members, killed and wounded from rifle and machine gun fire directed on it from the front and both flanks, the enemy broke and retired. The survivors of the Squadron then established themselves in a position where they were joined after much hand to hand fighting, by Lieutenant Harvey's party. Lieutenant Flowerdew was dangerously wounded through both thighs during the operation, but continued to cheer his men. There can be no doubt that this officer's great valour was the prime factor in the capture of this position.[5]

Over seventy Germans had been killed by sword thrust outside the wood, and inside the wood opposite Flowerdew's squadron another two or three hundred had died fighting, for they refused to surrender. All over the wood there was severe fighting, sword against bayonet, pistol against rifle, rifle butt against pick helve. The Bavarian infantry holding Moreuil Wood fought as bravely as the Canadian cavalry, and one German soldier refused the assistance of stretcher-bearers saying that he would rather die than surrender. The dismounted squadrons of Lord Strathcona's Horse, fighting their way through the un-

[4] Brigadier Harvey is now the regimental colonel of Lord Strathcona's Horse.
[5] Seely, *op. cit.*, pp. 303-304.

dergrowth, received a terrible mauling and might well have been thrown back had the Germans not been afraid of being cut off by the remnants of Flowerdew's squadron hanging on along the southern face. Newcomen's squadron of the Royal Canadian Dragoons, still in position on the edge of the wood above Moreuil village, were unable to move either forward or backward, and the Fort Garry Horse were ordered to gallop a squadron back across the Avre and onto the high ground beyond Moreuil, from where they could enfilade the Germans still holding the southwest corner of the wood. Over three hundred men had been killed and wounded, and over eight hundred horses had fallen between 9:30 A.M.—when the first squadron of the Royal Canadian Dragoons had charged up the slopes of the Moreuil Ridge—and 11:00 A.M. when all German resistance ceased except in the extreme southern corner of the wood.

The Canadians were still in grave danger of being driven back to their start line. They had lost between a third and a half of their strength in officers and men, while the casualties to their horses had been crippling. The Germans were still entrenched in the southern corner of the wood and were dribbling forward reinforcements, and Seely had no reserves left. The whole of the Fort Garry Horse were now engaged with the enemy, and a German counterattack seemed imminent.

It was at this moment that a British cavalry brigade arrived to support the Canadians. In the lead were the 16th Lancers commanded by a great cavalry soldier, Lieutenant Colonel (later Major General) Geoffrey Brooke. He had been brigade major of the Canadian Cavalry Brigade before his appointment to command the 16th Lancers, and the Canadians regarded him as one of themselves. An Irishman, and imperturbably brave, Brooke could see that German reinforcements were infiltrating into the Moreuil Wood and extending their right flank outside the wood. The 16th Lancers were ordered to make a dismounted attack against the southern corner of the wood, with the 4th Hussars operating mounted on the lancers' right to protect the flank. The attack went in successfully, but there was a considerable amount of fighting inside the wood. Geoffrey Brooke had the reputation of being completely unmoved by enemy fire, but not every soldier was as stouthearted. In his account of this attack, he says:

> I had just passed the word down the line to advance, when a soldier, who had temporarily lost his nerve started to run back. I had a large pair of wire-cutters which I hurled at him and hit him on the knee. This may have restored his equanimity as he then carried on—or it more likely may have been due to the remark of an old soldier seeing the German machine guns ripping up the grass in front of us. "God," he said, "it reminds me of old Nobby cutting up the billiard table!" [6]

The capture of Moreuil Wood did much to turn the tide and save Amiens. Captain Liddell Hart, writing of this brilliant action, has said:

> Even so, there was a moment of crisis when the Germans captured the Moreuil Wood ridge, which was not only a joint between the French and British but commanded the crossings of the Avre and Luce where they joined. And these covered the main Amiens-Paris railway. But the menace was warded off by a swift counterstroke of the Canadian Cavalry Brigade, made on the initiative of and led by General Seely, ex-War Minister turned Murat. [7]

The Germans were fully aware of the vital importance of Moreuil Ridge. Throughout the rest of March 30 they launched counterattack after counterattack in an attempt to recapture the wood. Towards evening their shelling grew heavier and heavier, and gas shells were mingled with the shrapnel and high explosive. By then the Canadian and British cavalrymen had withdrawn to the outer edges of the wood and thus escaped the worst effects of the gas, but the numbers of killed and wounded were growing. The high elation of the morning had passed, but the exhausted Canadians hung on grimly, deter-

[6] Letter to the author from Maj. Gen. G. F. H. Brooke, dated November 28, 1959.

[7] B. H. Liddell Hart, A History of the World War 1914-1918 (Faber & Faber, London, 1930), p. 507.

mined not to give up the ground they had wrested from the enemy.

Away to the north the Germans were hammering at Villers-Bretonneux, only five miles from Amiens. Had they been able to consolidate their position on Moreuil Ridge during March 30, they would then have been able to outflank the Villers-Bretonneux position. The charge of the Canadian Cavalry Brigade had blunted and turned aside the spearhead of the final German thrust against Amiens, and at 2:00 A.M. on March 31 they handed over the blasted and reeking Moreuil Wood to the infantry of the 8th Division, who had come up to relieve them.

As the Canadians stumbled back through the darkness, reeling with fatigue and pounded by the unceasing clamor of the guns,[8] they passed scores of silent and shadowy figures stretched out in the stubble. For the most part these were dead horses, but here and there a rider lay torn and twisted beside his mount. Three officers and seventy-two soldiers would never return to Canada, and one officer and seventy-five soldiers were missing. Twenty-four hours later what remained of the brigade was called upon to attack again, this time on foot at Rifle Wood, and by the end of it all, the wounded amounted to nearly 350. The price had been high but the German advance had been stemmed.

Field Marshal Haig subsequently described the action at Moreuil Ridge as "a brilliant counter-attack carried out by the Canadian Cavalry Brigade, supported by the 3rd Cavalry Brigade," and he went on to say, "Without the assistance of mounted troops, skilfully handled and gallantly led, the enemy could scarcely have been prevented from breaking through the long and thinly held front of broken and wooded ground before the French reinforcements had had time to arrive." [9]

The commander of the Fourth Army, General Rawlinson, who had taken over the defense of Amiens from the Fifth

[8] General Weygand, chief of staff to General Foch, told Seely later: "While you held on to that ridge I got ninety-five batteries of Seventy-fives into position, and during the ensuing thirty-six hours they fired one million three hundred thousand shells."

[9] Seely, *op. cit.*, p. 311.

Army, went in person to the Canadian bivouac and told the
survivors:

> Your recapture of the Moreuil Ridge was a great feat of
> arms. It did much to turn the tide and save Amiens. But
> that is not all. It was vital to the saving of Amiens that
> Rifle Wood should again be in our hands, but there was
> no infantry force at hand for the purpose. I knew that you
> were depleted in numbers and very tired, and that you had
> already done more than your share; but I called upon you
> for the task, as I felt that there was no one else available
> who could do it successfully. I have asked that a cable be
> sent to Canada informing the Canadian people of your
> splendid deeds.[10]

Canada has not forgotten the bravery of her cavalrymen at
Moreuil Wood. The charge of the Canadian Cavalry Brigade
will always remain one of the most famous incidents in the
history of the Canadian cavalry, and each year on the anniversary of the charge Lord Strathcona's Horse commemorates
the matchless courage of Gordon Flowerdew and the Strathcona's Horsemen he inspired to follow him to certain death.
The regiment has distinguished itself on many a battlefield
since the days when it charged at Moreuil Wood—in Italy, Holland, Germany, and most recently in Korea—but for Lord
Strathcona's Horse, Moreuil Wood will always be a battle set
apart.

It is well that this should be so, since the successful charge
of the Canadians at Moreuil Wood illustrates a side of war
which we may be in danger of forgetting. It is this: Theoretically Seely's plan was doomed from the moment of its incep-
tion, for he was pitting men on horseback, armed with swords,
against men in trenches, armed with machine guns. But the
theory of war is often a very different thing from its practice
because the human factor, which plays such a dominant part
in battle, is an uncertain and ever-varying quantity. The Seelys
and the Flowerdews of this world have proved this time after
time, and we should honor them for having done so.

[10] *Ibid.*

CHAPTER ELEVEN

Fondouk

APRIL 9, 1943

W HEN General John Hale died at Guisborough in Yorkshire it was said of him that he bequeathed to posterity "seventeen children and the Seventeenth Light Dragoons." That was in 1806, and nearly fifty years had passed since he brought to the Court at St. James's the news of Wolfe's death in the moment of victory at Quebec.

Hale was a close friend of James Wolfe, and as lieutenant colonel of the 47th Foot he particularly distinguished himself during the battle. The mortally wounded Wolfe had named his friend to carry back to England the dispatches which told of the victory, and for his services Hale received a grant of £500, ten thousand acres in Nova Scotia, and King George III's commission to raise a regiment of light dragoons.

All this happened in 1759, "the year of victories," and Hale's

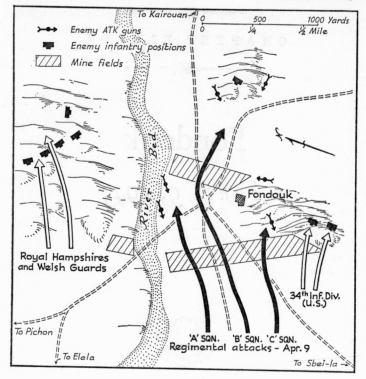

To Kairouan

Enemy ATK guns
Enemy infantry positions
Mine fields

0   500   1000 Yards
0   ¼   ½ Mile

River Bed

Fondouk

Royal Hampshires
and Welsh Guards

34th Inf. Div.
(U.S.)

To Pichon

To Elala

'A' SQN.   'B' SQN.   'C' SQN.
Regimental attacks – Apr. 9

To Sbei-la →

commission to raise a regiment was worth many hundreds of
pounds a year. From the outset, however, he was determined
that his regiment should be not so much a source of personal
revenue as a lasting memorial to the sickly and eccentric genius
who had fallen at Quebec. Hale remembered the General Order
published by Wolfe the day before the battle—"The officers
and men will remember what their country expects of them.
. . ."—and he was determined that the 17th Light Dragoons
should be a perpetual reminder of his friend.

Hale chose for his regiment's motto a Death's Head [1] with
the scroll "Or Glory," and in doing so bestowed on them the
best-known and best-loved nickname in the British army—

[1] The Death's Head with the scroll "Or Glory" is always referred to as
the regimental motto, and *never* as its badge.

"The Death or Glory Boys." [2] He also selected white facings
for the uniform, either to signify mourning for Wolfe or because white was the recognized color of the French army, which
had been so signally defeated by Wolfe at Quebec.

The 17th Light Dragoons became lancers in 1823, and it
was as the 17th Lancers that the regiment charged at Balaklava
on October 25, 1854. The charge of the Light Brigade is probably the most famous of all cavalry charges, not so much on
account of its military merits as because Tennyson later immortalized it in his verse, and the story has been told so often
that it is not intended to do more than sketch the outline here.

The charge was the result of a misunderstanding between
Lord Raglan, commander in chief of the British army in the
Crimea, and Lord Lucan,[3] who commanded the Cavalry Division. Much of this confusion was due to an order indifferently
drafted by Raglan's chief of staff; to an excitable aide-de-camp
who galloped with the order to Lucan; and to Lucan's own
failure to reconnoiter properly before ordering his division to
advance. The result of all this was a charge which may have
set the standard for gallantry for all time, but which in every
other way was an appalling waste of valuable human lives.

The Russian infantry had attacked the Causeway Heights
above the Balaklava valley and were dragging away some naval
guns which the British had emplaced there. Raglan intended
the cavalry division to drive off these Russians and so save the
guns, but unfortunately he failed to make this intention clear
to Lucan. Raglan and his staff were on the high ground looking down into the valley, but the Cavalry Division were drawn
up in the valley itself. From where he was sitting on his horse
at the head of his division, Lucan could not see the Russian
infantry on the Causeway Heights, but he could see a considerable Russian force drawn up across the valley, about two miles
to his front. They were unlimbering their guns preparatory to

[2] Some of their more irreverent sister regiments, although recognizing
the superb record of the 17th Lancers, have been known to refer to them
as the "Dog's Dinners" on account of their skull and crossbones.

[3] Lord Lucan had formerly commanded the 17th Lancers. He had then
been Lord Bingham and was such a martinet about dress that he earned
for his regiment the nickname of "Bingham's Dandies."

bringing them into action, and Lucan conceived that these must be the guns that Raglan wished him to charge. He therefore gave orders for the Light Brigade to lead the advance under Lord Cardigan, while Lucan followed behind in support with the Heavy Brigade.

The valley was narrow and flanked by hills, and in Lucan's opinion there was only room to deploy two regiments abreast. Cardigan thought otherwise, but then Lucan and Cardigan, even though they were brothers-in-law, never agreed on anything. Lucan was the senior and his orders had to be obeyed, and the Light Brigade therefore advanced with the 17th Lancers and 13th Light Dragoons leading, the 11th Hussars behind them, and the 4th Light Dragoons and 8th Hussars bringing up the rear. Out in front rode the Earl of Cardigan in the cherry-colored overalls of the 11th Hussars—as brave, as arrogant, and as stupid an officer as has ever led cavalry into battle.

The 17th Lancers were wearing "marching order"; in their case this meant blue double-breasted coatees piped with white, lance caps without plumes, tight blue overalls with double white stripes, and white pouch belts. The red-and-white lance pennants were furled beneath the points of their lances, and the officers carried swords.

Cardigan gave orders for the Light Brigade to trot, and the light cavalrymen moved off in perfect alignment down the valley. So perfect was the drill that it might have been a military review instead of a battle, and Cardigan was constantly checking men whose horses were pressing forward and spoiling the straightness of the line. Raglan was watching the advance from the heights above, and at any moment he expected Cardigan to wheel to the right and attack the Causeway Heights, where the Russian infantry had stopped trying to drag away the naval guns and were hurriedly forming squares to meet the expected cavalry charge.

But to Raglan's surprise there was no alteration in the direction of the Light Brigade's advance. With all the stateliness of a minuet the Light Brigade trotted on "into the jaws of death," and as they did so every Russian gun and rifle within range opened up at them. The range was only eight hundred yards and at that distance even the Russians could not miss. Man after man, and horse after horse, fell in a bleeding, kicking, thrashing mass, and yet Cardigan still trotted on, and the ranks closed in on the center.

Only when they were within a few hundred yards of the Russian battery did Cardigan urge his horse into a canter, and almost immediately after this his trumpeter sounded the "Charge." The lances of the 17th came down to the "engage" and they charged home, knee to knee and boot to boot. The Russian artillerymen held their fire until the oncoming lancers were less than eighty yards from them, and then they fired all their eight guns in one salvo.

When the smoke cleared there was no longer a line of charging lancers—only a confusion of small groups of smoke-blackened and battered men, blood streaming from their wounds, fighting and slashing their way forward, and receiving back as good as they gave. Soon it became clear that either the Light Brigade must retire, or remain to be annihilated in close combat, and the trumpets sounded the withdrawal. The remnants of the Light Brigade galloped back down the valley, reeling in their saddles from wounds and exhaustion, and shot at from every side; it may have been magnificent, but it was still a disaster.

At roll call that night only three of the ten officers with the 17th Lancers were fit for duty, and out of 135 rank and file only thirty-five answered their names. Ninety-nine horses had been killed in the 17th Lancers alone, and every other horse in the regiment had been wounded. Eighty-nine years were to pass before the regiment was called upon to endure similar casualties.

Never again could there be anything which would quite compare with the charge of the Light Brigade; like the Taj Mahal, or the Hanging Gardens of Babylon, it defies comparison. Yet at Ulundi in South Africa in 1879, the 17th Lancers charged home with almost equally spectacular results, even though no Poet Laureate saw fit to commemorate the battle in deathless verse. It was at Ulundi that the 17th Lancers smashed the Zulu impis which had been menacing Natal, and finally broke the

Zulu power. There have been few braver fighting men than the Zulus, but they could not stand up to lances, and it is interesting to speculate how Custer would have fared against Crazy Horse and the Sioux had his 7th Cavalry been armed with lances. There seems to have been something about charging lancers which affected the morale of savage peoples, but the United States army never had any use for the weapon.

During the South African War the 17th Lancers enjoyed the doubtful distinction of being surrounded by a Boer commando led by Jan Christian Smuts. Smuts later became a British field marshal and an elder statesman, but on the day when he surrounded C Squadron of the 17th Lancers he was only a Boer attorney with a genius for war. More than half the squadron were killed and wounded, and after the battle Smuts wrote a letter to the commanding officer which is now one of the regiment's most treasured possessions:

> How gallantly those boys fought against us, many being killed because they knew not how to surrender. That fight . . . ought surely to be reckoned always among the most precious records of that great regiment.[4]

It was also during the South African War that a certain Lieutenant Colonel Douglas Haig arrived from England to command the 17th Lancers. Haig subsequently became a field marshal, commander in chief of the British armies in France during World War I, an earl of the United Kingdom, and colonel [5] of the 17th/21st Lancers;[6] of all his many distinctions he is on record as saying that he valued most of all the colonelcy of his old regiment.

[4] R. L. C. Tamplin, A Short History of the 17th/21st Lancers (Combined Service Publications, London, 1959), p. 19.

[5] In the British army each regiment has a colonel who is usually a distinguished ex-officer of the regiment. Although the appointment is an honorary one, colonels of regiments can exercise considerable influence on purely regimental matters, such as selection of officers, dress regulations, and choice of commanding officers.

[6] The 17th Lancers have always had a remarkable record for producing high-ranking officers. In World War I the regiment produced both the commander in chief and the chief of staff of the British armies in France, and as recently as 1957 the regiment had one lieutenant general and one major general on the active list.

After every war Britain has reduced her army to below the acceptable minimum, and the United States of America has never been backward in following her bad example. In 1922, as part of this reduction, the sixteen junior cavalry regiments were paired off, and then amalgamated to make eight regiments, this curious arrangement going some way towards satisfying the twin deities of Britain—Tradition and The Treasury. Two squadrons were taken from the senior regiment, and one squadron from the junior regiment, and the three squadrons then comprised the new regiment. In the course of this reorganization, which led to a great deal of heartburning and dissatisfaction, the 17th Lancers and the 21st Lancers were amalgamated to form the 17th/21st Lancers.[7]

The 21st Lancers had enjoyed a somewhat diverse existence. Like many other British cavalry regiments they had been raised and disbanded on frequent occasions, and although they claimed to trace their descent from a regiment of light dragoons raised by the Marquis of Granby in 1760, in fact they were really descended from an East India Company regiment which had been raised in 1857. The Indian Mutiny had shaken the Company's faith in its native troops, and it therefore increased the number of European regiments in the Bengal army. Within a year of doing this, however, the British Crown took over the government of India from the East India Company, and the Company's European regiments were either absorbed into the British army, or disbanded. The 3rd Bengal European Light Cavalry became the 21st Light Dragoons, subsequently the 21st Hussars, and in 1897 the 21st Lancers.[8]

In that year the regiment started on its march from Cairo to Khartoum under Kitchener. The object of the expedition was to avenge Gordon, whose death at the hands of the dervishes

[7] The so-called "fractionalized" British cavalry regiments were a constant source of puzzlement to American officers during World War II.

[8] French gray had always been the distinctive color of the light cavalry regiments of the East India Company. The 21st were the only British cavalry regiment to wear French-gray facings, and there was much heartburning in 1897 when the regiment became the lancers and the facings were changed to red. Queen Victoria personally ordered a return to French gray when she heard of the regiment's conduct at Omdurman.

had shocked English public opinion, and to free Egypt from the ever-present menace of a dervish attack from across the Sudanese frontier. It would be foolish to pretend that any nation is actuated in its international dealings by anything other than self-interest, but there are undoubtedly occasions when such self-interest is more "enlightened" than at others. Kitchener's expedition to free the Sudan from dervish tyranny comes into this category, since seldom has any rule been as brutal and as negative as that of the Khalifa Abdullahi, the Mahdi's successor in the Sudan.

Kitchener's ponderous advance across the desert ended within sight of Omdurman on September 2, 1898. Khartoum, where Gordon had been cut down on the steps of the governor general's palace, was still hidden from view, and although it was early in the morning, the heat haze already made it difficult to tell where the desert horizon ended and the mud walls of Omdurman began. The landscape was burned the color of yellowochre and dominated by the vast bulk of the Jebel Sorghun, and the only green came from a few desiccated bushes struggling for life in the wadi beds. It was a barren land, and a land of blood.

Kitchener's army consisted mainly of Sudanese and Egyptian regiments, and his only British cavalry regiment was the 21st Lancers. Service with the 21st Lancers on the Nile Expedition had been much sought after by young and ambitious cavalry subalterns, and among them was a young lieutenant who had managed to worm his way past Kitchener's gruff and ungracious guard. This was a certain Lieutenant Winston Spencer Churchill, whose own regiment, the 4th Queen's Own Hussars, was engaged in humdrum garrison duties in India. Kitchener, who always had a weakness for the British aristocracy, had agreed after some hemming and hawing to Churchill's attachment to the 21st Lancers, and Churchill, whose instinct for being in the right place at the right time was as marked in his youth as it was to be later, was given a troop in the 21st Lancers.

The dervishes were the first to attack at Omdurman, but they were driven back by the point-blank fire of Kitchener's artillery and infantry. As they withdrew in considerable confusion towards Omdurman, Kitchener suddenly realized that they might retire into the city itself, and he would be faced with having to fight his way through one of the biggest native cities in Africa. His tiny army would be swallowed up in a maze of narrow alleys and courtyards, and it would be highly dangerous to launch it on such a hazardous task. It was therefore vital that the dervishes should be intercepted before they withdrew behind the city walls, and the 21st Lancers were ordered to work round the enemy right flank and cut off their line of withdrawal.

The regiment cantered forward to carry out its task, but it had only gone a short distance before it was fired on from the flank. The commanding officer assumed that this fire was coming from skirmishers, and he decided to charge them before continuing the advance. Accordingly he ordered his trumpeter to sound "Right wheel into line," and in that formation the 21st Lancers broke into a gallop. No sooner had the "Charge" been sounded than a dense mass of white-shirted dervishes rose out of the ground ahead, almost as if they had come up on an elevator, and the startled commanding officer then realized that a deep wadi lay directly in the path of his regiment. Several thousand dervishes had been lying concealed in this wadi, and they rose to meet the British cavalrymen with all the exaltation of religious fanatics who regarded death in battle as a one-way ticket to paradise.

There was no time to halt the charge or to change the direction. With a tremendous crash the dervish swordsmen and spearmen and the 445 lancers locked in combat. For a moment in time the contest swayed backwards and forwards, and then the lancers galloped on, leaving behind them twenty-two of their own dead and many times that number of the enemy dead.[9] The dervishes, like the Zulus at Ulundi, were unable to stand up to the shock action of the lance, and were thrown into utter confusion; their rout was completed later when the 21st Lancers dismounted and engaged them in enfilade with carbine fire.

[9] Many of the lancers' casualties were due to horses falling when jumping the wadi. Any man on the ground was cut to pieces immediately.

Trumpet Major Malcolm Norris of the 21st Lancers has re-
counted this story of the charge:

> I was nineteen years old when the regiment went to the
> front and took part in the famous 21st Lancers' charge at
> Omdurman. Mr Churchill was attached to the regiment
> and was posted to my Troop in "A" Squadron. He was a
> daring and efficient soldier.
>
> The battle of Omdurman started about 5:30 A.M. on
> September 2nd, 1898, when we were ordered to recon-
> noitre and entice the Dervishes on! I remember Mr Church-
> ill being dismounted with sword in one hand and a re-
> volver in the other, the dervish bullets flying all around
> him. Colonel Martin ordered him to mount again and join
> the regiment.
>
> When the first part of the battle was over, we were again
> ordered out to keep the remainder of the Dervishes from
> getting to the River Nile. This is where the 21st Lancers
> played their part in the battle.
>
> As we advanced, we saw at a distance a large body of Der-
> vishes. Colonel Martin knew that this was a decoy so he
> had the "right wheel into line" sounded, followed by the
> "Charge." To our surprise we were in the thick of it. It
> was estimated that there were about three to four thou-
> sand Dervishes there, but we had to go through—there was
> no going back.
>
> Some of our horses had their tails cut clean off, and some
> their forelegs—it was a horrible sight to see them.
>
> I am glad to say I got through without a scratch, but
> some of my comrades in the rear rank dropped out.
>
> After we had marched into Omdurman that night we
> had to picket our horses down. When I was going to put
> in the heel peg I happened to kick a bundle of rags; in it
> I found a Dervish baby, I should say two or three days old.
> As Mr Churchill happened to be passing I asked him to
> take it to the Sudanese lines as they had their wives with
> them.[10]

[10] It was not to be the last time that Winston Churchill was to find
himself left holding the baby.

Queen Victoria was so delighted when she heard of the charge by the 21st Lancers at Omdurman that she conferred on them the title of "Empress of India's." She also restored their French-gray facings and ordered that all ranks in the regiment would wear her Imperial cipher on their shoulder straps —a unique distinction.

These then were the two regiments which came together in 1922 to form the 17th/21st Lancers: the 17th with a record of more than 150 years of gallant service all over the world, and the 21st with a shorter but nonetheless equally distinguished past. With such a brilliant record to inspire them, it is not surprising that the offspring of this union has more than lived up to the standard set by those who rode knee to knee at Balaklava and Omdurman.

The 17th/21st Lancers were mechanized in 1937. Never again would a lancer, waiting in the shivering dawn for the order to mount and ride to battle, feel as Julian Grenfell [11] once had felt, and described so well in "Into Battle":

> *In dreary, doubtful waiting hours,*
> *Before the brazen frenzy starts*
> *The horses show him nobler powers:*
> *O patient eyes, courageous hearts.*

From now on the 17th/21st Lancers would drive into battle in their tanks or armored cars, and the day might come when their tanks would give way to helicopters, or even space ships. Their heritage was that of the mobile arm, and although their weapons played a vital part in battle, the spirit with which they fought was even more vital.

To begin with, however, their mobility was more theoretical than practical. Returning to England from India in June, 1939, the regiment was to find that the army which first employed the tank in battle had lacked sufficient vision to produce tanks in significant numbers. Consequently there were not enough tanks to equip the 17th/21st Lancers to go to France with the British

---

[11] Julian Grenfell was himself a cavalryman and a lancer. He won the Victoria Cross with the 9th Queen's Royal Lancers in 1914 and was killed later in the war.

Expeditionary Force, and after the British army had been driven
out of France in May, 1940, they were given a curious assort-
ment of equipment to repel the anticipated German invasion.
This equipment consisted of a few ancient tanks and a number
of commercial trucks in which were mounted machine guns.
How they would have fared against Guderian's *Panzers* is anyone's guess; fortunately they were never put to the test.

By 1942 the regiment had been fully equipped with modern
tanks, although the British tanks fell far short of the German
tanks in gunpower and armor. Nevertheless, they were a considerable advance over machine guns mounted in trucks, and
the regiment was as proud of its tanks as once it had been of
its horses. In October, 1942, it loaded them onto the tank land-
ing ships and sailed for North Africa with the rest of the
British First Army. With it in the 26th Armored Brigade of the
6th Armored Division were the 16th/5th Lancers and the 2nd
Lothians and Border Horse; all three regiments were to remain
together for most of the war.

"Operation Torch" was the first real venture in Anglo-
American co-operation on the battlefield. Recently there has
been a tendency to belittle the success of that co-operation, to
magnify the differences which will always exist between allies,
and, by ignoring the successes, to stress the failures. Critics of
Anglo-American co-operation during World War II might well
reflect on Dr. Johnson's comment about the dog that could
walk on its hind legs. When the great man was asked whether
he thought the dog did this well, he replied that it was im-
material whether the dog walked well or not—the remarkable
thing was that it could do so at all.

The aim of "Torch" was to land an Anglo-American army
under General Eisenhower in Morocco and Algeria, and then
join up with the British Eighth Army, which was advancing
westward from Egypt. It was planned that the two armies would
meet somewhere east of Tunis, and so complete the encirclement and destruction of the German-Italian forces in North
Africa. This plan was considerably slowed down by a number
of factors. Bad weather, mountainous country, and lack of
battle experience slowed down the First Army's advance. The

Eighth Army always just failed to accomplish the encirclement of Rommel's retreating Afrika Corps. And Hitler did the unexpected and flew in thousands of German and Italian reinforcements from Sicily and Italy.

By the first week of April, 1943, the Anglo-American forces under Eisenhower had reached nearly to Tunis after a winter of bitter fighting through the mountains and the mud. A week earlier Montgomery had driven Rommel from his strongly defended position at Mareth, and was following him up towards Gabès. It was considered essential that the Afrika Corps should receive a knockout blow before it could link up with the German-Italian forces defending Tunis, and a plan was therefore prepared whereby the First Army was to force its way through the mountains. It was then to seize Kairouan and Sousse on the Mediterranean coast, and thus block Rommel's line of retreat, while at the same time the Eighth Army would attack Rommel at Gabès and drive him back onto the First Army. The First Army's part in this plan was entrusted to the 9th Corps, which consisted of the British 6th Armored and 46th Infantry Divisions, and the 34th U.S. Infantry Division. The 17th/21st Lancers were serving in the 6th Armored Division.

They were a different regiment from the one which had landed at Algiers on November 13, 1942. During the winter they had acquired their battle experience the hard way, fighting their way through the rain-soaked valleys and up the steep slopes of the Tunisian hills. They had learned that their Valentine and Crusader tanks were outranged by the formidable 88-mm. antitank guns of the Germans, and they had also discovered the effectiveness of the German antitank mines. In March they had been issued with a new tank which mounted a 75-mm. gun, and which became known in the British army as the "Sherman." This American tank was a firm favorite with the British till the end of the war, and its gun was capable of firing both armor-piercing and high-explosive shells. Probably no other tank in the world has been so consistently reliable and so easy to maintain as the "Sherman," the all-purpose tank of the American and British mobile forces; it merits an honorable mention in any book about mobile warfare.

The route from central Tunisia to the coastal plain around Kairouan ran through very hilly country. The road crossed these hills by way of a pass called the Fondouk Gap. The Gap itself was about one thousand yards wide, flanked by rolling hills to the north and by a steep ridge to the south. A wide wadi wound its way through the Gap, in several places extending almost from one side of the pass to the other; a series of shallow water channels ran along the bed of the wadi, with a few bamboos and trees growing along the banks. Apart from these there was no cover. The ground was covered with long, coarse grass interspersed with wild flowers, and a small mosque stood at the western entrance to the Gap.

The Germans had blocked the way through the hills by laying a series of mine fields across the entrance to the pass. These mine fields were covered by artillery batteries firing from east of the pass, and by antitank guns cunningly sited to take in enfilade any tank which succeeded in negotiating the mine fields successfully. The high ground on either side of the Gap was held by German infantry in well-prepared positions, and they provided excellent observation over the plain to the west, from which direction the Allied attack must come. General Crocker, who commanded the 9th Corps, knew that he would have to seize the heights dominating the Fondouk Gap before he could move his armor through the hills and out into the plain beyond.

He accordingly ordered the 46th British Division to clear the hills north of the Gap, and the 34th U.S. Division to capture the ridge to the south. This attack went in at 8:00 A.M. on April 8, and at 10:00 A.M. the 17th/21st Lancers were placed at thirty minutes' readiness, and moved up close to the entrance of the Gap. It was thought that the infantry would soon be in possession of the heights.

The Welsh Guards had in fact captured the first hill by walking straight up it in the face of withering fire. After losing over one hundred casualties they were forced to take cover for a time, but they called up artillery support and then advanced again behind a creeping barrage. But there were other hills beyond, and progress was slower. Meanwhile, to the south the Americans found the ridge a very tough nut to crack. They had still failed to find a foothold on it when at 2:30 P.M. the 17th/ 21st Lancers were ordered to move forward into the pass.

There was still no definite information about the extent of the enemy mine fields or the location of their antitank guns. The commanding officer was understandably reluctant to commit his entire regiment until he knew more about the situation, and he therefore ordered B Squadron, under Major Nix, to move forward and reconnoiter the gap. This it proceeded to do, led by the squadron leader, and almost immediately the Germans opened up with everything they had. Clouds of dust thrown up by the tank tracks and bursting shells hid B Squadron from the anxious view of the rest of the regiment waiting outside the Gap, but it did not hide the British tanks from the artillery observation posts looking down on them from above. The bombardment increased in intensity and accuracy, and four tanks were destroyed in quick succession. To continue the advance would be to court disaster, and the squadron was ordered to withdraw and rejoin the rest of the regiment. No further advance seemed possible until the infantry had cleared the heights.

All through that night the infantry went on attacking in an attempt to drive the Germans off the high ground. The hills were steep, and in some places precipitous, and the German positions were well prepared and bravely defended. In the north, the British made a little progress, but the 34th U.S. Division was still held up to the south. At dawn on April 9 the southern ridge, commanding Fondouk village and the entrance to the pass, was still in German hands, while to the north the Germans were counterattacking fiercely and the British were in difficulties. Meanwhile, east of the Gap, Rommel's troops were streaming back from Gabès on their way to new positions south of Tunis. The Allied air forces reported that the roads on the coastal plain were full of tanks and trucks heading north, and soon it would be too late to intercept them. Once again the Afrika Corps would live to fight another day.

It was with this in mind that General Crocker visited the commander of the 26th Armored Brigade early in the morning of April 9. Crocker told him that the infantry had failed to capture the high ground and that there was no longer time to repeat the attempt to clear the pass for the armor to pass through it. Instead the armor must itself force a passage through the Fondouk Gap, and this was to be done regardless of cost. If need be, a regiment would have to be sacrificed on the mine fields as targets for the antitank guns in order that the remainder of the brigade could break out to Kairouan and beyond. Casualties must be accepted—time was vital.

Brigadier "Pip" Roberts commanded the 26th Armored Brigade. He was an almost legendary figure in North Africa. Aged only thirty-seven, he had won his spurs fighting in the Eighth Army, and his reputation as a commander of armor was second to none in the entire British army. But on that sunny April morning he was faced with a decision that even the most war-hardened commander hates to make; he was going to have to order one of his regiments to advance to virtually certain destruction, and at that moment no man could say whether or not their sacrifice would be in vain. He chose the 17th/21st Lancers.

When they learned of the brigade commander's order, they started up their tanks and moved off. Some of them knew what it had been like in the Gap the previous afternoon, before they had been ordered to withdraw; it seemed crazy to go back again with the hills still in German hands. Others must have remembered another valley running through the hills, and a day in October eighty-nine years before when a similar kind of mission had been entrusted to the regiment. It would be "Death or Glory" all over again, but this time the horses at least would be spared.

It was just nine o'clock as B Squadron turned into the Gap and entered "the jaws of death." The jaws closed on it rapidly, and within a few minutes the squadron was snarled up in an enemy mine field. This stretched from one side of the Gap to the other, and consisted of tellermines buried in the loose sand and scattered in considerable depth. In between were antipersonnel mines designed to kill or maim the crewmen as they jumped from their wrecked tanks. There was no cover behind which the tanks could maneuver their way forward, and the regiment was a sitting target for the antitank guns. Tank after tank went up on the mine field, and as each one lurched to a standstill the enemy artillery plastered it with high explosive shells.

The operation had become a turkey shoot. Amid scenes of mounting horror, B Squadron struggled forward into the Gap, but it was no longer capable of operating tactically. At such short ranges the German armor-piercing shot went through the tank hulls as if they were made of paper, and inflicted ghastly wounds on the crews inside. Many of the tanks "brewed up" and men were either trapped inside the blazing inferno, or they "baled out" only to find themselves pinned to the ground by enemy machine-gun and shell fire. Across the battlefield drifted thick black smoke from the burning tanks and dust thrown up by exploding mines; one eyewitness described it later as his conception of Hades.

Nix led on his squadron until he too was killed. He was standing up in his tank turret, calmly directing the advance of what remained of his squadron, when he was shot through the head by an enemy sniper. Two of his gallant troop leaders carried on without him, and Lieutenant Micholls actually succeeded in leading his tanks through the second mine field and out into the Kairouan Plain beyond. There he was killed and his troop destroyed by antitank guns positioned to cover the exits from the pass.

When, finally, there were only two tanks left in B Squadron, the advance could no longer continue. Corporal Melling commanded one of the two remaining tanks, and he stubbornly refused to retire. Regardless of danger, he remained in action fighting his tank, and affected not to hear the repeated orders for withdrawal which came over the wireless. He was later decorated for gallantry and promoted to sergeant, but he never lived to see the victory for which he had fought so hard. He was killed in action.

The other two squadrons had been following behind B Squadron, and soon they too were bogged down in the mine fields. A few of the enemy antitank guns were located and destroyed, notably several which had been concealed in the wadi, but it was growing increasingly difficult to continue the advance. Within thirty minutes of entering the Gap, over half the regiment had been put out of action; eight tanks had been destroyed by antitank guns, and twenty by mines. Only a handful of tanks remained by 11:00 A.M. and they could do little to damage the enemy.

At this stage Brigadier Roberts moved another of his regiments into the Gap. The 16th/5th Lancers were ordered to make their way along the wadi bed, which afforded some protection from enemy-observed fire and which had been cleared of antitank guns by the tanks of the 17th/21st Lancers. By dusk the 16th/5th had found a way through the enemy mine fields, and it leaguered the night of April 9 out on the plain beyond the pass. For the first time since the previous December, the First Army was out of the Tunisian hills.

That this was so was due entirely to the 17th/21st Lancers who leaguered that night in the Fondouk Gap and counted the cost. Three officers and eleven men had been killed, and three officers and thirty-two men wounded. Out of some fifty tanks, thirty-two had been put out of action.

Fondouk had been the regiment's sternest test since Balaklava, and it had risen worthily to the occasion. The courage and dash which for so long had been a characteristic of the light cavalrymen had been given fresh impetus by mechanization. That mechanization had given back to the 17th/21st Lancers their place on the battlefield, and as armored cavalrymen they had added fresh laurels to the many they had won in their horsed days.

There had been those who believed that the cavalry spirit could not survive the disappearance of the horse. There were others who believed ardently in mechanization, but who considered it impossible to graft the new technique onto regiments with their roots in Balaklava and Omdurman. The new type of warfare required an entirely new approach—an approach which was beyond the comprehension of the old-style cavalryman.

Both schools of thought were wrong. The spirit is greater than the machine—and much more important. Many of those who fought at Fondouk had begun their career with horses and had hated the thought of giving up those horses and accepting tanks in their place. But they had shown at Fondouk that what mattered was their regimental spirit—that alone had carried them forward in the hills of Tunisia, and that alone had carried them forward in the hills of the Crimea.

Happy the soldier who can fight with such glorious traditions to sustain him in adversity, and foolish the army which ignores them.

CHAPTER TWELVE

The Future
of the
Mounted Arm

"The man is the first weapon of battle: let us then study the soldier in battle, for it is he who brings reality to it. Only study of the past can give us a sense of reality, and show us how the soldier will fight in the future."

ARDANT DU PICQ

WAR has changed beyond all imagination since Kellermann's *coup d'oeil* saved the day for France at Marengo. It has become infinitely more complicated and immeasurably more terrible. We are now on the threshold of even more remarkable developments, and the new weapons coming off the drawing board are certain to revolutionize strategy and tactics. Their inclusion in the armories of the nations will entail vast changes in organization and attitudes of mind, and may well invalidate long-cherished theories concerning the art of war. But the requirement for mobility will not be changed; if anything, its importance will be enhanced, since on the atomic battlefield an army which cannot concentrate and disperse rapidly will never live to fight another day.

A danger lies in the tendency to equate mobility with speed. True mobility is inseparable from flexibility. What is required is the ability to deploy rapidly, to grasp a tactical situation quickly, and then to possess the necessary speed into action which enables a commander to seize the fleeting opportunity— an opportunity which may never come again. There is nothing new in all this, but the steadily increasing killing power of modern weapons has made mobility a paramount requirement. The cavalry have been presented with a great opportunity, providing they are prepared to adapt organizations and techniques to keep pace with the developments in weapon systems.

In what manner the cavalry of the Twentieth Century will differ from the hussars and cuirassiers of the Nineteenth is undoubtedly, from the military point of view, one of the most interesting and momentous questions of the day [wrote the biographer of Stonewall Jackson in 1902]. Of the three arms, cavalry has undergone the least change since the introduction of gunpowder. The load upon the horse has been gradually lightened but defensive armour has not yet been altogether discarded; and although the carbine and revolver have been added to the equipment of the trooper, there are armies in which weight, of both man and horse, is reckoned a more important attribute than either marksmanship or activity. Shock-tactics, the charge, and the hand-to-hand encounter are still the one ideal of cavalry action; and the power of manoeuvring in great masses, maintaining an absolute uniformity of pace and formation, and moving at the highest speed with accurately dressed ranks, is the criterion of excellence.[1]

Colonel Henderson was accounted one of the profoundest military thinkers of his time, but it is doubtful whether he foresaw a day when his hussars and dragoons would be as much an anachronism on the battlefield as the bow and arrow; and he could hardly have visualized a time when the cavalryman would be compelled to abandon his horse in the interests of mobility. The modern cavalryman is probably less blinkered by the lessons of the past; he has experienced so many scientific wonders in his lifetime that he has come to think there are no limits

[1] Colonel G. F. R. Henderson, *The Science of War* (Longmans, London, 1913), p. 51.

to what may happen in the future. Nevertheless, it is difficult for the armored cavalryman of today to imagine a time when the tank will be as obsolete as the horse, but he will be foolish if he deludes himself that such a time will never come. The march of time is inexorable and one must keep pace with it or go under.

This is easier said than done, since change often will entail a break with traditional forms and ideas. The military is the profession above all others which sets the greatest store by tradition, and with good reason. This is true not only in Britain, "the home of tradition," but in most other countries to a greater or lesser degree. When, after the Bolshevik Revolution, the Russians swept away all traces of the former regime, they abolished tradition in their army. Yet in 1942, when the Germans stood at the gates of Moscow, it was not for the "Dictatorship of the Proletariat" that Stalin appealed, nor even for the need to safeguard the "Glorious Revolution," but for the sacred mission to defend the soil of Holy Mother Russia, and no czar would have appealed any differently. And when the Germans had been held and driven back, the Red army had restored to it regimental designations and traditions which linked it directly with the armies of Peter the Great, Suvarov, and Kutuzov.

Although most armies acknowledge the value of tradition, it is not always easy to graft tradition onto some newly raised organization. Charlton Ogburn, describing the formation of the 5307th Infantry Regiment, better known as "Merrill's Marauders," was not a professional soldier, but he appears to have had little doubt of the value of tradition:

> In view of the American tendency to regard change as in itself a good thing—a condition precedent to being up to date—you cannot expect our army always to understand that an enduring continuity suggested by a name like the Queen's Own Royal West Kent Regiment (the heroes of Kohima) can do something for an organization that a mobile snack-bar cannot—not that we had a mobile snack-bar either. In time we grew attached to our unhandy appellation, the hopeless inappropriateness of which came to seem in itself appropriate. The back-handed pride the

organization developed as the record of its iniquities and accomplishments grew apace found expression in the syllables Five-Three-Oh-Seventh pronounced with indulgent exasperation. But that was with time. At the outset the name seemed depressingly of a piece with the one (as I recall) regimental formation we had, of which the most conspicuous feature was the lack of all insignia, guidons, flags, and as much as a single drum to march by.[2]

By no means every soldier and civilian would agree with Ogburn. There are those who confuse tradition with militarism, and who therefore want to abolish all insignia, bands, and anything else which may be considered to glamorize war. The newly raised German army has turned its back on tradition for a totally different reason, arguing that the weapons a soldier has been given today demand a completely fresh approach and that anything which ties a soldier to the past will teach him false lessons. The Bundeswehr is not going to be given guidons or colors, and no attempt will be made to link its regiments with those that fought for Frederick the Great, the Kaiser William II, and Hitler.

There is unfortunately a good deal of truth in the argument that tradition can become reaction, and therefore a barrier to progress. In far too many instances tradition is confused with sentiment, as was undoubtedly the case during the bitter horse-against-tank controversy of the nineteen-twenties and -thirties. An excellent example of the blinkering effects of sentiment is to be found in the story of the 5th Royal Irish Lancers. In 1921, the British cavalry were to be reduced by four regiments of which the 5th Lancers was to be one, and as an alternative to disbandment the regiment was offered the choice of being converted to a battalion of tanks. The offer was unanimously rejected, the regiment preferring oblivion to the exchange of the horses it loved for the tanks it despised, although in less than twenty years the entire British cavalry would be mechanized. After that mechanization had taken place, many of the younger officers were bitterly critical of their seniors for their failure to deduce the right lessons from their

[2] Charlton Ogburn, Jr., *The Marauders* (Harper, New York, 1959), p. 61.

experiences in World War I; and yet, had the roles been reversed, it is doubtful whether the younger officers would have acted any differently. Sentiment often has a myopic effect.

Slavish adherence to the past must obviously be wrong, but there should never be any need to bolster tradition artificially —if it is worth anything it will survive of its own accord. It is only when it is used by those unable or unwilling to accept change as an argument against change that it becomes a menace, for the army which fails to adapt itself to modern conditions will be defeated long before it leaves its peacetime garrisons. And yet modern weapons and organization are not in themselves sufficient. Weapons change but man does not, and in the final analysis it is man who wins or loses the battle.

The soldier of today is no braver, nor less brave, than the uhlan who charged at Mars-la-Tour or the trooper of the 6th Cavalry who rode down the Confederates at Brandy Station. War is a brutal affair, and death is death however it may come—slowly from radiation sickness or an arrow through the lungs, or instantaneously from a bullet or a shell. Men are just as frightened in the face of mortal peril as they always have been, and their bodies are still as vulnerable. For the comparative few who are genuinely elated by the thrill of combat, there are thousands and thousands who are desperately afraid. Man's natural instinct under such conditions is to escape—either by running away or by cowering in the bottom of his foxhole or even, in the ultimate resort, by taking his own life. Something more than the latest thing in weapons is needed to sustain the soldier when all hell is breaking loose around him, and over the centuries it has been found that this is best achieved by creating an *esprit de corps*—working on the theory that it is easier to be brave in company than it is to be brave alone. And since men are more likely to give of their best for a small community which their imaginations can comprehend, the size of the group has been purposely kept small:

> The army in general is an entity so vast that its members can hardly visualize it as such. But the regiment can be seen, can be measured, can be understood. A man has his own place there. He can be recognized there among

others. Of a soldier, the first thing one says is "he is in such and such a regiment." Moreover, the emotional side of the profession finds something to feed upon in this organic grouping. The desire which is felt by the weak, mediocre, transient individual to participate in the power, the greatness, the permanence and the splendour of a famous regiment is exciting and satisfying. In addition, the aesthetic character of military affairs which appeals most strongly to the senses is most clearly seen by the soldier in the regiment; impressive spectacles in which he is allowed to take part, thrilling symbols which he is privileged to see and to touch, stirring bugle-calls, and music in which sings a soul with which his own mingles.[3]

The truth of this has been proved on battlefield after battlefield. Those regiments and corps which believe the most profoundly in the value of tradition have proved it time after time. How much of the incomparable courage displayed on the blood-soaked beaches of Tarawa was owed to those who had gone before and made the traditions of the United States Marine Corps? Some armies have nurtured tradition to a greater degree than have others, in the conviction that the soldier, no more than man, can depend on bread alone. A soldier who fought at Cassino had this to say about *esprit de corps*:

> Under supplied, without sufficient time to prepare, these few fought a lonely battle in the mountains and no one in the rest of the army had any idea what they were fighting. They had nothing to sustain them except that potent imponderable their regimental identity. It mattered to the Rajputana Rifles that they were Rajputana Rifles. It mattered to the Royal Sussex that they were Royal Sussex. In the end it was probably this alone that enabled them to hang on.[4]

It was this potent imponderable which led the officers of the 3rd Light Dragoons, all of whom had been wounded at

[3] General Charles de Gaulle, *The Army of the Future* (Hutchinson, London, 1940), p. 102.

[4] F. Majdalany, *Cassino* (Longmans, Green, London and New York, 1957), pp. 155-156.

Dettingen in 1743, to conceal the fact from the authorities lest they be needed to charge again the following day; and when they were reviewed some days later by King George II, who asked with some asperity why they were so weak and where were the rest of their men, they replied, "At Dettingen, your Majesty." The same imponderable led Pickett's Virginians forward to certain death on that last terrible day at Gettysburg, and inspired Flowerdew's squadron of Lord Strathcona's Horse to achieve the impossible at Moreuil Wood. It is something which cannot be measured because it is of the spirit, but it is a pearl beyond all price.

This book began with an account of the last soldier in the British empire to ride in battle in a mounted attack. It has ended with the story of a cavalry regiment which exchanged its horses for tanks but yet retained the spirit of dash and chivalry of the mounted arm. The cavalry spirit inherited from his forebears by the armored cavalryman of today will in time be handed on to the cavalryman of the future. We do not yet know how that cavalryman will be mounted—perhaps in a helicopter and possibly one day in a spaceship. He may emerge from the depths of the ocean in an atomic-powered submarine which will take to the land as some form of amphibious tank. The mount from which he will fight is still hidden in the future and it would need the imagination of a Jules Verne and an H. G. Wells to predict its precise shape and size. All that we do know is that one day the tank will give way to some other form of war machine and that man will still be required to crew it. He will still be the same kind of individual as the man who rode the horse and who drove the tank, and he will still require the same characteristics of dash, boldness, and independence if he is to measure up to the requirements of the mobile arm.

Man still remains the first weapon of battle. We may girdle the earth with spaceships, bombard the moon with rockets, and invent increasingly terrible weapons, but when all has been said and done, it is the things of the spirit which will prevail. The cavalry spirit is a proud inheritance which we who fight mounted will do well to preserve.